EASTER ISLAND

THE GODS OF DOOM

So they stood on the burial platforms before the collapse of the world's most mysterious culture. (From a reconstruction)

EASTER ISLAND

Home of the Scornful Gods

BY

ROBERT J. CASEY

Author of Four Faces of Siva

ILLUSTRATED

Indianapolis

THE BOBBS-MERRILL COMPANY

Publishers

First Edition

Printed in the United States of America

PRESS OF
BRAUNWORTH & CO., INC.
BOOK MANUFACTURERS
BROOKLYN, N. Y.

In memory of

Shirley Short

Richard Peck

Lewis Rice

and

Robert Gormeley

the crew of *The Blue Streak*

CONTENTS

CONTENTS—*Continued*

CONTENTS—*Concluded*

APPENDICES

ILLUSTRATIONS

ILLUSTRATIONS—*Concluded*

Facing page

COMPLINE

The surf pounds itself into opalescent mist against the cliffs of basalt. The island shakes, and the bones of the ancient dead stir themselves in their rocky vaults. Clouds wreathe the gaunt peaks and haste furtively away on their journey to nowhere.

Unfelt winds move lightly down the treeless slopes and make ghostly footprints in the tundra grass and fill the torpid valleys with ominous whispering.

From the summit of a dead volcano gigantic gods of stone leer across a landscape as desolate and forbidding as the craters of the moon. Their long ears seem attuned to the moan of the distant breakers. Their scornful faces, made animate by the sun, mock the wreckage of all that man has done, while they survey the epic futility of his glamourous past and his hopeless future.

The rolling zone of the burned-out fires quivers amid the heat-waves—empty, lonely, terrible—a vista that carries the eye to distant gray cones and loses itself in the veils of the Pacific. And everywhere, broken only by the occasional low moan of the sea, is brooding silence that stuns the ear.

Fear is abroad in this land of death. . . . Fear and Peril and Despair. Thousands of men and women lived here and loved and reared children and vanished into the burial cairns that fence the island from the snarling ocean. But if their ghosts walk by night, a wailing concourse whose inbred bitterness denies them peace even in death, they must always be less terrifying than the obscene spirits that they evoked and left behind them in their passing.

Easter Island! a pin-prick on the chart of the South

Pacific . . . a spike of rock rising up sheer twelve thousand feet from the floor of the ocean . . . one lone pinnacle about which spin the empty horizons.

A region, this, of evil mystery and forbidding legend. Scores of ships have broken their aging backs in the black shadows of its headlands. Other scores have sailed away to find a more wholesome resting-place on the bottom.

The island stands as Nature's greatest monument to the loneliness of man and the failure of his works. . . . Cut off from all communication with the outside world save for the ship that once a year comes venturing from the Chilean coast to make sure that its naked mountains still rise above the sea, it is now and always has been, one of the most inaccessible spots in the world.

Year by year its history becomes more baffling; its clues of stone more indecipherable. Its ancient culture is vanished. Its script, the only written language of the South Pacific, has been long forgotten. The remnants of its people, sullen, harassed, despairing, to-day look into the face of Death, to-morrow will be gone. Only the gods are permanent—the gods and the Fear and the bones of the ancient dead which the pounding of the surf stirs in the crumbling tombs.

EASTER ISLAND

EASTER ISLAND

Chapter One

THE VANISHING ISLAND

Where Are the Peaks of Davis Land?

The tail of a hurricane beat in her rigging. Her square black canvas—what was left of it—billowed against a thin blue sky above stained and battered decks. And with a ballast of loot in her hold, *The Bachelor's Delight,* the tall ship of Davis the Buccaneer, drove on and on into the endless loneliness of the Pacific.

A sullen crew, garbed in the fraying clothes of unfortunates who lay here and there on the bottoms of two oceans, manned the wheel and kept watch aloft, or diced for women's trinkets in the forecastle. In the cabin aft sat John Davis studying a chart which save for thumb-prints and the stains of spilled wine was an empty white space. Wafer, his lieutenant, a hawk-eyed man whose scarred face told of the luck that had preserved him in a perilous calling, leaned across the table and stared at the spot where rested Davis's gnarled forefinger.

"Our position," announced the captain.

The mate grunted and looked more closely as if expectant of seeing some legend or cabalistic mark spring into being beneath his chief's broad and dirty nail.

"Latitude twenty-seven degrees, twenty minutes, south," went on Davis. "We are due east about five hundred leagues from Copaipo."

Wafer listened with some concern. *The Bachelor's Delight* had been following a course in which navigation played no part for the past several days. There had been a raid on Panama—one of the customary raids—and there had been excellent prospect for loot in the cities of the South American coast. But there had been a tidal wave and a great storm and where the crew had once been hopeful and enthusiastic, they now were in panic and glad to be alive.

"And the course?" inquired the mate.

"Due west," answered the captain.

The mate grunted again.

"West she is," he said with gruff resignation. "But I'd like to point out that we could just as well head south with a beam wind and we may have some trouble with the crew if we keep on running all over the Pacific. We haven't had a tot of rum since we left the Galápagos and it's many a long month since we saw the Dover cliffs."

Davis swore and straightened himself as if to leave his chair. The mate slowly moved back.

"Don't mistake me," he urged. "I'd just as soon be out here alive as anywhere else dead. There's nobody waiting for me at home except maybe one or two hangmen. But I just thought I'd mention the crew. Some of the boys don't know their luck and besides the tub is leaking and the water is beginning to crawl."

Davis settled back in his chair again.

"If any critic gets too loud, toss him overboard," he ordered casually. "And if he's too big for you I'll attend to the matter myself. In the meantime you might spread the news about that we're getting out of a hurricane. The boys may not have noticed it. And we don't know much about what's between us and the coast of Chile. We might run into bad weather or a hostile war-ship. And wouldn't that be too bad?"

"What about the towns over there waiting to be looted?"

"The hunting has been fairly good and the season is just about ended," returned Davis. "And with things as they are I don't care to take any chances. There's a little place I know just outside of Plymouth and I want to get back there to spend my declining years. The sea isn't what it used to be. It's getting too crowded.... The course is due west."

"West she is," agreed the mate. And he went out on deck.

All that night the tall ship drove on with the singing wind in her black sails and the Southern Cross on her port bow. And two hours before the break of dawn the lookout set up a cry that brought the crew tumbling out of their bunks.

"Breakers ahead!"

Davis himself scrambled forward and ordered the ship to lay to. Little could be seen in the darkness ahead but the presence of land was unquestionable. Somewhere not far off the port bow surf was crashing. Its hollow drumming went on interminably.

Two hours later came the sunrise and the men gazed in awe at the miracle growing out of the misty dawn. Before them, turning from pink to yellow, stretched a long sandy beach fringed with coconut-palms. The sea was breaking on it in a feathery tide.

The captain shouted a command to the man at the wheel and altered his course to the south, approaching the land at a cautious angle. The sandy beach stretched southward for miles without a sign of inlet or harbor but marked for its entire length by the white ruff that gave a constant warning of danger.

The ship skirted a low cape and swung west again. Clouds of sea-birds approached from over the horizon.

"There is no land like this on the chart," observed Davis to the mate. "We seem to have discovered something."

"And also something else," added Wafer. He pointed

off to the west where a gray patch was taking form against the fading black of the sky.

"Peaks," observed Davis. "A high island. What do you make the distance?"

"About twelve leagues," said the mate.

Davis nodded.

"Not more than that," he agreed. "And that island isn't on the chart either."

The ship rode on to the west and the sun rose higher and the saw-toothed ridge of the mountainous island stood clearly defined above the horizon.

"Are we going ashore to take a look at this place?" inquired the mate.

The captain was silent for a moment. His belated answer was a harsh negative.

"We are not taking any chances," he said. "Nobody can say what may be over there. . . . Men-of-war, hostile natives . . . anything. We risk a shipload of loot if we go over there and we don't stand to gain anything."

"You take the words right out of my mouth," concurred Wafer. "And where do we go now?"

"Around the Horn and home," answered the captain. And he gave suitable orders to the helmsman after which he went back to his cabin to plot a new course.

This was in 1687 when skippers were discreet and chronicles of the sea were compiled largely through the aid of guess and hearsay. Captain Davis got home to England and presumably settled down in the little place outside of Plymouth that had focused his sentimental regard while he was cutting throats on the Spanish Main. Little enough is known about him and that little is a puzzling mixture of romance and conjecture.

His exploits as a buccaneer were not well advertised in his homeland and in a generation might have been forgotten

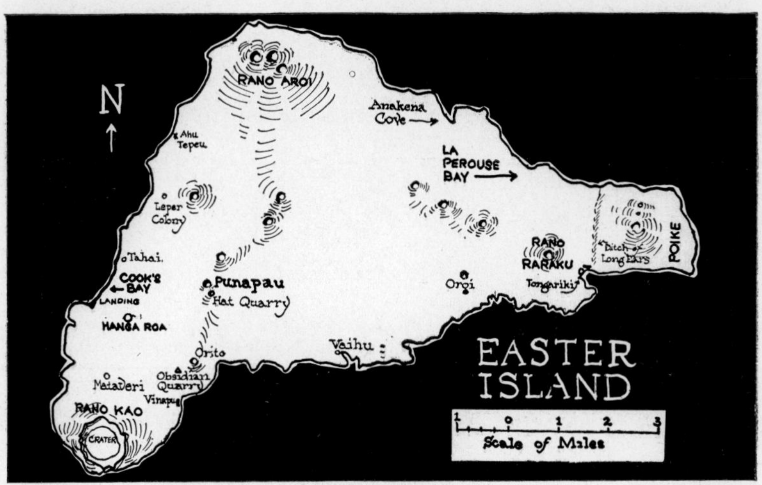

EASTER ISLAND

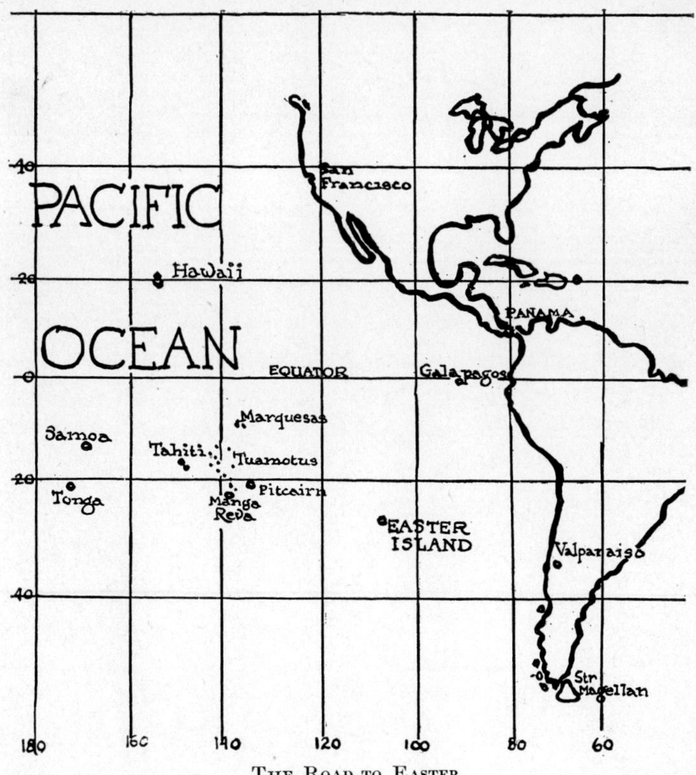

THE ROAD TO EASTER

Tahiti

Here always have come the ships, small and great

save for one incident to which during his life he probably never gave a thought—his report of the sandy beach and the "fair high island" that lay in the Pacific in latitude 27° south and some five hundred miles west of the South American coast. This land was duly marked on all existing charts and given the name of the discoverer: "Davis Land." It was so designated for some fifty years and might keep his name alive on the broad white plans of the South Seas to-day save for one thing. . . .

It vanished.

There came other adventurers through the Strait of Magellan and into the Pacific: freebooters, explorers, naval men and treasure-hunters from every nation under the sun. Dreams of empire and illusions of grandeur were stirring every petty monarch in Europe. In all quarters of the globe were discoverers spreading the gospel of civilization with the hoisting of strange banners over the heads of unimportant natives. And the legend Davis Land on the Pacific chart was a constant challenge to navigators who knew that nobody's flag had ever been flown there.

Eager searchers roamed the twenty-seventh parallel of latitude for a distance of a thousand miles west of the Chilean coast and in the end were forced reluctantly to an unpleasant conclusion. Davis Land, if it existed at all, was certainly not in the place where the buccaneer had reported it.

There was never any doubt among these voyageurs—nor is there much question to-day—that Davis actually sighted the fair high island. In five or six decades, however, the investigative sailormen began to wonder where he had seen it. Perhaps his low-lying sandy beach was really the coral reef of Crescent Island and the high ground at a distance of twelve leagues was the Gambier Archipelago something over two thousand miles from the point of his reputed discovery. A buccaneer's navigation when he is being chased by hurricanes might have in it certain elements of inaccuracy. At any rate Davis Land became one of the mysteries of the South Seas, and remained an object of popular speculation until fifty years later when the Dutch admiral Roggeween came through the Strait of Magellan on the historic course of the freebooters.

Roggeween swung west along the twenty-seventh parallel but unlike his predecessors in the quest for the vanishing island he failed to turn back after the first thousand miles. And he had his reward. On Easter Sunday, 1722, the sun came up to reveal an island on the horizon ahead of him—a high island with formidable peaks. The admiral landed, named his discovery in honor of the day and revealed to the world one of the most amazing puzzles in the history of man.

It was conceded by Roggeween himself that Easter Island was not the high land that Davis had seen. No low-lying beach could be found within twelve leagues of it nor for that matter within a thousand miles of it. The rocks of Sala-y-Gomez stick above the surface about two hundred and fifty miles to the east but it is evident that they were never part of a flat sandy island. Nor could they possibly have been considered part of a picture that included high peaks as a background.

The chart of the South Pacific to-day is a businesslike sheet, covered with notations of soundings and currents and compass bearings and spattered with dots representing islands whose latitude and longitude have been carefully compiled and checked. A novice glancing at it must feel that no single square inch of these seas remains to be mapped, and he permits himself to smile at the haphazard navigation of Captain Davis's day. And yet . . .

Three years ago a round-the-world tourist ship steamed

into Papeete harbor. She was a big ship . . . close to twenty thousand tons, and her staff included two officers of the British Naval Reserve. All officers came to the bridge each noon for the shooting of the sun and each calculated the position independently, submitting his figures to a conference which carefully checked the result. It would seem that all possibility of error had been eliminated from navigation on this ship so the world gave unquestioning attention when the captain reported:

"We have passed over the latitude and longitude of Easter Island without finding a trace of it. Probably the island was sunk in recent seismic disturbances noticeable along the South American coast."

So—temporarily—ended the history of the strangest island in the South Pacific. A race born in the shadow of death had finished with a cataclysm. A great mystery had been absorbed in a greater. The news was circulated and universally accepted. And then a gunboat put out from Valparaiso to investigate.

Ten days out from the Chilean coast the lookout picked up the headland of Rano Raraku just where it had always been. There had been no earthquake on Easter—no tidal wave—no disturbance. The stone gods still leered at the sea. The brooding silence still enveloped the dead craters. The natives still huddled in their wretched village and talked of their ghosts and of dooms yet to come.

The captain of the gunboat was not interested in the promise of dooms yet to come. He checked carefully to make certain that a granitic spike twelve thousand feet high had not shifted its position on the ocean floor, and then he went back to his home port. The error of the liner's officers has not yet been explained.

One might pass over this incident—charging it to a lack of proper observation and a mistake of say fifty miles in dead reckoning—were it an isolated case. But there is something almost uncanny in the fact that it is a mere repetition of what has happened many times since Davis brought back to England the story of the islands that afterward vanished.

In 1802 Captain Gwyn returned from a voyage with the news that the rock of Sala-y-Gomez had been improperly charted. He had visited its stated location—26° 27′ S., 105° 28′ W.—and had found no trace of it. But he had persisted and in the end had reaped his reward of diligence by rediscovering it some three hundred miles west. Captain Gwyn's new charting placed the rock about fifty miles south of and almost within sight of Easter Island.

So mariners who for thirty years had been seeking Davis Land gathered once more in this isolated corner of the world and searched for an island which apparently had no existence. In the end Sala-y-Gomez was found securely anchored in its old position and there was no sign that there had ever been land in the locality where Captain Gwyn still insisted he had seen it.

With the standardization of shipping lanes and the mapping of ocean currents and compilation of information about compass errors, the chart of the South Pacific became more accurate and navigators who had been graduated from a stricter school than the one which had given tickets to the whaling masters laughed at the mistakes of the Davises and the Gwyns.

New reports of mysterious tracts of land freshly risen from the sea and of disappearing islands received little credence. Then, in 1912, the steamship *Glewalon,* a big English freighter with a full complement of officers and men came into Valparaiso with news that land had been sighted at 34° S., 82° 10′ W., fairly close to the South American coast.

There was no questioning the accuracy of this shipmaster's observations. His own calculations had been checked by his first officer and the result as analyzed by the harbor authorities seemed to be correct. It was generally believed throughout Chile that some submarine volcanic activity had thrown up a new island near the coast. The training ship *Baquedano* was sent out to search for it.

The *Baquedano* was gone three weeks. She returned to report that she had cruised for miles about the supposed position of the new land and had found no soundings shallower than ten thousand feet.

So new mystery takes place with the old. Somewhere—possibly on his own fair high island—the spirit of Davis the Buccaneer may find time to smile at the efforts of modern navigators who work so manfully to keep his memory green. Ships still come home from distant seas and strange tales are still whispered in water-front taverns. And one who stands amid the black rocks of Easter, helpless, alone, apart from the world, can not but realize that the story of the South Pacific is not yet written.

Chapter Two

OVERTURE TO TRAGEDY

"Women Lived Here Once"

For two hundred and ten years since Roggeween sailed home to Rotterdam, Easter, the Island of the Dead, has been the great puzzle of the southern ocean.

The Dutch admiral brought tales of tall stone gods who wore red hats and cast their spell over a tropic paradise. He hinted at great engineering works done by a people who, apparently, had neither tools nor equipment. And it is to be regretted, but none the less true, that many of his countrymen doubted him. Stories of Inca treasure and flowering Edens had been in circulation long before the advent of Roggeween. Great galleons had set forth in quest of them never to return; and adventurers who had gone out fired by youth and hope found their way back to port, aged, empty-handed and palsied by disease. Europe in 1722 was still romantic, not to say gullible, but its faith in the accuracy of navigators was beginning to waver.

So Roggeween's report was received politely but without enthusiasm. . . . One might believe that stone gods thirty feet high could be manufactured by a savage people and set up on platforms of basalt by some miracle that dispensed with tools. But that these gods should wear hats—and furthermore, red hats—must, of course, be charged to the admiral's imagination. It was conceded grudgingly that Roggeween had discovered some sort of island about 27° S. Lat. and two thousand miles west of the Chilean coast. And so, for fifty years, the matter rested.

Then came Cook, and La Pérouse, and Gonzalez to look at the weird landscape of Easter and to verify, in most of its details, the story of its discoverer. On this pinnacle of rock in the middle of the stormiest corner of a stormy ocean, hundreds of miles away from the nearest land, a wretched and isolated people had come close to culture if not to civilization. Monuments whose construction seemed beyond all natural explanation stood in grandiose pride to mark their moment of power and accomplishment. That the twilight was now falling about the massive gods seemed not the least puzzling feature of their mystery.

Hundreds of men have looked on Easter since and have brought back to the world facts and theories and stone carvings from the graveyard of the gods. And scientists have puzzled over the epic story of a continent now racking its bones like Lyonesse at the bottom of the sea. Hydrographic survey ships have traveled for thousands of weary miles over the South Pacific questing some trace of an archipelago in which Easter might have had a place. Linguists have searched and still are searching for a Rosetta stone by whose agency they may one day decipher the island's hieroglyphics—characters that resemble nothing in the world so much as the inscriptions of ancient Crete. Imaginative writers—no more puzzled, probably, than the practical-minded investigators whose reports they have seized—invest the weird altars of Easter with the curse of the lost Lemuria. And so through the years has been built up the tradition of mystery and fear.

Few men in recent years have seen Easter Island. Once, perhaps, the whalers made it a port of call and disinterested souls from New Bedford cast an appraising eye upon its disdainful images. But even before the collapse of the whaling industry these calls became infrequent, for there was a wide-spread rumor among sailors that Bad Luck had taken permanent residence on this island. Somewhere in its craters, so competent authority had it, was an entrance to hell. And many an Anglo-Saxon shared with the natives the belief that the stone gods were the handiwork of supernatural and evil beings.

To-day the island is cut off from the world save for one ship a year that anchors as far as possible from the wreck-strewn coast and hurries back to Valparaiso at the earliest opportunity. It may be that the old curse is still alive, or it may be that the high velocity winds in this region have a habit of shifting suddenly, but it is a fact that things happen to vessels that loiter in the resonant shadows of Easter's cliffs. Now and then a bank of lights against the night or a streamer of smoke on the horizon marks the passage of a freighter hurrying by on its way to some port thousands of miles over the rim of the sea. But no one stops here who does not have to.

The known history of Easter during the past century has been evil enough to foster a belief in its curse. In December, 1862, Peruvian slave-traders raided the island and carried off half of the population to die in the South American guano fields. In 1867 Dutrou Bornier, a soldier of fortune, obtained three-quarters of the land between the east and west headlands in exchange for red calico and other trade goods. He established a sheep ranch, possibly to supply fresh meat to ships passing the island on their way from the Strait of Magellan to Tahiti and other points in mid-Pacific; and he was promptly murdered.

Remnants of the populace taken off by the Peruvians came back to Easter after numerous countries had raised a protest, and with them they brought smallpox. Only a small percentage survived the resultant plague.

Chile proclaimed her sovereignty over the island in 1888 after buying out the interests of the Brander family of

Tahiti who had inherited Bornier's land. It was a complicated proceeding. Easter had been discovered by a Dutchman. Bornier, the first white settler, had been a French citizen. The Branders had flown a British flag from the masthead at the ranch-house. Chile's rights in the matter were extremely questionable had any one bothered to argue. But no one bothered.

Most of the surviving natives sailed away to work in the sugar plantations of Tahiti. Years later, homesick, dispirited and hoping for death, they straggled back again—some to reach Easter, others to end their lives on Manga Reva in the Gambier. The proud history of the image builders was ended. At Hanga Roa on the island's west coast the remnants of an intelligent, powerful and warlike people huddled together in a squalid village, ignoring at last the differences of birth, breeding and tradition that had kept them for hundreds of years in distinct castes. Sullen, morose, and—with good reason—distrustful, they sat down in their rotting huts to consider the blessings that a white civilization had brought to them: clothes, moral axioms, firearms and disease. They may have been actively conscious of their none-too-distant relationship with the scum of the seven seas that had manned the whaling schooners for they displayed in their lighter moments a highly developed homicidal mania. In time, from Tahiti, or from some indigenous source, came leprosy to occupy the public mind.

The sardonic smile of the stone images would seem to be explained.

Chapter Three

UP ANCHOR!

Three Thousand Miles to Easter

The mail boats had gone from Papeete, and Tahiti had dropped once more into the dolce far niente. Through the tunnels beneath the intertwining branches of the flame trees the dancing-girls and the guitar-players and the sellers of leis were wandering out to jungled retreats on the far side of the island, there to rest until next month when there should be more mail boats. Quiet had descended upon the water-front and on the straggling town. Barefooted girls moved silently through the spangled dust. Chinese merchants drowsed in their shop-fronts. Brown-skinned men with moist and glistening bodies burrowed into the warm and dizzy twilight of the customs sheds and stretched themselves to sleep on piles of sacked copra.

No wind stirred the palms. The surface of the harbor spread a million facets over deeps of blue and mauve and green out to the shining mist that marked the barrier. Thin streamers of gauzy cloud hung motionless about the blue-black peaks of distant Moorea or trailed lazily into the mysterious valleys.

The air was thick with jungle scents and the heavy odor of tropical flowers. And it was deadly silent save for the whisper of little waves lapping about the piling of the dock and the distant artillery of the Pacific beating against the reef.

At a table in the shadowy coolness of the Cercle Bougainville sat the Little French Captain, the Vanilla Planter, the Pilot, the Archeologist, the Artist, and One Other whose identity is of no importance . . . an inquisitive person from up yonder.

"Got a charter yet?" inquired the Vanilla Planter.

The inquisitive person nodded.

"What boat?"

"The *Ramona.*"

The Artist came to life.

"Do you expect to get to Rapa Nui in a boat of that size?"

"She's a good little boat."

"She's about thirty-four tons and seventy feet long and she was named after a phonograph record."

"She'll make the trip all right," contributed the Pilot.

"She'll have to make it," observed the inquisitive person. "The question of a voyage to Easter Island resolves itself into this: take the *Ramona* or swim."

"You'll probably swim anyway," stated the Vanilla Planter hopefully.

"Who's captain of this splendid scow?" inquired the Archeologist.

The Pilot told him. "He's a good man. But he won't do the navigating. He hasn't any long-tour certificate. Louie Wilmot has been signed on for that job. . . . I just heard about it over in the harbormaster's office."

The Archeologist slumped back in his chair.

"I'd make sure about the navigation if I were you," he advised. "It's about twenty-four hundred miles to Easter on the chart and you'll have to sail about three thousand to get there. . . . And what a Tuamotu skipper doesn't know about navigation is plenty."

"It is simple to navigate the Tuamotus," observed the Little French Captain. "The skipper start out. He point his hand. He say: 'We go zis way.' So they set the course. In the morning he sees an island. He look. He say 'It is one coconut, it is Pukapuka. It is two coconut, it is Fakahina.' And if he is not sure he go ashore and ask somebody what island is it."

The inquisitive person looked pained but before he could make a comment there arrived Alec Stergios, founder, house committee, president and manager of the Cercle Bougainville, to set out some concoctions of lime and ice and other ingredients.

"Just to wish you good luck on your journey," he said. "The Insurance Man was coming up to join the farewell committee but it seems he has a better idea. He's down at his office making a book on your chances for coming back. . . . He's betting you won't."

"He always was a shrewd lad," observed the Vanilla Planter encouragingly.

The hurricane season was still in progress. The docks were a leafless forest of tall masts where schooners from the Tuamotus and the Marquesas were tied up waiting for better weather.

It had seemed that none of them would ever dare to hoist a hook again, but after all it is an axiom of the sea that where one man will not venture, others may be willing . . . a policy that accounts in part for the fine graveyard of ships on the Tuamotu reefs.

The *Ramona*, loading for a voyage into the Dangerous Archipelago, had suddenly become available. . . . All morning trucks had been rolling to the wharves with drums of fuel oil. Her usual stock of trade goods had been altered to suit her new requirements. Her deckload of lumber, destined for some lonely atoll to the northeast, had been taken off, and a fine store of corned beef, canned salmon and the like had been dumped into the yawning hatch.

The blackboard attached to the forward rail had been relettered with names that seldom appear on the billing in these parts: Manga Reva, Pitcairn, Rapa Nui. And such of the populace as remained in Papeete came down in twos and threes to look at this message and marvel. To the native imagination Rapa Nui, the mysterious Ile de Pâques, has all the romantic allure of far places like San Francisco. A Tahitian looks upon it as the end of the earth—and so indeed it is.

The *Ramona* had been scheduled to sail on Tuesday at five P.M. But things never happen according to intention in the South Seas. The port authorities demanded some new manifests and declarations, and the mainsail had to be fixed, and there wasn't enough fuel oil on board, and besides there didn't seem to be much reason for hurry. Departure was postponed for twenty-four hours.

Wednesday at one o'clock the skipper decided to get away at two. . . . And the difference of three hours is considerable when one has to pack a motion-picture outfit, a suitcase and three trunks, collect one's belated laundry, pay the bill at one hotel and arrange for the storage of one's relics and chattels at another, obtain the blessing of the gendarmerie and rush one's baggage to the so-called boat. But eventually all of these things were done. And then came the voice of Louie the Navigator protesting that something was wrong with the chronometer. . . . Something wrong with the chronometer. The phrase made no impression at the time. It was to be recalled many a time afterward with the decks awash and the glass falling and a half-sick crew trying to pump the Pacific out of the hold.

By half past four somebody returned with the chronometer and reported it in good repair. The compressed air whistle tooted a shrill farewell. The *Ramona* cast off and headed for the west pass through the cannonading reef with the sun hanging low in the sky behind her and at least twenty-four hundred miles of the lonely ocean in front.

Long shadows had picked out the shaggy valleys of the Tahiti upland. They rose from the feathery ruff woven and rewoven by the surf on the coral, and stepped away through trailing folds of green to wreathe themselves in a thin veiling of cirrus clouds.

The schooner turned slightly north after leaving the pass and moved within sound of the breakers along the side of the island. Schools of luminous blue fish were in the wake. Porpoises leaped across the bows. Far astern the saw-toothed mountains of Moorea turned quickly from green to bluish gray and then to black in silhouette against the pink of the sunset.

The night came suddenly and with it a lazy breeze, damp and cold from the high valleys of Tahiti. The sailors who had been active enough an hour before disappeared or froze themselves into silent statues along the rail. One became conscious of the swishing of water and the rumble of the little Diesel . . . the strained creaking of pulleys, the flap of canvas, and one other sound that was to be the leitmotiv of this symphony, the iron clang of the pump.

The little after deck which had seemed almost roomy by daylight shrank to no size at all. There seemed to be no room in which to stretch legs already cramped . . . no place to set a canvas chair among the clutter of boxes and rope.

Six o'clock. . . . Papeete less than two hours behind. . . . And the day's end seemed to have blotted out the world. There was nothing to do. If one could have stood the nauseous mélange of Diesel fumes and bananas and copra one might have found a place in the cabin where one could read by the reflected glow of the binnacle lamp. But the schooner had begun a combination of pitch and roll that was agitating a diaphragm quiescent for twelve years. One could only wrap one's self in a blanket and lie on top of the deck-house and recall the gaiety and comfort of the liners and wonder why Easter Island had ever seemed the Port of Great Desire.

The *Ramona* was a strange little ship with a strange history. She was built in France to serve with a polar expedition and had actually reached Sydney when the war ended her scientific career. Rebuilt for the copra trade she had been fitted with an engine fished up from the bottom of a Tuamotu lagoon out of the wreckage of another schooner and sent to brave the reefs in the Cloud of Islands—the Dangerous Archipelago. Originally she had been called *La Curieuse*. But when she left the ways after her remodeling the hills of Tahiti were echoing to a refrain about mission bells and the poetic owners rechristened her *Ramona*. The natives of the coral islands gave her another name: *The Ghost Ship*. . . . And a seasick passenger found much to trouble him in that unofficial title.

The crew, as observed hastily in that brief interval between the pass of Papeete and darkness, mustered eleven men, a puzzling surplus for a boat of the size. It was to be learned later that sailoring in the waters of French Oceania runs largely to muscular oarsmanship in the landing of the long-boat on coral reefs and the handling of trade goods and sacked copra. The men were all Tahitian. They talked to one another in beautiful French that shifted without notice to a Polynesian dialect and was difficult to follow. Only one spoke any English . . . Louis Wilmot, Louie the Navigator . . . who was somewhere forward when the night came down.

From the motionless shadows came hushed voices barely audible above the whisper of the sea—voices speaking in a strange tongue, adding to the unreality of a situation that seemed like something out of the Red Queen's dream. One lay on one's back on top of the deck-house and looked at a sky white with stars but unlike any other sky that one could remember ever having seen . . . a sky quivering with the explosive brilliance of the Magellanic cloud but a sky from which the Dipper and Polaris had been tossed below the north horizon. Off the starboard bow the Southern Cross leaned crookedly on its side . . . poignant reminder, if one were needed, that the last link with a familiar world had been broken. Even without the roll and pitch of the ship and the attendant miseries of the flesh, one could not escape the night's abysmal loneliness.

It is an amazing thing, the art of navigation in the South Pacific. The sea is the natural playground of the Polynesian as it has been for hundreds, perhaps thousands, of years. The native science of marine survey has vanished and the sons of the hardy adventurers of Captain Cook's time can no longer make charts of ocean currents with sticks of wood nor calculate their positions from a single look at stars near the horizon. But the directional instinct is strong in them and mariners who never saw a sextant nor heard of a logarithm range up and down among the Perilous Isles of the Tuamotus, risking their lives on every reef, fighting surf and tide in every lagoon, in order that the palpitant world may have its supply of coconut-oil and lip-stick and soap . . . carrying on while their little ships rot under their bare feet and eventually fall to pieces.

The Polynesian sky was a bowl of blue stone inverted over the land and sea. Across the arc of it flew the sun, moon and stars like brilliant birds. Some supernatural destiny had decreed that these flights must take place at a certain time and consume a definite period. So holes were provided at the edge of the world where luminous bodies could rest after their journey. Presumably they tunneled underground until they came to another hole that would let them out again at the proper time next day.

The winds also came from holes and to this day if you ask a true Kanaka sailorman what is the direction of the breeze he will identify it by the hole of its origin.

Presently came Louie the Navigator to find an unoccupied space on the deck-house roof and to roll himself up in a mat of pandanus fiber for sleep. The lonesome voyager ventured to ask him about this matter of the blue stone bowl. His tone betrayed the smile that the darkness concealed.

"That is an idea that the old people had," he explained. "It was wrong but it was good enough for them. They went everywhere in their boats just as we do now when we know the sky isn't stone. Maybe better we had a stone sky and no chronometer. . . . This chronometer is just an alarm clock but has no bell."

The wind seemed to have become suddenly chill and the swish of the sea more ominous.

"Do you think you can hit Rapa Nui with this chronometer as it is?" inquired the passenger.

Louie the Navigator grunted and slid farther into his roll of matting.

"If we miss it," he said, "we must surely hit the coast of South America . . . if the engine doesn't quit. . . ." He went to sleep.

Louie the Navigator in brain and body is one of the finest types that the South Sea Islands have produced in generations—a genius for mathematics, a navigator for whom the ocean lanes seemed to be marked by sign-posts that he alone could see and read. By day he pored over charts and tables and studied the cabalistic markings of a slide rule, cursing in three languages the deficiencies of his equipment. But by night, under a full moon, the blood of forebears, who had been sailoring men for centuries before Magellan, stirred within him and the cares that one might express in terms of tangents and cosines and logarithms seemed of no moment. The ancients of Polynesia stood at his elbow and whispered to him the old philosophy. At such a time he would willingly have undertaken to reach Easter Island in a bathtub. And one who looks back shiveringly over a vista of some six thousand miles of tempest and wave is ready to admit that he probably would have brought his tub to port.

Chapter Four

CORAL ROSARY

Down through the Perilous Atolls

For nearly a thousand miles southeast from Tahiti lie the Tuamotus—the Perilous Islands—coral atolls which Nature in a jestful mood strewed across the water to be the playground of hurricanes and a graveyard for ships. There are scores of them—low-lying banks fringed with coconuts and pandanus, scarcely visible above the horizon by day and discoverable at night only by the crash of the breakers that constantly threaten to engulf them.

Even outside of Polynesia, in a region where time has a value and watery miles have length, these islands would be close to each other . . . "like beads of a rosary," Hippolyte the Supercargo described them, as he set his finger at the end of their straggling course on the chart. And there is something more than pretty poetry in that. Seldom is one separated from the next in the long chain by more than forty miles of water, and inter-island communication by means of open cutters and outrigger canoes is too common to arouse discussion.

And yet one knows as one goes dreaming down the long monotony of the atolls from Tahiti to the Gambier that one has come upon a different phase of life from that in which developed the Polynesian culture of Tahiti. From the moment when, a day out of Papeete harbor, the lookout shouted land ho! and pointed to what seemed only a spreading cloud on the horizon, one has been aware of the difference. The few leagues of sea between the great high island and the first of the coral rings is a barrier as real and as indefinable as that which in other and dryer climes divides the desert from the sown. One has come overnight from a land of prodigal fertility to a zone where Nature is an inhospitable old crone with a tight purse. One is aware for the first time that even in the languorous tropics there may be such a thing as a struggle for life.

With the coming of the white man and the rise of the copra trade in the South Seas, these islands have prospered in their fashion. The coconut grows well enough in the thin chalky soil. It is no harder to pick and dry here than in other places and the supercargoes on the trade schooners will pay a price for it in calico, and sewing-machines and tobacco and matches and sugar and tea and canned beef. Starvation has gone—and with it cannibalism. The natives live in a close approximation of Tahitian indolence and at times could approach Tahitian gaiety were it not for the threat of the sea.

Not an island of the entire eighty but shows gaunt mementoes of the last hurricane. . . . Not an inhabitant in all the group but looks forward to lashing himself to a coconut tree as a last desperate gesture when the storm comes back again to toss this portion of Polynesia into the sea.

Of the islanders alive to-day who saw the tidal waves march across Faaite and Hikueru and Anaa in 1906 not one escaped save by roping himself to a treetop and hanging there battered and drenched for the better part of three days. And only a percentage of those who reached the trees lived to tell of their experience. . . . For trees went as well as stone buildings and native huts and terrified men and women and children. Ahead of the wind came a cliff of blue water to spill across the atolls and to leave vast stretches of reef and beach as bare of vegetation as they

The Ramona
After thirty-one days of storm the schooner dropped anchor off Tongariki

Easter as Cook Saw It

Erosion of statues is exaggerated in this memory sketch by Hodges from *Three Voyages*

were when the coral insects first started to build. To this day these gaunt barriers extend from the reclaimed plantations, denuded of their thin layer of soil, incapable of growing anything save weirdly colored algæ, totally worthless save as instruments for breaking the backs of ships which erratic currents bring to them in the dark.

It is only natural that such an environment as this should have produced a type of people entirely different from those who live in the comparative freedom and safety of the high islands. For all his proximity to Tahiti the Tuamotuan was a savage until not so long ago. The British admiralty chart on which one marks one's course from one death trap to another has almost as many notations regarding dangers from natives as from winds and tides and submerged reefs. . . . "Pukapuka. . . . Natives hostile here." "Angatau. . . . Natives low and barbarous" and so almost through the entire roster of the islands. The pilot book makes frequent mention of dog-eaters and cannibals and "people who wear no clothes." One, reading these things by candle-light in the little cabin of a rolling schooner, could not but feel that one was well on a journey to the Land-of-Never-Come-Back.

The picture is changed now. The natives of the Tuamotus are not so demonstrative as those of Tahiti or the Leeward Islands. To one who has made no deep study of them they seem sullen and none too friendly. But they are certainly not hostile; they govern themselves with every show of success. They live in harmony with one another. They dress in the modes popularized by the trade schooners. And cannibalism—even ceremonial cannibalism—is too far back in their history to be even a memory.

The old school geography—from here it seems a document old enough to have been inscribed on the bricks of

Babylon—pictured the South Sea atoll as a strange and wonderful thing. One recalls a woodcut illustrating the somewhat vague text—a little doughnut of land perhaps three hundred feet in diameter, rising from a placid ocean. Palm-trees grew on this doughnut, tall and straight and neatly spaced. And the open water in the center—the lagoon—was connected to the sea by a sort of canal whose sides were straight enough to have been diked with concrete.

The reading matter below the illustration mentioned that these atolls were held in great favor by mariners because of the splendid anchorages furnished by their lagoons which were deep, calm, fresh-water lakes. Alas for what one knows to be true! . . . It is so generally wrong.

Basically the picture in the geography is fairly close to fact. An atoll in its broad sense is a ring-shaped island surrounding a lagoon. But some of the Tuamotu atolls are thirty-five miles in diameter and no matter where one stands on such an island the opposite side of it is always hidden below the horizon. The lagoon which stretches as far as one's vision can reach seems like any other section of the Pacific, and so indeed it is.

The safety of an anchorage inside the ring of coral is something that never existed outside the geography. In calm weather it is more comfortable than a berth in the open sea, for the ground swells are broken by the reefs. But the lagoons are shallow and filled with coral heads, and vast rocky flats, and gales which sweep unhindered over low reefs and through straggling coconut groves have torn more than one ship to pieces while the tardy skipper was trying to hoist his anchor. Nor are the lagoons fresh-water lakes. They are as salt as the ocean to which they are tributary. Fresh water is one of the most serious problems on such islands. It is generally obtained by conserving the rainfall in cisterns and is subject to all the hazards of supply and conservation that obtain in a desert.

The ring of coral about the lagoon is not always one solid piece. Sometimes it is made up of a chain of a score of islets with numerous passages to the sea. Sometimes the ring is a continuous wall, portions of which lie just below the water-level. Generally there is one navigable pass into the lagoon, but not always. On numerous islands in the Tuamotu Archipelago one must land on the reef itself, a process to which even more than to storms and currents may be ascribed the high mortality among schooners engaged in the copra trade.

Probably no one has ever looked at a coral island without marveling if only for a moment at the tremendous outlay of life that went into the building of it. Billions of tiny insects have lived and died—leaving their carcasses in tremendous heaps whose pattern science is still attempting to explain. Any atoll gives evidence of a more magnificent organization, more prodigal energy and greater accomplishment than the most striking of man's works in the South Pacific. The busy coral is still one of the puzzles of the universe. On island graveyards the insect is still alive and carrying on endlessly the work that began thousands of years ago. But to date no one can determine why it is working or where it started.

Possibly the intelligent coral picked the craters of sunken volcanoes for his foundation. But if that is true why should he build all around the cone of a sunken mountain whereas he builds his reefs only on the lee side of those that are standing? Why should the Society and Cook and Leeward Islands have coral necklaces when the Marquesas have none?

One gets a fair idea of a coral atoll at Fakahina where the dazzling sand stretches back for some yards from the reef. It looks like a bone-yard—which it is—with white chunks of fantastic lime growth stretching as far on either side as the eye can see. There are flowery pieces here tinted with pink and occasionally a spray like something taken from a frosty window-pane. But for the most part the pieces are short and broken and suggestive of skeletons long fallen to bits.

It is a dangerous reef—if that description may differentiate one reef from another in the Tuamotus. A lantern hung on a flagpole warns of its presence by night—the tall masts of a wrecked schooner scattered on the gleaming beach give testimony to its peril by day.

The *Roberta*—apparently a three-master—went up on to the coral one evening and stayed there. She was broken up for her planking and probably solved the housing problem of the island for many years to come. But her skeleton still bleaches where she grounded. . . . The boats of the copra traders ride the swells to a precarious resting-place alongside her rotting keel.

On the reef itself where the wash is continually passing and the coral is always alive and always wet, the scene is ever changing. There one walks from the long-boat over what is alternately a flower garden and a beautifully made mosaic flooring. The coral flowers are at their best in this shallow covering—rosebuds, violet clusters, fantastic arrangements of red-veined leaves. And close beside them stretch areas of closely packed color, as smooth as a tiled courtyard and much the same in appearance.

Queer fish lie in the crevices awaiting the feet of the unwary. One spiky creature like a sea-urchin is equipped with nature's finest imitation of the hypodermic syringe. Each spike is a hollow tube in which is a needle. If one steps on the spike the tube is pushed back while the point remains stationary, bringing an irritant substance into contact with the wounded foot. Sometimes, say the natives, the result is fatal. Another odd specimen is a shell-fish with a protruding cylinder in which a large part of his anatomy is enclosed. The unfortunate pedestrian steps on the cylinder and cuts a section about the size of a dime out of the sole of his foot. The fish retreats into his shell and creates a vacuum. The bit of flesh is drawn into the cylinder after the fish who then has rations for a day or two. The victim spends a long and painful period abed.

Nature seems to have provided the natives with an instinct to avoid these perils, a thick sole which guards when instinct fails, and a blood factor which minimizes the results of careless encounters. But they are not entirely immune. Paradise still collects its taxes. The coral itself is omnipresent and unavoidable and when it is alive its sharp edges make deep suppurating cuts that heal only after months of treatment and leave jagged white scars.

It was calm enough during the first few days among the Tuamotus—which is to say the wind uprooted no masts and the decks were never completely under water. The queer roll-jerk-pitch motion of the schooner continued to defy will-power and experience. But one became used to the quaint aromas of Diesel oil, bananas and copra. And one suppressed effeminate yearnings for dry clothes and comfortable bedding.

There was always rain. It drove under the awning of the after deck and made sleep impossible on top of the deck-house. It sprayed through the open hatches and collected in puddles on the cabin floor. It trickled through crevices and uncalked ports into one's bunk.

Night after night, no matter what time one chanced to wake, the scene was always the same. . . . In the light of the binnacle the half naked body of the helmsman glistening like metal in the wet—and forward, a shadow dimly visible through the forward hatch, another metal figure—bending, straightening with the rhythm of a pendulum and as oblivious to the water that coursed over his straining muscles—the man at the pump.

One morning came Louie the Navigator.

"You know the north wind and the south wind and the other winds?" he inquired.

The answer was yes. Louie seemed cheered.

"Well then what else does this word wind mean in the English language?" he pursued.

"It might mean a variety of things," suggested the puzzled voyager. "If a man loses his breath he is winded."

Louie nodded.

"That might be it," he admitted. "This thing surely has lost its breath. But that doesn't seem to make any sense either. I'll look." And the puzzle remained a puzzle until he had burrowed into the box above his berth and extracted the chronometer.

"There it is," he said, and he pointed to the two dials one of which marked the passage of time and the other showed a knob under which was the somewhat elementary instruction "Wind."

The pronunciation of W-I-N-D with reference to a clock was explained to him. He twisted the knob a few times and shook his head sadly.

"Even with good English the chronometer is bad," he sighed. "I am afraid for the chronometer. . . . And last night I check the compass and I don't think it is so very good either."

Chapter Five

BLOWING WEATHER

The Saga of Louie the Navigator

TEN passengers came aboard at Fakahina journeying to Pukapuka—old men, old women, girls, babies, dogs and bicycles—a silent docile group that made no protest against being herded into the narrow spaces between the *Ramona's* rail and deck-house. It was raining a little and the rising wind had a bite in it, but not even the babies seemed to mind. Wind and a dripping body are phenomena not without precedent in the Tuamotus. The passengers wrapped themselves in their mats or bits of sail-cloth and made the best of it.

Down in the cabin Louie the Navigator was still tinkering with the chronometer and giving attention occasionally to the barometer. The slim bronze hand was sliding steadily to the right—entering a region whose significance was marked by labels such as *orage* and *tempête.*

"I think it will be not much," he said encouragingly. "Maybe a squall . . . a little wind . . . some water. It always happens when you have many people on the decks."

The ship heeled over to the starboard and shook herself like a wet dog.

"It is rolling, I think," he commented. "Maybe it is better you strap yourself in your bunk. If you fall out you hit your head on the steps and maybe break your neck."

Up forward pulleys creaked as the foresail went up into

the breeze. The bell in the engine coop jangled and the schooner got under way.

The roll was unbelievably bad at six o'clock. Darkness had come, thick and soggy, and there was no room on deck to walk about. One could only remember the advice of Louie, strap one's self into one's berth and stay there.

At nine o'clock the rain changed from a drizzle to a cloudburst, a torrent of water that seemed to have no end nor direction. It sluiced along the space beside the deck-house and drove the passengers into a huddle on the roof, then found an opening under the awning and forced them aft to the deck again half drowned and miserable.

Sailors came to close the forward hatch and the fumes of the engine exhaust rolled up through cracks in the floor, a dense sickening cloud. The supercargo shouted something in Tahitian. The sailors reopened the hatch. The wind had veered and as the cover slid back the sea came in. The schooner plunged, took a tidal wave over her bows, shivered and plunged again. Trunks, film boxes, sea chests and trade goods broke loose from their moorings and slid across the floor with a crash that sounded like an automobile wreck. The table overturned. The charts and instruments slid from a rack near the ceiling and dropped into the mess on the floor.

The supercargo shouted again and two or three of the crew, naked save for shorts and *pareus*, and dripping as if they had just emerged from a surf, came tumbling in through the forward hatch to tie up the trunks.

For a moment the scene was reminiscent of Victor Hugo's account of the loose cannon. . . . Boxes sliding and rolling, two chairs smashing to splinters, the sea cascading in sporadic jets through the open door and agile sailors leaping skilfully to avoid a crushing against the bulkhead.

At ten o'clock the water on the floor was four inches deep

and rolling in imitation of the parent ocean, swirling about the stanchions that upheld the tiers of bunks and breaking with a fine little surf in the corners of the room. A man who seemed to have been just rescued from drowning came down the ladder with a baby boy about a year and a half old. One had time to notice that the baby was almost blond and the man as black as a Melanesian, his skin oily and glistening in the light of the binnacle. Then the ship heeled to port and the pair went down out of sight below the sideboards on the berth.

The deck erupted another startled parent and another child—a little girl this time. She was sick and frightened and cold, her brown skin showing beneath the wet calico that encased her. They slipped and fell in the water on the floor just as the earlier arrival picked up his baby and got back on to his feet.

Both men, bewildered at finding the storm almost as bad indoors as out, stood helpless and loose-footed among the dangers of falling furniture. They refused offers of a bunk and blankets for the children, explaining that no baby could stay in a berth when the ship was threatening to turn upside down. Louie, whose bed was nearer the floor, got up and wrapped the little girl in his mat. The black man still clung to the boy who whimpered and shivered by turns.

Some more men came down from the deck and lay on top of the moving trunks or in the swirling water on the floor. Then came a period of rhythmic turmoil that seemed almost a calm. . . . A bedlam that stunned the ear until the world was on the verge of silence. . . . Only as a background came the pistol-cracking of cordage, the creak and clang of the swinging boom, the howl of the wind, the grumble and rush of the water . . . and the clang of the pump. Louie the Navigator crawled into the potato bin at the forward end of the cabin to find a bed.

There was reassurance in Louie's calm acceptance of the situation. The deck passengers lost their hunted look and closed their eyes. The baby quit crying and went to sleep.

So for an hour the ship drove on through the storm—sometimes above the water, sometimes half submerged—climbing up the steep slopes of the rollers, shaking herself on the crests and tumbling with sickening speed into deep ravines. At eleven o'clock she took a breaker over the side and heeled with a thump that strained her planking. As she came slowly back to an even keel Louie crawled out of his bin.

"It's full of copra bugs," he announced. "I think maybe the water is better." His further comment was lost in the wailing of the awakened children. The little girl had bumped her nose on the side of the berth. Her father was making a vain effort to get to her side over the constantly sliding furniture.

Louie, with his superior training in the hazards of the sea, reached her first. He spoke to her soothingly, rubbed her nose and crawled into the berth beside her. She quieted.

So went the night—a series of watery flashes impressing themselves vividly and painfully on a numbed consciousness. . . . Men standing up and falling down. . . . Things that should have been stationary leaping about as if suddenly animate. . . . Frightened faces in the halo of the binnacle. It was like the dull ache of an impacted tooth dramatized for pantomime and enacted by an enthusiastic cast.

At one o'clock the baby boy woke up and screamed. The father who had been hanging, half asleep, to the companionway ladder released his hold. The ship dived into another roller and threatened to somersault. The black man's face glowed for a brief instant in the light, gray as ashes.

Then his feet went out from under him and he shot head first across the room.

A sea-chest stopped him as he was about to crack his skull against a stanchion. He tripped, fell sideways, and, still falling, brought up against another chest. He threw out his hands and swung the baby down with a crash on to the table top.

Louie the Navigator raised himself up in his bunk.

"I think maybe that kills the baby," he commented. And he leaped out.

The baby wasn't dead. A blow that should have broken his back had done him no harm whatever. He quit crying and looked about him with renewed interest in his surroundings. The forlorn father carried him back to the dubious security of the ladder.

Out on the deck the women, old and young, lay bundled up in sail-cloth, perhaps more comfortable, certainly no worse off than the males who had sought the presumably drier refuge of the cabin.

In the dawn, recognizable by a reddish-gray hole in the sodden cloud-bank, the palm fringe of Pukapuka serried the horizon. The streaming sailors were swinging the boat outward on her davits preparing to fight the sea to the reef.

The barometer had started to crawl upward again. Louie gave it an unfriendly glance.

"Just a squall," he said. "I knew the glass would go up again. One day he goes down. The next day he goes up. It is like a tide. To-morrow we have better weather. Next day, maybe we have worse."

The day was momentous for reasons other than the fact that Pukapuka's reef smoothed out some of the swell and Pukapuka's tall palms broke some of the wind: that afternoon the captain surveyed the corpse of the chronometer and decided that nothing but a miracle could restore it to a semblance of life. He called his battered passenger to hear the news.

"We must go back to Tahiti," he said. "We can not find a longitude without a chronometer and we can not find Rapa Nui without a longitude. . . . *Voilà!*"

Louie glowered at him.

"Go back to Tahiti," he repeated. "What for? We are six days from Papeete. It takes us another six days to get back. Then six days more to come here again. . . . We waste eighteen days. And in the end do you think we have a better chronometer than this one? . . . Where do you think they get another chronometer in Papeete?"

"You must have a chronometer," repeated the captain. "I myself never need one cruising around these islands. But I know that if you want to know what your longitude is you look at this clock and it tells you."

Louie the Navigator sniffed. "You brought me to navigate," he said. "Then let me navigate. I say, let's pull up the hook and maybe get going while we have the wind."

"But Ile de Pâques is a small island. If we miss it."

"We don't miss it. I can find Ile de Pâques without a chronometer."

The captain turned helplessly toward the passenger. It was obvious that all of this was beyond him. In his eyes one could read a yearning to abandon this senseless venture and return to the sort of navigation he could understand—a navigation that required no timepieces and implements for sun-gazing—and for that matter no compass. And the passenger, bruised and racked in a night of storm, was more than half inclined to admit the soundness of his idea. On the other hand there was Louie the Navigator—Louie, whose magnificent gesture was wasted on those who did not understand what it meant—calmly undertaking to find an island ten miles long after a quest across a possible two thousand miles of open water in the hurricane season.

The passenger turned to Louie and spoke to him in English.

"Do you mean that?" he asked.

"I do," said Louie.

"You know what you are doing of course?"

"I know what I am doing."

"How do you expect to work out your longitude?"

"You brought me to navigate the schooner. I tell you I can find the longitude. I can find Rapa Nui. That is what you want me to find—Rapa Nui. Isn't that enough?"

"Yes," the passenger admitted. "That's enough. I shall enjoy seeing how this business finishes. Advise the captain to pick up his hook."

So once more the *Ramona* put her nose into the rollers on the long trek down through the Tuamotus. . . .

Days of wind and raging water. . . . Nights of rain and storm and wet blankets. . . . Hours that were years when the ship was rolling and one's back was pounded black and blue against the sides of one's berth.

And always the islands—the endless islands—rising like a mirage out of the sea when one was close enough to hear the breakers on their reefs, and sinking again below the horizon while the smell of the coral still clung to the schooner. . . . A vasty graveyard that began with the infinitesimal remains of insects and fattened by turns on the carcasses of lost peoples and lost ships.

The forecastle was flooded. The crew came aft to cluster wretchedly in the drip of the deck awning or to sprawl uncomfortably on boxes above the wash of the cabin floor. The cook by some miracle kept a fire alight in his galley . . . not that it mattered.

One day came to pick up the monotony where another had left it. Bones ached in protest against the maddening confinement. Sleep came in brief snatches interrupted by the racketing of loose gear and the straining of timbers and the hissing of water. And one woke always to see the same picture framed in the dripping square of the open hatch—the brass-bound spokes of the wheel, rain-beaded, scintillant in the aura of the compass light, and above them a wet brown face peering wide-eyed into the murk.

From the gloom ahead there came, forever and ever, the clang of the pump.

Chapter Six

MANGA REVA

The Empire of God

THERE came a lull in the tempests. By day there was sunlight. By night with the Antarctic winds in her sails, the schooner swung down the cold pathway of the moon. And one afternoon the mountains of the Empire of God came up over the horizon like gray scallops pasted on the fringe of a blue-gray sky. Staggering away on either side the lesser peaks of the Gambier Archipelago fenced the sea with a saw-toothed barrier.

Here, with a scant third of the journey pricked off on the maps, was the threshold of emptiness—the jumping-off place in the long ocean trek to Easter. One approached it in awe born of the knowledge that one would leave it with regret. One stood speechless at the sheer beauty of its materialization from the tumbling water. Its gray became iridescence as if it had come out of the ocean encrusted with pearls. Sunlight reflected from the clear green depths of an unseen lagoon was thrown back against the sky to produce an effect like the top-lighting of a stage. The islands seemed to be taking shape out of shimmering green dust. . . .

The Gambier Archipelago consists of a large coral reef surrounding the tall cones of half a dozen extinct volcanoes. Manga Reva, the principal island, has had a weird history since questing buccaneers and whalers first snatched it from isolation. It has been a religious stronghold with no great faith; an independent community with no reason for independence; an empire with no population. And always it has been a treasure chest of pearls about the edge of which has loitered a people content with lazy poverty.

Only a few days ago the curé, now the sole staff of the old cathedral, marched down the beach road under the coconuts and orange-trees with cross-bearers, candle-bearers, acolytes and choir. The distances echoed with muffled chanting while the thin melodies of Polynesia tinkled across the lagoon. The priest stopped to pray at many a crumbling shrine and to drive his bent and weary body over many a mile of jungle-grown pavement. And so for a moment was revived the pageant of Manga Reva that died with the burial of the last king in his mountain tomb. So were brought back with tragic realism the glories of the day when the spires of the vast church rose in a magnificence of gold leaf above the tallest palms, and a Spanish city, carved from blocks of pink and white coral, spread itself along the shore of the lagoon.

The old priest prayed and the graybeards remembered. And then the procession moved on to the little grass-covered pier about which lay at anchor a fleet of little white boats—the pearling luggers. Stalwart boys with red *pareus* about their brown bodies, stood on the decks of the boats listening to him. Tall slim girls in simple white frocks with flowers in their hair and babies at their breasts stood on the shore to watch in silence.

The fleet sailed out to the coral flats near Aka Maru where the Gambier reef is broken by the southeast pass. And so began a new era for this capital of loneliness.

Here have come hard-bitten pearlers from the seas where skin-divers brought up jewels for Cleopatra's wine, and from the Solomons and New Guinea and the Persian Gulf.

Here is Pedro Miller with a navy such as French Oceania has seldom seen. Across the coral flat from him is the camp of Victor Berge, perhaps the best-known pearl fisherman in these parts—a pearler who knows the charts of ocean floors from personal experience better probably than he knows the maps of the islands on the surface. And with them dozens of minor fortune-hunters set out each morning at the call of a drummer beating on a gasoline tin to lose themselves in coves and inlets until a lull in the wind at sundown warns them that it is time to come home.

Manga Reva's history began a hundred years ago with the arrival of its pearls in distant markets and the growth of the legend that its lagoon was paved with jewels. Until then the simple natives had lived the typical life of Polynesians, more interested in fish than in pearl oysters and more concerned with shell-hooks than with pretty beads of nacre. Food was abundant. The sun was warm. If pearls were numerous so were the pebbles on the mountainside, and one seemed about as useful as the other.

The white man came on two great missions: to gratify the vanity of fine ladies who had never heard of Manga Reva; and to save the immortal souls of the Manga Revans. Where the island had had no past save in the hazy memory of natives too tired to think about such things, it acquired almost overnight a set of amazing traditions, a modern graveyard, a tremendous and startling acreage of ruins and an atmosphere of tragedy.

To-day as one glances past the pearling fleets and the village on the shore of the lagoon one loses sight of the new Eldorado at once and beholds a Spanish cathedral town virtually deserted and encompassed by jungle.

On distant islands across the opal water rise pillars and arches against the sunset. On the sky-line of Manga Reva itself one sees the dome of the tomb of the king and traces the gradient of a royal highway cut through dense foliage and rock to the summit.

As one turns to the left from the mole one moves through a green gloom beneath the orange-trees and comes at length to the white façade of the cathedral—a huge Spanish church built of coral block and probably the finest structure of any type in all the South Seas. It is as always a ghost cathedral. It has no bishop. A lone priest, more interested in the welfare of his dwindling flock than in the magnificence of the church, says mass unassisted to a congregation of perhaps a hundred. Untrained voices raise a thin quaver of native tunes to the distant vaults. Echo shivers and dies and the long pillared nave becomes an empty silent tomb—appropriate mausoleum for a visionary's dream of empire.

To-day a man is dead—an old man whose passing has been scarcely noticed even by his immediate family. The ancient priest and a diffident choir are bidding his soul God-speed. The flames lean lazily from the peaks of the tall candles. The black vestments blot out momentarily the soft glow of mother-of-pearl that flows over the face of the high altar. Weary chanters raise their lifeless voices and the echoes stir again:

"Dies irae . . . dies illa. . . ."

"Oh, day of wrath!"

And one forgets the hot sunlight at one's back in sudden consciousness that the ancient church is damp and cold. One is no longer alone. All about are ghosts—familiars of the temple who will be here till the last pillar falls . . . thousands of them as real as if their bare brown bodies filled every shadowy recess from apse to porch . . . the men who gave their lives to build this place. . . .

"Oh, day of wrath . . . oh, fated day!" It is no wonder

that the rising melody of the funeral chant has acquired a thunderous volume.

In 1836 a priest came to Manga Reva filled with missionary zeal in pursuit of a magnificent vision. It is difficult to classify the good Père de Laval. From the point of view of the twentieth century one sees him as a shadowy figure scarcely more tangible than the ghostly creatures that inhabit his great empty church or wail by night in his crumbled shrines. In Polynesia where the eternal languor comes down from the mountain tops like a cloak it is easier to doubt his existence than to explain him. Among the pitiful remnants of a dying people it is simple to condemn him. . . . And yet . . .

He must have been a genius, this man. Perhaps nowhere else in the world is the power of one brain, the relentless force of one will, so definitely proved. He worked with the poorest raw material on the face of the earth, the sweat and strength of a semi-savage people, and he wrought a magnificent work. . . . Crazy perhaps, but still magnificent. He forced the outward forms of civilization upon a race that knew nothing of them. Out of a nation which lived in huts of pandanus matting he fashioned a race of builders that went to death in carrying out his commands. And he left to the South Seas a mass of ruins more remarkable when one considers their source and evolution than those of ancient Egypt. One stands in tongue-tied awe before the evidences of his achievement.

One pictures him as a thin-lipped ascetic with smoldering fires in his gray eyes. A visionary in whose sensitive ears voices from heaven shut out the plaints of a tortured humanity. One senses the pride of autocracy that enveloped him. One sees him walking with bare feet over sharp rocks, sleeping on the floor of a stone cell, starving himself on a simple meager fare, torturing himself body and soul with sufferings that he could not recognize in his people. And one realizes that he was mad. His heavenly voices, like his genius for organization, engineering and architecture, came from somewhere in his cracked brain.

Père de Laval found on the island a population variously estimated at from two thousand to five thousand—a population unsuited by tradition, training and natural choice for any sort of manual labor. These were people whom Nature had always fed with tropic prodigality. They had only to stretch out a hand for food. Palm-leaves sheltered them from the weather and provided them with what few clothes they cared to wear. They were far from threat of war. Their lives were an idyl of sunny days and warm moonlit nights.

But Laval had seen a vision and his tremendous driving energy was too much for the resistance of the lackadaisical natives. They found it easier to do what this strange creature wanted done than to argue about it.

They arose in sleepy puzzlement to quarry coral blocks where he told them to. They carried stone as he directed. They sweated up the long slopes of the mountainside and they laid rock pavement in the roads they had graded according to his engineering. They saw the tall towers of the church rise up above the palms of the beach . . . and they must have marveled at their own handiwork. They built dikes out into the lagoon to make elaborate mazes for fish-traps. They constructed little chapels at intervals all through the village of Rikitea so that proper ceremonials could be held to celebrate the journeying of the king from his new palace to the cathedral.

They hauled their rocks to distant islands in the Gambier and there built large buildings called monasteries. On other islands they erected convents and on still others

THE LAST OF THE CANOE MEN
Boat made of short slabs as pictured in La Pérouse's chronicle

A Surf-Boat Lands in Bounty Bay, Pitcairn Island

schools for boys and girls. The foundations of a larger and more important school were laid in Rikitea and a huge house was constructed to shelter the makers of tapa-cloth and the weavers of matting. The king—destined to be the last of a long line—embraced the Christian faith. So his subjects gave him a suitable palace on the water-front after which they carried masses of coral up the long stone road to the hilltop where they made for him a residence close by the shrine-like tomb one day to preserve his bones.

Buildings—incredible masses of buildings—all of them squarely, massively and skilfully put together, made of Rikitea the strangest capital in the South Seas. The fame of them spread to the ports of the world where skeptics denied their existence. To-day, in their ruinous state, they are scarcely more understandable. Lack of care and the quick ravages of tropical weather have taken most of their roofs and rotted much of their timbering. But their walls still stand as Père de Laval intended them to stand. That the priest could have held in his dizzy mind the pictures of these buildings—their architectural and structural details—is almost beyond belief. That he could have translated his ideas into tangible form through the medium of the Manga Revans implies a force close to the superhuman.

He established a theocracy—a despotic government in which the king was only a nominal ruler. He organized a department of ecclesiastical police whose exploits still figure in the dark legends of the island. He expounded his own ideas of law and what is more remarkable got the sad-eyed populace to listen to him.

The bubbles of nacre, once in low esteem throughout the Gambier, poured into the treasury of the church. Some of them poured out again to bring vessels of gold and fine oil paintings from Spain. Native fingers not yet made spatulate by hard labor were trained to contrive delicate flowers and delicate glowing inlays of mother-of-pearl. The altars of Manga Reva and Aka Maru stand to-day unique examples of an art that had a hurried beginning and an abrupt end.

De Laval was undoubtedly a fanatic but he had a strange gift for impressing his fanaticism on others. The history of his régime has not yet been written and the tradition of it is sketchy, not to say reticent. But there seems to have been no resentment against the priest as a builder. There are stories that some of the royal family rebelled against his interference—notably a princess who offered a schooner captain a treasure of pearls to take her away. But there is no record of any wide-spread dissatisfaction among the workers who quarried the rock and erected the lofty towers.

The religious spirit fostered by the mad organizer apparently was something like that of the Middle Ages in Europe whence sprang the great cathedrals. Certainly there were Polynesian women who sought service in cloistered sisterhoods. And there were Polynesian men who cheerfully abandoned their three-fingered gods to enter upon a life of prayer and self-denial in the new monastery.

Somehow the priest found time to teach school, preparing other teachers to carry on the work. It was part of his plan that the blessed isles of the Gambier should have the greatest educational advantages in the South Seas. The appointment of a bishop was in prospect and the Golden Age seemed about to begin.

At which point a French man-of-war arrived in the harbor and an astonished functionary looked over the capital of the new empire and admitted that its like was not to be seen anywhere else in the world.

"But," he announced, "I am more interested in your

vital statistics. I should like to study the ratio between births and deaths."

These records showed one important fact: the birth-rate had dropped, and this it was easily seen was not due to new and more stringent marriage regulations so much as to the fact that most of the population had gone either to the new graveyard or to other islands where the building program was less ambitious. The Polynesian physique had failed to survive the strain of rock-hauling in the hot sun.

The city of God was finished but only a handful of men and women remained to live in it. Père de Laval was taken to Tahiti and placed on trial. The tribunal found him mad and he was kept in Papeete until he died. His body was brought back to Manga Reva and sealed up in the crypt of his church but even before that the disintegration of his great work had begun. His successors found themselves embarrassed by all of his splendid buildings and eventually sold them or allowed them to fall to pieces. The ruined populace shivered at the lonely echoes in the empty corridors and came in time to walk with ghosts—the most superstitious people in the South Seas.

To-day only the great church of Manga Reva and two lesser chapels remain intact to mark that mad period. Despite the difficulty of keeping such vast edifices in repair with so small a congregation the present pastor has succeeded in it. In little his work has been that of another De Laval for he has had virtually no help from the outside. . . .

The British pilot book dismisses Manga Reva with a brief note: "The natives are generally untrustworthy and lazy, and the population has fallen off because they pick up all the white man's vices and none of his better qualities." . . . One of the unacquired qualities being, presumably, an ability to haul rock.

CHAPTER SEVEN

PEARLS

The Footprints on the Ocean's Floor

GOLDFIELD in the days of its prime plus a vista of slowly waving coconut fronds and an obbligato of plaintive song; Spindletop after the first gusher stopping to rest by the opal waters of a coral basin; the Klondike, snowless and warm, against a back-drop filched from some musical comedy. . . . One must imagine all of these to envision Manga Reva.

The islands of the Gambier have been known as pearl sources since their discovery by Captain Wilson in 1797. Early travelers frequently visited them and the legends of fortunes carried away by the captains of whaling ships in exchange for a few glass trinkets or bits of cutlery are still in circulation throughout the Tuamotus.

Manga Reva ceased to be the name of a place and became a descriptive term in the ears of the adventurer of the early nineteenth century. To him the word meant pearls, just as Easter meant mysterious images and Tahiti meant women. When the missionaries came to the archipelago in 1834, the casual traffic must have been considerable—enough, perhaps, to warrant the belief that the tall ships would one day crowd the lagoon as they were beginning to crowd the harbor at Papeete.

But Manga Reva, the languorous haven of a people born to be gentlefolk in an environment that fostered the idea, lacked the equipment for making an Eldorado. Its visionaries were at least a hundred years ahead of their time.

Even to-day, with fortune at its threshold as fortune lay in the pebbles of Kimberley, it gives one the sense of melodrama being enacted in the wrong theater with the scenery left over from an extravaganza.

Wealth comes ashore with the pearl fishermen, in little tobacco sacks hung to belts inside their shirts—or perhaps in rolls of flimsy paper francs in their pockets. But there hasn't been a murder in Manga Reva within the memory of man and robbery is generally considered tabu as would be anything requiring so much energy.

There is no prohibition here. Wines and rum are brought down in quantities from Tahiti on every schooner. But there are no saloons or cafés or dance-halls. If the pearl-divers, after wandering about all day on the ocean floor, have energy enough left for roistering, they can always find a place for dancing, singing or even fighting, in one of the dark avenues where the palms or orange-trees arch overhead to shut out the moonlight.

And when the master pearlers meet as they sometimes do ashore and far from their camps, they show none of that distrust so prevalent in the atmosphere of the world's treasure towns. Here is Pedro Miller, born and bred in Manga Reva, smiling a greeting to his principal rival, Victor Berge, citizen of the world.

"I am glad you have come over from Aka Maru," he says. "I have some new babies to show you."

Both of them pause to tell the uninitiated visitor that a "baby" is not an infant in the local argot but a pearl of exceptional size or luster.

"Good," agrees Berge. "I've got one or two of my own. We'll compare notes."

So they sit down on the deck of the schooner or on the porch of Miller's house and examine the luminous beads that pour from tobacco pouch or paper envelope.

"This button is thirty-five grains," says Miller, rolling on to the table a thing of glowing light. "It would be better except for the cloud on the top."

Berge looks at it closely.

"There are two French operators in New York who can remove that," he says. "It's a slight surface bruise. . . . New York is the place for that kind of pearl. You won't get the price for it anywhere else." And so goes the conversation concerning men who can buy jewels and women who will wear them.

Presently there is a knock at the door. There enters Matura, Berge's Number Two Boy.

"You left this in camp," he says. "I thought maybe you want to show . . ." And he drops on to the table another pearl . . . a perfect sphere, clear and lustrous.

"Wonderful," says the admiring rival. "Murders will be committed for that pearl some day."

"Yes," admits the proud owner. "Murders have been committed for worse pearls. . . ."

But it occurs to the disinterested bystander that the murders which will be committed for these pearls are peculiarly the right of civilization. Here such jewels are topics for conversation, things to be carried about in the pockets of native boys. Nothing happens to them or to their owners. This part of Polynesia has its own code about such things.

On Manga Reva small talk divides itself into a discussion of two general subjects—pearls and *tu-pa-paos, tu-pa-paos* being ghosts. Of the two the pearls seem the least important, possibly because there are fewer pearls.

Much has been written about the Manga Revan *tu-pa-pao.* The natives believe implicitly in a spirit world less than a hair's breadth removed from their own. They walk in constant terror of the restless dead. They speak of ghosts as people of another and less mysterious community might speak of close acquaintances and so manifest are their beliefs, so vivid their accounts of supernatural visitations, that one feels the contagion of their fears and in time, perhaps, comes to see the things that they see or think they see.

White men are not immune. It is startling to hear them declare how on nights of the full moon they have heard the voices of long-dead Polynesians conversing in an ancient tongue—of the ghouls they have encountered in graveyards and of the terrible faces that have come to their windows on rainy nights.

No matter how skeptical a person may be he finds it a little difficult to laugh at these stories. He can not but feel the presence of the dead in Manga Reva. The whole creation of Père Laval is one vasty tomb in looking at which a person sees evidence not so much of builders who once lived as of a people who died. His imagination, if he is at all sensitive, repeoples the flower-grown paths with the men and women whose bare feet made them—as eery and intangible a crew as ever wailed by night or tossed fire balls across the burying-ground of the kings. And having evoked ghosts of his own he is on precarious ground when he comes to denying the experiences of other souls perhaps more psychic.

Manga Reva may not be the most superstitious spot in the world but it would be difficult to find another like it. A person may sit all day and listen to tales of black magic until the hypnosis of the recital dims his senses and focuses his vision on that world of shadows where every Manga Revan spends at least half his time. Not a native but has seen a ghost with his own eyes. . . . Not one who has not received his word of warning from those wandering ones who must long ago have realized the futility of warnings.

If he is unable to see these things for himself he probably has only himself to blame. Certainly if he is looking for ghosts he could not find a place where the supply is more lavish.

When a person is about to die in Manga Reva everybody knows it, for on such occasions the Old Man and His Dog come out of the lagoon. On a bright sunlit morning you can see their footprints coming up the beach of coral sand out of the water. They are clearly defined, these footprints, but not deep as would be those of a living man and dog. Several persons, including two Americans, who saw them state that the marks represent a pressure of not more than five pounds. And if this is taken to indicate that ghosts weigh five pounds it is undoubtedly an important scientific fact.

The prints follow the beach to a point opposite the house of the person about to die. Then they turn inland and are lost in the shrubbery. After the expected death occurs the Old Man and His Dog return to the lagoon and resume whatever work is done by ghosts in lagoons. No more is heard of them until another death is imminent.

Another tale, so often repeated that it has become virtually an article of faith, has to do with a conclave of men in white *pareus* who also have their residence in the opal waters. They stand in ranks on the coral floor against the face of a submerged cliff near Aka Maru, silent and dead with their white loin-cloths knotted about them like belts of stone. They were discovered there years ago, so the story goes, by pearl-divers; and numerous other pearl-divers have seen them since. The story of such encounters was to be heard in every pearl camp—repeated endlessly day after day and month after month until the rank of sunken dead men became as much a part of the Gambier's population as the living contributors to the census records.

With the coming of compressed air helmets and Victor Berge's gasoline-pump diving machines, the corpses in white *pareus* became less and less a matter of moment. A man in a helmet has more time to look about him than a "skin-diver" who must get down perhaps a hundred feet, pick up his oysters and return again while he is able to hold his breath. The machine divers worked in many sectors of the lagoon without finding evidence to support the old legend . . . but nothing is so difficult to kill as a ghost. So the tale survived.

A fairly hardened trader now in Papeete investigated the matter two years ago and returned with an inconclusive report.

"You'd wonder how so many divers came to tell the same yarn," he said. "About the time you think that the widespread circulation of the legend is just a local habit, some boy from a distant island comes up from the bottom with the same old description, the men in white *pareus* waiting there in the seaweed at the foot of the coral cliff.

"After you've heard that sort of thing repeated often enough you get to wondering if there might not be something in it. You know all the time it's impossible . . . but . . .

"I got quite interested in Manga Revan history and legend. It's very rich in incident and, of course, leads back eventually to the cannibalism that once obtained in all these islands. That may or may not give a clue to the story of the men in the white *pareus*.

"It is quite conceivable that the bodies of the chiefs were taken out into the lagoon and dropped over the coral shelf to prevent their being taken up and eaten by religious fanatics who hoped to obtain their qualities and rank. Old men have told me that such things were done. And admitting that much one doesn't have to strain one's imagination much to picture some process of petrifaction which preserved these bodies under water."

Then to Manga Reva came Victor Berge with the pearl fields of the seven seas behind him and the folklore of Polynesia at his finger-tips. His men had been diving some three months when he first heard the story of the sunken chiefs.

"I'll respect any man's belief in anything," he said. "I've been around enough to know that some people can see things that I can't see. But I'll say this: I've never seen a ghost and I've never yet heard of a yarn like this that would stand investigation. We'll take a look into the matter."

He called to Teora, his Number One Boy in command of one of the diving machines. And personally he piloted a course to the rim of the coral shelf.

"Hop off here," he directed. "Go down till you hit bottom and then come up and tell me what you see."

Teora went. Two minutes later the alarm bell rang—four quick strokes. . . . "Pull me up at once." And then another signal rapped out with the quick nervous energy of panic. . . .

His drawn face came into the sun a brown-gray as the helmet was lifted from his shoulders. He swallowed several times and sank to the deck.

"Did you see any men in white *pareus?*" demanded Berge.

"No, sir," answered Teora. . . . "No *pareus*. . . . I saw footprints on the floor of the lagoon. . . . The marks of many feet where men have walked away from the cliff."

And at that moment the ghosts of Manga Reva seemed very real.

There remains one more tale of ghostly manifestation.

The passenger to Easter had been ashore at Rikitea developing some test samples of moving-picture film. The schooner lay anchored about a hundred feet from shore, her boat drawn up on the sandy beach. It was one of the nights of the full moon when the spirit populace of Manga Reva is at the height of its restlessness. The lagoon was placid and frosty white as a sheet of aluminum but under the trees the shadows were dense and black and shapeless.

Midnight had long since passed when the developing was finished and the passenger began his long walk from Berge's headquarters to the mole. But he met no ambulant spirits on the road and heard no strange voices in his ears. Not until he had come to the corner where one turns to go down to the quay was he conscious that something unusual was going on. From the far end of the village came mutterings and then a whispering sound as if many people were stirring themselves.

The mole was deserted. No sailors were at hand to man the boat and the tide had run out. For five minutes the passenger worked to get some water under the keel. The noise in the village was increasing but he paid no attention to that. In another two minutes the boat was launched and the developing apparatus aboard and he was sculling back toward the schooner. He turned at the sound of running footsteps along the pier, came in close and stopped long enough for a breathless youth to leap over the gunwale. The panting one was revealed in the moonlight as Louie the Navigator.

"I waited for you a long time but then I missed you," said Louie as he took an oar. "I am very sorry."

Lamps had begun to shine in the houses of Rikitea and some one had lighted a fire in the road. Even from the deck of the schooner one could discern figures dashing to and fro under the palms.

In the morning a terrified populace was still clustered about the water-front and one heard authentic stories of the island's most recent visitation. An army of ghosts had swept through the town turning people out of their beds, wailing in their ears, and chilling their bones with the cold winds that generate in graveyards.

The passenger heard all of this and when he had the opportunity to speak in private he turned to Louie.

"What were you doing last night?" he inquired.

Louie grinned.

"I waited for you a long time and it was very lonesome," he said. "So I played ghost. I started in a house up near where you were. There are no locks on these houses so I got in very easily. I did not make any noise. The people were sleeping on pandanus mats with sheets over them. I made sad noises and I pulled the sheets off. They were frightened. So I went to the next house. I went to every house in the village. I am very sorry I was late."

"They'll murder you if they find out," mentioned the passenger.

Louie shrugged.

"It is no matter," he said. "They like ghosts here. I give them one. I have made them very happy. . . . Besides, now, I am going to pull up the hook and get out of here."

Ashore the fires of the night still smoldered and the terror of the rampant *tu-pa-pao* still hung heavy over the beach.

Chapter Eight

PITCAIRN

The Breed of the "Bounty" Mutineers

They came out of a crack in the sheer wall of the cliff—a cast from Treasure Island—in a surf-boat as long as a Viking galley.

The surf was rolling so high that they seemed to break right out of the sea and alternately they came into sight amid clouds of spume or disappeared in the caverns of water. Always their oars lifted and fell with mechanical precision like streaks of metal across the fading sun. They shot alongside the schooner, threw a rope and presently were clambering over the rails.

Up they came, as strange an assembly as ever was released from Neptune's graveyard. . . . Old whalers out of the New Bedford prints. . . . Mariners with square jaws and roast-beef jowls who might have just returned from fighting the Spanish Armada. . . . Dark, lantern-jawed men whose half-closed eyes undoubtedly had seen strange things done on the pirate main. . . . And humorous-looking lads who seemed to be on the point of proceeding with the opening chorus from *Pinafore*.

Their costuming was somewhere between bedlam and a white-elephant sale . . . coats emblazoned with gold braid . . . coats of white duck . . . coats of dungaree . . . coats of a mode that Fifth Avenue and Piccadilly knew before the war . . . trousers of pongee silk or wool or linen or broadcloth . . . shirts, sometimes dispensed with, of a pleasing and endless variety . . . head-gear, mostly of pandanus fiber but occasionally and effectively of the variety worn by officers on British liners. Virtually every line that flies the Union Jack was represented in the flag and wreath arrangements on these cap bands.

An amazing lot of people. Their faces belonged to a race of Englishmen unknown to the world since the British Navy shaved off its whiskers and adopted the svelte outline. Their clothes seemed to be part of an impromptu masquerade. And when they cleared the rails and started to speak English in accents that may have been known to the American colonies at the time of the Revolutionary War one doubted the evidence of one's eyes and ears.

Pitcairn has lived up to its heritage of race. The white strain, only fifty per cent. to begin with when the island was settled, is now dominant. The strange crew that pushed for space along the narrow deck of the schooner, save for one or two isolated examples, is white—made to look a little more villainous, perhaps, by the piercing black eyes of the Polynesian, but none the less white.

The boarders—one discovered with surprise that they were armed with baskets instead of cutlasses—grinned in toothless friendliness at the visitors and began a breathless cross-examination.

"Where are you from?"

"Tahiti."

"Where are you going?"

Out of habit one answers:

"Ile de Pâques."

"Where is that?"

"Easter Island."

"Easter Island! The man is going to Easter Island! Oh, brother, take me to Easter Island!"

There was an immediate clamor to this effect. It became evident that one could, with very little persuasion, cause the entire male population of Pitcairn to go a-voyaging to that outer rim of the world called Rapa Nui. With difficulty this new and interesting movement of an entire people was halted. With care one explained that the charter would not permit the carrying of passengers. The men of Pitcairn sighed and turned to other subjects.

Have you any bananas? Would you care to trade a flat-iron for a bunch of bananas and a pineapple? Do you carry any pearl shell? Have you any old clothes? The snarl of the sea was lost in the roar of many voices.

Pitcairn is possibly the best known of the South Sea Islands—certainly the one which has exercised the greatest influence on popular imagination. For generations its name has been a synonym for isolation, its people the children of loneliness. A little world that sprang into being amid violence and bloodshed it worked out its own destiny. A tiny cone of rock thrust up from a wide ocean it fostered a race which, in little, became a nation.

In December, 1787, H.M.S. *Bounty*, a sloop-of-war, sailed from Plymouth in command of Lieutenant William Bligh. George III was King of England. The American colonies had just accomplished their independence.

Britain, deprived of one source of revenue and trade expansion, was looking about for the improvement of others, in keeping with which policy it was decided to transplant the breadfruit tree on islands in the West Indies. For this purpose the *Bounty* with a crew of forty-five including a gardener was dispatched to Tahiti. Lieutenant Bligh was under instructions to obtain suitable shoots, carry them around the Horn, plant them in designated islands and return to England. The *Bounty* never came back.

The voyage to Tahiti was uneventful. The work of

gathering the breadfruit shoots was simple work and the natives—especially the women—were over-kind to their visitors. The chapter in the *Bounty's* history immediately following this pastoral idyl is common enough in the South Seas. The crew spent six months in the clasp of soft arms or gazing into smoldering eyes and found no thrill in the thought of putting to sea again.

Lieutenant Bligh recognized the signs of revolt. In April, 1789, he ordered his men aboard the *Bounty* and sailed out of Papeete harbor. In the Tubuai Islands he took on the provisions he had intended to obtain in Tahiti and set his course due south. Two days later—on the twenty-eighth of April, 1789—the crew of the *Bounty* mutinied.

Fletcher Christian, master's mate, was the leader of the uprising. He had been reprimanded shortly after the departure from Tahiti and a desire for revenge even more than the sybaritic lure of Tahiti ended the honorable record that night of a man long distinguished in His Majesty's service. Fletcher Christian gave the signal for the mutiny that he had planned and fortunately was denied a foresight of the destiny that he was preparing for himself. The crew broke into the commander's quarters as he lay in his bunk. They trussed him up and carried him on deck where they held a convention to separate friend from foe.

There was no bloodshed, no particular animus against Bligh or his fellow officers. A vote was taken and every one on the ship was given the privilege of joining the mutiny or putting to sea in a long-boat. Eighteen men were set adrift with Bligh. The *Bounty* sailed back to Tahiti with Christian in command.

Bligh's journey from that moment until he landed weeks later at Kupang, a Dutch settlement on the island of Timor nearly four thousand miles away, is one of the epic voyages of the South Pacific. He steered a course at once to Tofoa, an island thirty miles from the scene of the mutiny, encountered hostile natives and went away again leaving one of his men dead. Thence he struck southwestward over a poorly charted sea, through tempest and blistering sun, with only such provisions and water supply as could be obtained on hostile islands. And so he came one day to Kupang a gaunt shadow in command of seventeen other gaunt shadows, to move on via Batavia to England and turn the British Navy on a quest for the mutineers.

The *Bounty* in the meantime proceeded to Tubuai which had seemed like a comfortable hiding-place. Christian vetoed a plan for immediate colonization when he discovered that the supply of animals was small. He took the ship to Tahiti to stock it with pigs and food plants and returned to discover that the Tubuai natives had tired of him. They came down to the shore en masse to prevent a landing and so once more the *Bounty* went back to Papeete harbor.

All but eight men deserted Christian in Tahiti. Those who remained with the *Bounty* took Tahitian women as wives and six native couples as servants, after which they sailed away to the southeast looking for a place of settlement. In this fashion they came to Pitcairn where they landed in January, 1790.

Of the mutineers who remained in Tahiti fourteen were picked up by H.M.S. *Pandora* in the subsequent wreck of which four were killed. Ten were rescued and taken to England for trial. Four were acquitted, one discharged on a technicality, and five condemned to death. Of the five found guilty two were pardoned and three were hanged at Spithead.

The men with Christian were never to know the fate of those they had left behind but they understood well enough what they could expect if they were ever found. They tarried at anchor long enough to make certain that Pitcairn, despite its luxuriance, was actually deserted and then destroyed their ship.

Thirty Crusoes, cut off from the world for ever, toiled up the cliff wall from Bounty Bay and laid out a town. To the twenty-one Polynesians brought into the party at Tahiti the incident may have had no significance, for journeyings to far islands were the traditional lot of the Kanaka. But the nine white men who stood on the rim of the precipice and watched the burning hulk of the *Bounty* dive to her end under the breakers must have seen the meadows of England fading beyond the horizon. They must have understood that they were under sentence of death just as surely as if they had placed themselves on the gallows at Spithead.

For two years they lived in a sort of stunned quiet, cultivating land, building shelters, gathering salt from shallow pools in the rocks of Bounty Bay. Their life was a species of communism in which all their possessions were equally divided. The mutual loss of the white men served to increase their mutual tolerance. They achieved a peace that approximated happiness.

Then one day the wife of Seaman John Williams set out along the cliff to search for birds' eggs and fell to her death. Here was a situation which Fletcher Christian had never foreseen in his plans. There was no surplusage of women on the island and Williams' grief over the loss of one wife was not sufficiently poignant to prevent his demanding another. Christian and the other whites needed no gift of prophecy to forecast trouble. But Williams refused to listen to advice. He took a woman away from one of the Tahitians and so ended a brief sojourn in Arcadia.

The Tahitian men banded together against the whites. The sympathies of the women were divided. One wife

The Daughters of the World's End
(Pitcairn Island)

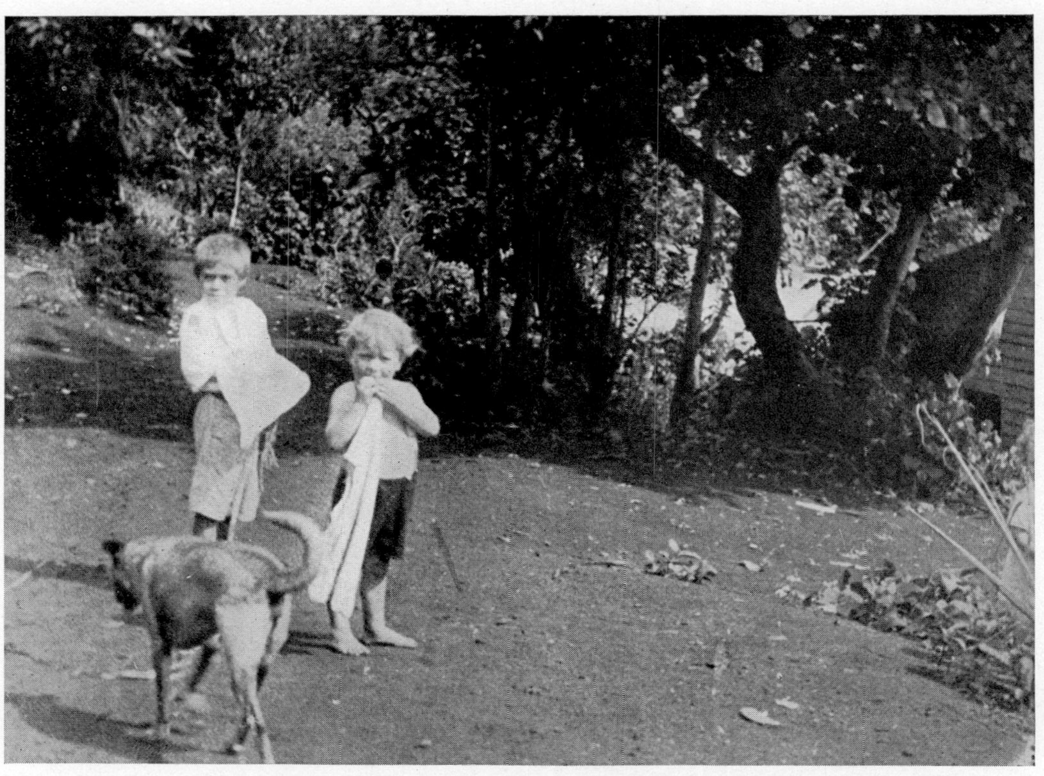

The Returning Dominance of the White Strain is Evidenced in the Children of Pitcairn Island

murdered Tulaloo her native husband as he lay beside her in a cave. Another gave the alarm when a concerted attack would have wiped out the mutineers. There were minor battles and skirmishes—bloody but without fatalities. The men slept in two armed camps with threat of death hanging constantly over them. The women sought to compel peace by flying from the island on a raft but were forced back from their suicidal venture by storms. One Timiti, a native, was captured and killed. And in this fashion went life on Pitcairn for another six months.

Until a few years ago a woman was alive on the island who had lived in this reign of terror. As a little girl she had spent days on end flitting from one cave to another with her white father and Tahitian mother sharing the fear that she could not understand. She had come to know hunger even in this paradise of plenty. And one dreadful night she had seen the final attack when the natives armed with axes came out of the bushes to murder the whites.

In the morning there were no more native men left alive, but few of the mutineers of the *Bounty* remained to celebrate the victory. John Williams, the cause of the trouble, had been slaughtered in the first rush and close to his battered body lay the corpses of Fletcher Christian, John Mills, Isaac Martin and William Brown.

William McCoy and Matthew Quintall had saved their lives by fleeing into the woods. Edward Young had been concealed by the women. John Adams had been wounded and left for dead.

The peace that might have been expected after this shambles never came. McCoy made a still of a teakettle and drank himself into delirium tremens with decoctions from native herbs. In his frenzy he killed himself by diving from the cliff on to rocks five hundred feet below. Quintall attacked Adams and was brained by Young.

Young died of tuberculosis. And so in 1800 Adams found himself the last survivor of the *Bounty*, alone on the island with twenty-five women and children.

The history of civilization on Pitcairn begins properly with Adams. He took a careful inventory of the results accomplished by the *Bounty* revolt, studied the well-filled graveyard near the settlement and had a vision. He saw in his dream that he would never return to England, a detail whose authenticity no one might have questioned. He saw himself atoning for the crimes of the dead by saving the souls of the living. He searched through the ancient chests of the *Bounty* until he discovered a long-neglected copy of the *Book of Common Prayer* and with this as a text-book he began the education of the children.

He taught them the advantages of peace and good-will and was immediately seconded by the tired widows. He instructed them in the rudiments of the Angelican faith and the English language and lived to see most of his charges able to read and write. When, in 1808, the *Topaz*, an American ship, visited the island the harmony of the colony was definitely established.

Shortly thereafter came a climacteric moment in John Adams's life. A British ship appeared off Bounty Bay and an officer came ashore to investigate the report of the *Topaz*. Adams made no attempt to hide himself.

"I am the last of the *Bounty* mutineers," he said. "I am willing to pay for what I have done. I'll go back with you and stand trial. The work I have started here will go ahead without me. I am sure of it."

But the captain shook his head. "I know nothing about the *Bounty*," he said. "I have seen nobody who had anything to do with the mutiny. I do not understand what you are talking about. And these children need you." He shook hands with Adams and went away.

There have been few additions of outside blood to the population of the island since that time. The descendants of the mutineers have multiplied rapidly—so rapidly that in 1856 an attempt was made to transplant them on Norfolk Island near Australia. Large numbers of them remained on Norfolk but three homesick families returned to Pitcairn in 1860. In 1864 twenty-four more people returned bringing with them missionaries of the Seventh Day Adventist sect. To-day, with a population of one hundred and eighty, the entire island is of that faith. Where Williams, McCoy, Young, Quintall and Christian fought the bloody fight their great-grandchildren stand on the cliff above Bounty Bay awaiting the end of the world. Many authorities would concede that it had already arrived.

Chapter Nine

ARCADY

A Life of Loneliness at World's End

Once—and not so long ago—Pitcairn was the most isolated spot in the Pacific. Not even Easter was lonelier. Far from the track of ships on regular voyages across the South Seas—without even a sheep ranch to insure the visit of one ship a year, the Pitcairners lived and died and waited for the end of the world with little or no outside assistance. Once every three or four years a British war-ship might pay a call at Bounty Bay to make sure that nothing had happened to the island. At intervals no more regular might come a mission ship to deliver gift packets and mail. But such events were so uncertain and so far between that they played no part at all in the community life. Mars could have seemed no farther from a normal world.

With the opening of the Panama Canal began a new era for Pitcairn. The island which had been merely a name in the vast white spot of the marine maps suddenly became a landfall on the route between Wellington and Auckland and London. Where once a stray schooner had seemed like a miracle there came great white liners and motor freighters and rusty tramps. Schedules that might have shown one sailing every half-decade now could be made out to show movements of two or three ships a week. The lonely island overnight found itself with the best mail service south of the equator and no list of correspondents.

There is no harbor at Pitcairn. For five miles—the entire circumference of the island—the sheer basalt cliffs rise like a wall from the sea. One little cove amid the rocks on which the *Bounty* was destroyed provides a dangerous passage for surf-boats and is the landing-place for Adamstown, Pitcairn's one village. Large ships calling at the island must anchor well off shore, ready to step away at the first change in wind.

So Pitcairn's release from isolation after a hundred and fifty years away from human ken does not mean that many new faces are seen in the settlement. The passengers of the mail packets plying between Cristobal and Wellington never leave their ships. They meet only those islanders who come out in the long-boats and the lonely plight of the women and children ashore is not much altered. From the edge of the cliff they see the ships come in and they see them go out, but any knowledge of what these miraculous things are like must come to them second hand.

The entire population was ranged along the path up the cliff wall when the surf-boat came back from the schooner carrying passengers. They cheered like a welcoming committee when the boat grated over the rocks and stuck her nose through the swirling spume on the steep incline of the landing. They cheered again when the bedraggled visitors had accomplished the four-hundredth foot of the dizzy path along the precipice. And they rushed forward to shake hands and to offer the hospitality of their homes.

It became evident here that the villainous appearance of the Pitcairn boatmen was not so much indigenous as acquired. The boat crews belong to an organization something like the volunteer fire departments of American villages. When a lookout sees a sail he rings a bell in front of the Adamstown church. Islanders close enough to hear the bell run for the cliff shouting "Sail ho!" The cry is taken up by householders on the outer edge of the village and by them is passed up through the barriers of jungle and rock to workers in fields far up on the mountain. In less than five minutes the message has gone completely around the island, and a hundred by-paths through groves of banana, pandanus, coconut and plantain are filled with running boatmen.

Just as they happen to be they come. In their work clothes, in their Sabbath best—sometimes in their wedding garments—they rush for the landing-place.

The boats are kept in thatched sheds which stand virtually on end on the side of the cliff. Runways made of saplings like a corduroy road run down from them to the black sands of a little beach. There are no rollers to facilitate the movement of the boat—no "ways" such as might be expected in a spot where the landing of a craft is equivalent to the placing of it in dry dock. Thirty or forty men seize the boat and drag it into the water or drag it out again by main strength—which after all is the keynote of life on Pitcairn.

When launched the boat is protected from the surf by one tall jagged rock. To reach the sea the boatmen have to steer past this obstruction and avoid another while they fight the waves over the saw-toothed threshold. When a breaker arrives with height and force enough to swamp them, they dive into it and are carried over the rocks by the swell.

Probably there are no better boatmen in the world than the Pitcairners. What they lacked in practise in the old days they make up readily enough now when ships are a regular sight on their horizon. Even so they do not always win the toss with the combers. . . . The little cemetery at Adamstown presents a dreary repetition in its headstones . . . John Young, Peter McCoy, Henry Adams . . . Died in Accident at Sea. . . .

Among the near-by islanders, particularly among the residents of the Gambier Archipelago, Pitcairn's closest neighbors in the southern ocean, there is a wide divergence of opinion concerning the descendants of the *Bounty* mutineers. One group—mostly traders who base their conclusions on past experience in the spread of thought and the creature comforts by means of ships—takes the position that the mail steamers from New Zealand and Panama have made of Pitcairn a community quite like any other under the British flag. Another group will tell you just as readily that the Pitcairners are now and always have been hermits whose simplicity is matched only by their woeful ignorance.

Both of these schools of thought are wrong.

The status of Pitcairn with regard to world trade has changed only slightly because Pitcairn can not produce enough of a surplus of anything to build up a market. The arrival of ships from the outside world has given the youth of the community no experience in travel inasmuch as funds are not available for the purchase of transportation and the steamships have no need to pick up crews at intermediate points. On the other hand the curiosity of the people has been aroused.

The watchers on the cliff see liners growing out of the smoke puffs on the horizon and they watch the same liners melt away into other smoke puffs. And they have heard much about such places as Panama and Cristobal and Wellington and Auckland and Sydney. They have resurrected the old geographies that a previous generation laid away in dust and mildew. And they have become conversant with the world's affairs.

One staggers up the cliff path under the weight of a heavy camera and is promptly relieved of the burden.

"The cinema!" says a pleasant voice. "We have never

seen one here. It would be too difficult to operate a projector. We have no electricity."

The voice belongs to a neatly dressed young man who identifies himself as a dental missionary of the Seventh Day Adventist faith.

"I have a brother in Wellington who is working on a new color process for film," he goes on. "Each frame is in three colors. In some of the former processes each frame had to be a separate color and the projection was done by means of synchronized filters working with the shutter. . . ."

The visitor gasps. This is not the Pitcairn he has heard about. Of course a dentist from Wellington may scarcely be classified as a native of Pitcairn . . . but the illusion is maintained by another voice, this time slightly accented.

"What is the speed of this lens?" inquires the newcomer.

He is told and responds with a flood of technical query.

"Have you a camera of your own?" asks the visitor.

"No. I have no camera. Sometimes we see them on this island but not often. It is hard to get supplies for them and we need our money for other things. But I picked up a book about optics on one of the mail boats and I am reading it."

Not all of the residents of the island are like that. But in the ascent of the cliff one hears much to evidence alert and inquiring intelligence. There is whispered speculation as to whether one may be English or Australian or American. . . . Then an occasional hesitant question concerning the popularity of Hoover or the likelihood of a federal enactment to enforce Sunday observance. These queries one learns later are echoes from the religious papers published in America by the Adventists and widely circulated in the South Seas. The papers were dry and republican during the recent presidential campaign and they stand against Sunday observance as an invasion of their right to observe Saturday.

On Pitcairn, as in every community whose inquisitive instinct has been aroused, one may find a wide variety of interest and an astounding fund of information on any given subject. The island is developing intellectuals who can and do think for themselves and on the other hand it is breeding as other communities breed a large populace of souls who fit their outlook to their environment. Pitcairn is the gossip shop of the Pacific. It repeats what it hears and it hears very little.

"You will be billeted with David for the night," said the young dental missionary as he turned from the cliff road into a by-path.

"Who is David?" inquired the visitor.

And the dentist smiled.

"I forgot," he said. "I should have told you that everybody here is called by his first name. There are now about two hundred people on the island and most of them belong to three families—the Adams, Young or Christian branches of the original settlers. You call them by their Christian names just to insure variety."

David turned out to be David Young, postmaster of the community, a quiet, soft-spoken man who in his day had traveled to Tahiti and beyond that to San Francisco and whose preference for the simplicity of the island was based on experience rather than hearsay.

"We shall stay at the house of a relative of mine who is in New Zealand," he said. "We could stay at my own house but I am afraid things would be a bit crowded there. In this house of my relative we shall have two bedrooms and a room to read in if we care to read. I have many fine religious periodicals with good reading in them.

"To-night for dinner we are going to a birthday party. Mrs. Brown's little daughter is two years old. But I suppose I should tell you before we go there that all this branch of the family are teetotalers."

The visitor hastened to speak his reassurances.

"I mean that we do not drink tea or coffee," explained David. "Some of our people drink cold water, although for my part I prefer it hot. Once this island grew large quantities of coffee. I have heard experts say that it was very good coffee. But I do not know much about such things because I do not like coffee and I think it is a good work to abstain from it.

"Men came here from New Zealand and even from London to look over our prospects for raising coffee and tobacco for export trade. We needed export trade, of course. We need it now. But our people felt that they should not grow and distribute things that they would not use themselves. If it is wrong to use them it is worse to distribute them."

David said this without pedantry, reciting history as he had seen it occur on the island. And one could not but contrast him and his fellow islanders with the ambidextrous reformers in other communities. Poor little Pitcairn, sorely in need of a revenue crop, is content to sacrifice her opportunity for a principle and to continue a hand-to-mouth existence which shows no likelihood of ending.

David led the way through a dark tunnel in a grove of banyans, plunged into a jungle of hibiscus and rose apple, and emerged into a clearing. He removed his cap and pointed his brown hand at a little fenced enclosure in which stood a headstone engraved with the name of John Adams, his birthday and the date of his death.

"So good came out of evil," he said. "Adams was a mutineer who had the vision and led our people back into the ways of light after bloodshed and murder and misery. And there must have been something about him that made him a leader. He wasn't afraid to speak up before the officers of the British ship that found him here. And the British didn't take him away in spite of the blood on his hands. . . ."

He sighed.

"He was different," he said. "I suppose that is why we are different. . . ."

And any one who has ever visited the island will subscribe to that.

From the very first day of its inhabited existence Pitcairn has been Crusoe's island with a steadily increasing number of Crusoes all of whom had to be fed, clothed and housed with what could be taken from one small rock pile in a vast ocean. It is Crusoe's island to-day, despite the fact that the great ships now pass by it to the leeward and generally drop anchor long enough for a deal in fresh fruit or yams.

"We lack iron here," was David's simple summary of the case. "That has always been the trouble with Pitcairn . . . no iron."

He led the way through another jungle of bananas, orange-trees and banyans and came presently to an open shed covering a forge. The air compressor was a simple leather bellows whose upper member was lifted up and pulled down by main strength without crank or pulley to aid. The forge itself was a pile of volcanic rock near which stood a small anvil mounted on a tree stump. At one side of the shed was a long bench made of squared logs with a strange-looking vise at one end of it.

"The vise came off the *Bounty*," said David. "It is all that remains of the smith's equipment. But it shows the foresight of the mutineers that they brought such stuff ashore. They were here twenty years before any one came to visit them so the only iron they had was what they had been able to salvage from the ship. At first they had to use up their tools to make nails and then when the tools wore out they had to use the nails to make tools."

Which in a way is the history of the island—a long experiment to prove the indestructibility of matter. For nothing ever wears out on Pitcairn. It is merely converted to some new use.

All of the houses are made of wood, which is scarce and difficult to get. Stone is more plentiful—in point of fact the island is a mass of it, loosely covered with volcanic ash. But one can not quarry stone without much more labor than is required to make a workable saw out of scrap iron on an obsolete forge.

When some one needs a house—and this phenomenon is not infrequent with a steadily increasing population—a group of volunteers, relatives or friends of the prospective householder, will go up to the mountain top and clear a patch of scrub hardwood. The logs are taken to a rude trench and laid across it lengthwise. Then one man gets into the pit and another stands over it to work the ends of a long saw—by which process the tree trunk is eventually cut up into boards.

The church and the administration building of the island, both of them two stories, are constructed of this hand-made lumber. To one who stands at the doorway of either building and glances across the pattern of saw-marks on the uneven floors, walls and beams, they represent an immensity of labor that recalls the ziggurats of Babylon. The gutters of the church are small logs, split and hollowed. On the hillside near the church where rapid drainage is necessary to prevent mud pits in wet weather, the emergency is met with wooden pipes. In a damp warm climate such as this, wood rots quickly. But when it goes there will always be more willing hands to make new planks and new pipes.

There are a few horses on the island, offspring of a pair sent by some experimental soul in New Zealand. They flourish fairly well until their arrival at an age when they might be of some use. At which time they generally contrive to break their necks. The Pitcairners feel no great sorrow about their going inasmuch as there is no place from the sea to the mountain top where a wheeled vehicle might be hauled. Such transportation as they require other than that provided by a sack carried on a pair of stout shoulders is made possible by heavy-looking wheelbarrows of a style that possibly dates back to the seventeenth century.

For many years there was no butter source. The Robinson Crusoes took ripe coconuts, grated them and added water to the pulp. The resultant milk made excellent baby-food and raised a cream like cow's milk. The cream could be churned into a fair butter substitute which in an emergency could be used for candle grease. And although bearing coconut-trees are few on Pitcairn and the necessity for vegetable butter making has been obviated by the regular arrival of such supplies from Australia, this primitive household chemistry is still carried on, perhaps out of habit, perhaps in fear of a day when something might happen to stop the boats.

Chapter Ten

DEATHLESS YESTERDAY

The Land of the Broken Hour-Glass

Fifty people sat down to dinner at the birthday party of Baby Brown—a set far different in appearance from that which had pulled the surf-boat out to the schooner. The young men were bathed and shaved and dressed in clean clothes which in their variety savored less of the masquerade than the costume of the boatmen.

The crowd was seated at a long deal table on a sort of enclosed veranda. As is usually the case on Pitcairn, the chairs of the household were few. But there was ample accommodation on benches that ranged along both sides of the table.

The menu was simple but plentiful: pea soup, cow peas, boiled chicken, rice pudding, baked plantain and such typically British items as currant buns and hot scones. Since the spread of the Adventist faith there has been a leaning toward vegetarianism, but some influence, perhaps an atavistic reminder of the lean years that were a part of the old isolation, has prevented the general adoption of the idea.

Darkness had come before dinner was served. The table was illuminated with kerosene lamps about which hung wisps of wood-smoke from the near-by kitchen. There was a crisp pungent scent of resin in the air, and save for the coconut-palms that stirred languidly outside, and the warmth of the breeze that came through the open windows, one might have imagined one's self a guest at a Thanksgiving celebration in Puritan New England.

"I think you will find the cooking very good here," remarked the dental missionary. "In a way these women are pioneers who must always be pioneers. They have to do the best they can with meager equipment and there is nothing like necessity to teach a woman how to cook.

"The baking is done in old-fashioned stone ovens—which nobody in civilization has been able to improve upon in two centuries. The ovens are merely boxes made with slabs of stone. When they are to be used wood fires are kindled in them and kept going until they are hot. Then the fire is withdrawn, the pans placed in the box and a slab set across the opening. Radiant heat does the cooking and does it as no baker's oven could do it."

A comment on the amount of work and expensive outlay of material to care for such a party as this brought a ready explanation.

"The women folk of the invited families bring along a lot of their own food," the dentist said. "That lightens the burden. These parties are a common thing. We have them on every provocation. After all, the social interchanges of a place like this are bound to be limited and we make the best of what we have."

The small talk of the table was as varied as the regalia of the boatmen:

"The schooner tacked twice before coming to anchor off the landing-place," announced one youth.

"She didn't tack at all," contradicted another observer. "She came straight in from the northeast."

"I tell you I saw it. . . ." This argument proceeds in subdued tones.

"There should be a cargo carrier in to-morrow, bound for Cristobal," says another voice.

And then:

"We should get a better price for pandanus baskets.

Two shillings isn't much when you have to prepare the fiber and bleach it."

After which:

"Well, if the kids want watermelon, give them watermelon. It won't hurt anything."

The dentist stirred himself suddenly from a discussion of automobiles he had seen pictured in the Wellington newspapers. "I'm forgetting how to talk," he said. "When you've been here a while you have nothing to talk about, so you just keep still. . . ."

The party adjourned to another room where such guests as could find chairs sat on them. The remainder of the party squatted on the floor. A brown maid played hymn tunes on a reed organ and sang a few verses to her own accompaniment. Then came David.

"Do you want to go to bed now?" he asked.

"Is it time?" inquired the visitor.

"Just as you wish," said David. "Here you can go to bed when you please and get up when you please. We have no rules."

He reached for his hat. So did the visitor. It was seven o'clock.

There was a good bed at David's billet, plenty of air from two open windows and a supply of blankets that became necessary during the night when the damp breezes began to wander up from the jungle along the cliff wall. But if a person is allowed to (or even persuaded to) go to bed at any hour that suits him, he is speedily aware that the arrival of morning on Pitcairn is something over which he has no control.

A bell rings. It is not yet daylight but there are promising streaks beyond the banyans in the direction of the sea. It may be, of course, that the bell is the voice not of a master but of a mentor. One need not get up unless one feels like it—such at least is the theory. On the other hand it certainly awakes one to the necessity for thinking about such things.

Housewives start wandering about the village for whatever reason is necessary to make housewives go from door to door at that hour. They stop at the corner in occasional knots and talk in loud clear voices, about the weather, the schooner, the whereabouts of James or John.

Dogs join them in conversation and chickens announce a readiness for breakfast. And after that even the most hardened citizen reaches wearily for his clothes. Sooner or later the sun comes up and confirms his conclusion that after all morn has arrived.

It was David's idea that his guest should see the hilltop farms and nothing that the guest could say tended to dissuade him. After a collation of bananas, pineapple, and bread and butter, he led the way along the cliff road above the landing-place and up toward the summit of the mountain. It was then only six o'clock and the boatmen were hauling their craft down the corduroy runway into the water. Out at sea the schooner was rolling and pitching after her fashion, and she had drifted so far away that she looked like an impromptu plaything tossed from the cliff. The boatmen themselves were scarcely more than amorphous dots clustered about a white chip.

Despite the earliness of the hour, the hill road was well traveled and not, as one might suppose, by men going to work. The farmers encountered on the upward climb were all coming down—all laden with bags of sweet potatoes and yams and bunches of plantain and bananas. Probably they had slept in the fields to be up at the first hint of dawn and have a sack of provisions ready for trade when the boat should put out to the schooner.

It was a heart-breaking climb up a slope of perhaps forty degrees. But it seemed to give David no trouble.

"You get used to the hills when you live here," he said. "You have to get used to them. There is no way to level the roads. And the steep grades give the lads the exercise they need to keep them in good health. The soil up here is very fertile although I must admit it's a little hard to get at."

The path came to an end after a time in a plateau that stretched about three miles in each direction toward the vast emptiness of the Pacific. Here the jungle had been beaten down and while an occasional path wandered across the countryside through arches of orange or groves of pandanus, the verdure seemed to be present on sufferance rather than through its own right and title to the land.

The flat top of the mountain was cut up into little plots of an acre or two each, closely planted and carefully tended. A few men were still in the fields when David brought his expedition safely to the top of the slope. They were working like figures from a Millet painting with hoes, rakes and wooden harrows.

"There are no such agricultural implements here as I have seen in other places," mentioned David. "But we do very well. Once, when the island had a population of one hundred and ninety, the British Government thought that we could not support ourselves any longer. So they moved the people to Norfolk Island. You probably have heard how large numbers came back. Now our population is nearly two hundred and there is still enough land left to support twice that number.

"The island is not, strictly speaking, a community enterprise. Before the mutineers died, they divided the land. Their children inherited and made other divisions to care for their children, and so it went on. Now everybody owns his little plot. But that doesn't mean much. If I can not raise enough on my land to keep me, I just go to my neighbor and tell him. He will let me clear some of his land and work it. A tenth of what we raise is taken to the tithe house and sold to the ships for the support of the church. Otherwise what we produce is our own.

"Of course this is the garden of the Pacific. We can raise anything here although, unfortunately, we haven't much of a margin left for trade after we feed ourselves. We never have a crop failure and this year the rats haven't bothered us much.

"I have heard that the rats came here with the mutineers. They probably came ashore from the *Bounty* when she was burned, and they never have had any trouble making the island support them. Last year they destroyed all our melons. This year we held a council and set traps for them. The traps didn't work so we trained dogs to hunt for them. When the dogs got lazy we made bows and arrows and we hunted them that way. This year, although we have plenty still with us, the pest is under control.

"That is how our people have been able to live on Pitcairn for a hundred and fifty years—by keeping vigilant and fighting their own battles. Within a few generations our population will be double what it is to-day and the island grows no larger. We are learning to conserve our resources."

Aside from the story of its romantic beginning, interest in Pitcairn Island is piqued by the fact that from its sadly jumbled ancestry is evolving a race that may be classed definitely as white. There is no doubt, of course, that the Caucasian strain in the Pitcairn breed is slightly less than the Tahitian. Elsewhere in the South Sea Islands, such a mixture has produced people with the brown eyes and brown skins of natives. Only at rare intervals does a half-caste show characteristics that might cause him to be mistaken for a white. In Pitcairn, however, brown skins have paled in six generations of close breeding. The types that one sees manning the boats or tending the farms are not much different from those one might find in similar situations in England or America.

A discerning half-caste woman of Manga Reva, well acquainted with the habits and thought of both sides of her ancestry, expressed this idea in puzzling over the fact that few of the Pitcairners wore shoes.

"It is so odd to see Europeans going barefoot," she said. "Of course we see natives going about all day that way and we think nothing of it because they are natives. But I have always thought that white people wore shoes." And she studied her own bare feet.

It never occurred to her that no amount of shoes could make the Pitcairners more European than herself any more than a supposed culture could make shoes without leather.

Scientists hopeful of fixing the status of eugenics in the development of the human race have here a laboratory ready to hand with a fine assortment of clinical material. Pitcairn's people are the brood of the *Bounty* with additions so slight as to be negligible. Very few outsiders have come here to stay since Fletcher Christian burned his stolen ship and began his great experiment in sociology—probably not more than ten in a period of a hundred and fifty years. There is little in the life of the community to attract one who has been reared outside of it. Only the cheerful hospitality of the people makes up for an austere Puritanism that began with John Adams as a reaction against bloodshed. So, while many men lingered for a moment at Pitcairn only one in a hundred stayed on. The

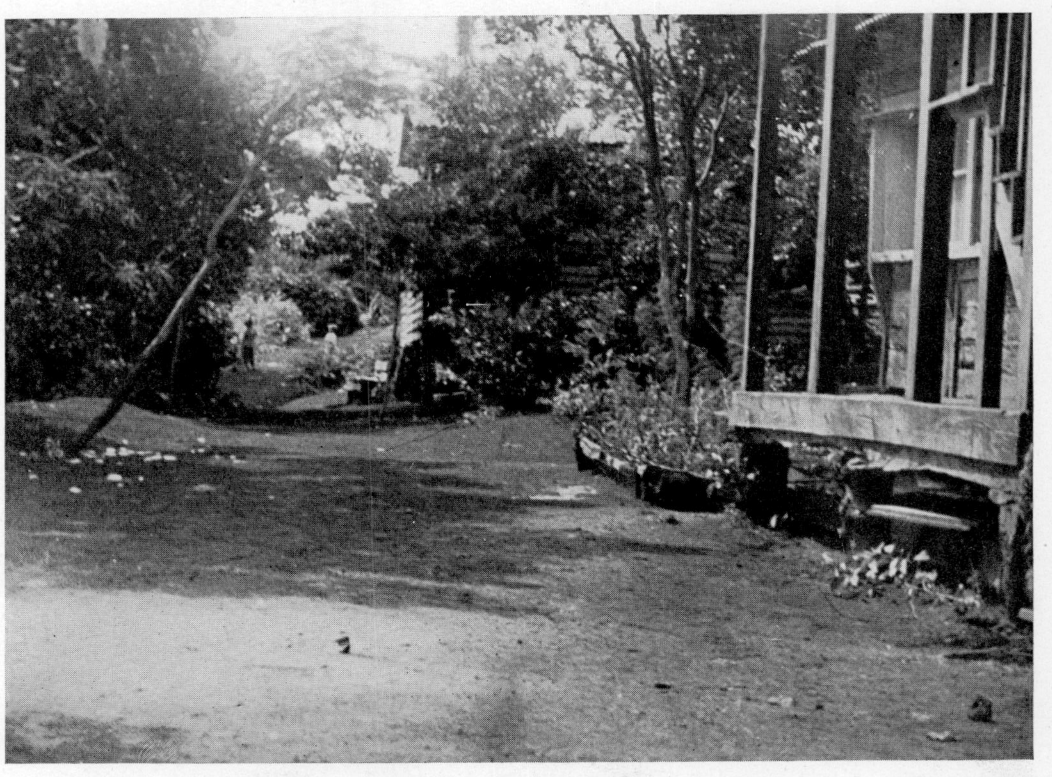

A Street in Adamstown, Pitcairn Island, Where Revolt Came to a Climax of Massacre

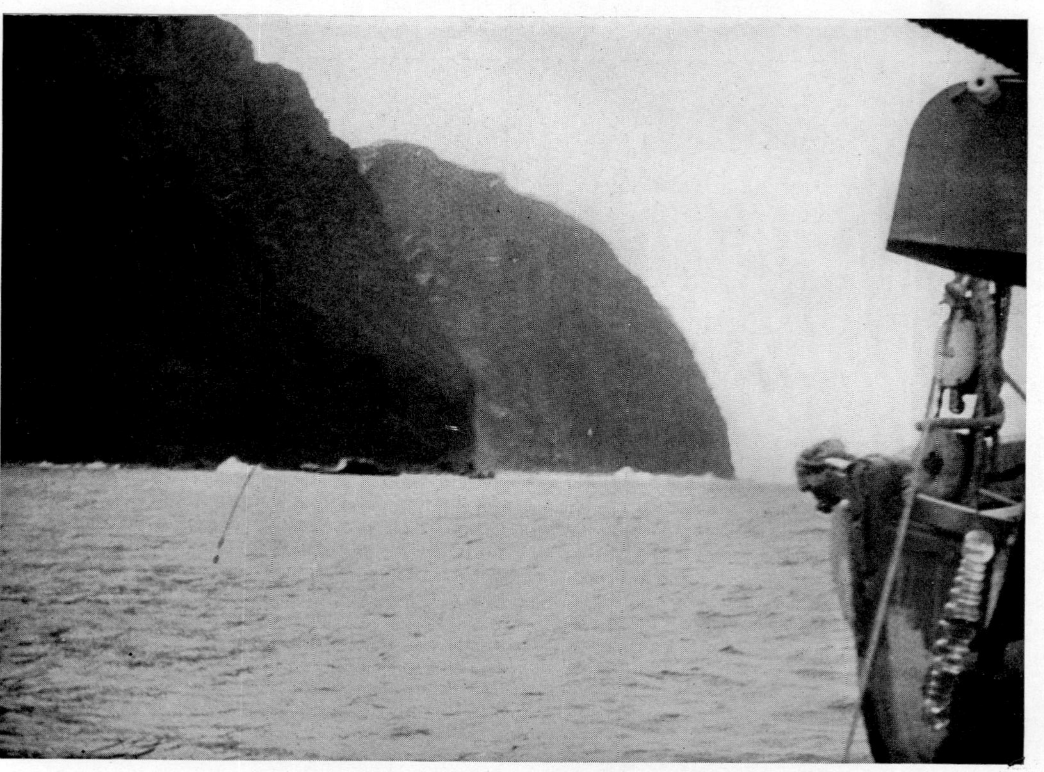

The Sea Road to Raraku, Easter Island

intermarriage of the families of the mutineers had been in progress for three generations before strangers began to drop their anchors off Bounty Bay and the influence of left-handed contributions to the strain is problematical.

Only the experts can say what has been the result of all this inbreeding. The casual visitor looks vainly for the signs of imbecility that such relationships are supposed to foster. A number of the islanders have no front teeth, and while this may be due to their ancestry it may also be due to an improper diet and ignorance in oral hygiene. One sees none of the physical freaks which are said to be the crop of a race gone to seed. The boatmen who push their craft through a roaring surf by sheer strength of back and sinew are normal specimens a little better developed than would be men of a similar age in a more critical and superior civilization.

Rose Young, who wrote a history of the island twenty years ago, mentioned as something odd enough to be worth noting, that some of her neighbors showed signs of mental irregularity. She reports, however, that this was only a passing affliction and never became epidemic.

Whether or not one may trust the accuracy of such an account, it is still possible to get an unbiased opinion about the islanders from one who has lived with them and yet is not one of them through any tie of birth or religion . . . an American who became acquainted with the community after a shipwreck and returned to it at a time of great sorrow.

"They're human," was his diagnosis. "They're just like any other human beings—not biological specimens. They've been kind to me . . . all of them. I'm not blind, of course. They have plenty of faults. They must naturally have a restricted point of view about most things. It strikes me that that is not so much a question of breeding as environment.

"And if you ask me I've seen just as many fools to the square inch in Los Angeles or Chicago or New York as I've seen in Pitcairn. Morally they're just about the same as other people. They're religious and they make some effort to live decent lives. We have a jail here and it's a waste of money to keep it in repair. There hasn't been anybody in it as far back as I can remember."

So rests the problem. Only the scientists can determine whether or not the descendants of Christian and Adams and Young are better or worse off for their circumscribed mating. It is difficult to judge the community by any standards common elsewhere in the world. The people of Pitcairn have never seen a moving-picture, an automobile, an electric light, a cake of ice, a street-car, a telephone, a theater, a shop, a miniature golf course, or an aeroplane. Save for such modern improvements as have been brought to them by the mail boats they are living in the world of the Middle Ages.

Yet somehow they contrive to talk intelligently about modern inventions whose lack, significantly enough, they seem to have survived with surprising ease.

CHAPTER ELEVEN

HURRICANE!

"Last Night the Moon had a Golden Ring . . ."

A WIND that promised to be a gale was roaring out of the northeast. Thirty Pitcairn Islanders, unmindful of the rain that streamed from their sodden clothing and splashed in the puddle at the bottom of their surf-boat, lay back on their oars and sang a hymn of farewell. Strong voices lifted the melody above the noise of the storm. Enthusiasm compensated for deficiencies of technique. And the words, jumbled now and then through lack of choral leadership, were all too easily understood:

"In the sweet Bye and Bye! In the beautiful land beyond the sky. . . . We shall part, never more, when we meet on the beautiful shore. . . ."

There was a hint of prophecy in that. A breaker came sizzling over the port bow. Another threw the surf-boat with a crunch of breaking wood against the schooner's side. And "the beautiful land beyond the sky" seemed much closer at hand than the dot on the chart which was labeled Easter Island. The hymn came to an abrupt end. The Pitcairners hastily pushed off and took an inventory of smashed oars. The foresail went up and the helmsman swung his wheel to port. The *Ramona* shivered and stuck her reluctant nose into the wind.

Pitcairn's rocky walls glowed briefly in the rain, then merged with the mists and presently were blotted out. Ahead lay some thirteen hundred miles of open water—a watery Sahara suddenly made animate with gray dunes rolling continuously from murky horizons—and at the end of the thirteen hundred miles a speck of an island ten miles long. Louie the Navigator, dripping wet as usual, came down the companion ladder and gazed sadly at the coffin of the chronometer.

From Pitcairn a course was laid southeast, and the schooner took her customary list to starboard. The weather, none too warm since Manga Reva, became definitely colder. One rubbed one's blue fingers and huddled wretchedly in wet blankets envisioning the ice-fields that stretched to the pole beyond the southern horizon.

The Tahitian sailors, suddenly aware of the distance they had come from their own warm island, went about over the slippery deck with bent bodies and chattering teeth. One by one they disappeared to emerge again in ill-fitting overcoats resplendent with brass buttons and gold epaulets and silver frogs. Their pandanus hats were discarded for officers' caps bearing the insignia of every steamship line known to the Pacific. And as they came aft from the flooded forecastle, they forgot the aches of the flesh and the perils of the sea. No weirder crew was ever seen on the deck of a ship—a beggar's opera in the setting of *Pinafore*. . . . Here were pursers, chief stewards, doctors and even captains of liners, scrambling over the deckhouse or reefing sail or clamped between the wheel and its gear-box—all of them wet and deadly serious and barefoot.

"Where did all this stuff come from?" inquired the startled passenger.

"Pitcairn," answered Louie the Navigator from the depths of a chinchilla collar. "We used to bring old clothes to Pitcairn and trade them for this and that. Now we bring shell and other things to Pitcairn and trade them for old clothes. The people of Pitcairn get the old clothes from the sailors on the New Zealand boats by trading the things we bring to them. Pitcairn is the second-hand store of the Pacific."

He glanced proudly at an overcoat that had once, no doubt, done service on the bridge of some New Zealand Shipping Company boat between Wellington and London. He shook himself with the effect of a collie emerging from a surf and looked appraisingly at the sailors clustered like a vagabonds' convention along the port rail—which at that moment was out of water.

"If we miss Rapa Nui and get to Valparaiso I wonder what the harbor master will have to say about our clothes," he said. The picture aroused by that thought was enough to make one forget one's troubles as, almost imperceptibly, the wet night succeeded the black day, and sleep followed bruised exhaustion.

One dreamed not so much of what might happen at Valparaiso as of the excitement in the neighborhood of Davy Jones's locker when this motley mob should step in full regalia from the broken hulk of the *Ramona* into the great concourse of the drowned. Even in sleep one was aware that there might be good reason for indignation among the moist spirits of the ocean. One recalled subconsciously that up in the north, now so much of a hazy legend, one greeted death in one's best clothes. It didn't seem to be quite proper to start upon one's career as a ghost in the rags and tatters of half a dozen oceans.

The next day the cook's galley was inundated and save for an iron ration broken out of cans in the cabin there was no food. The beef and biscuit were scarcely palatable but that seemed to make no difference. The sea was a region of cliffs with white edges eternally rising in menace at one's side. The cold increased. The wind held. There was no sun. It seemed to have been raining since the beginning of the world.

Over a table that refused to be anchored, Louie the Navigator spent long periods with slide rule and tables, and usually, at the end of his calculations noted his position on the chart with his thumb.

"Close enough," he would comment. "When we see the sun maybe we find out where we are. Right now we only know we are on the Pacific." And once, when a roller set the ship almost on her beam ends he picked himself from the wreck of a pile of dishes and amplified his statement.

"We are on the Pacific and I think we are still on the top side of it," he said.

Four days out of Pitcairn came the sun. Rain-clouds still banked the horizon to the west and south. But off the port bow was a band of light. And square in the track of the sun rode a ship.

She was a freighter of about ten thousand tons—a New Zealand boat—headed in a northeasterly direction presumably for Panama. She was well loaded and bucking a head wind and her speed was little greater than that of the schooner. For hours she rode along in an almost parallel track, moving gradually toward the rim of the world. The sanguine youth who had charge of the *Ramona's* little radio set signaled her repeatedly without result. Flags sent aloft with considerable effort brought no sign of recognition. There was no sign of life on her decks, no flash of glasses in the sun on her bridge. One watched her slide over the edge of the world and into the clouds without knowing more of her than if she had been the Flying Dutchman.

A passing ship. . . . The incident seems scarcely worth recording. But in the life of one who saw it there will never be an equal thrill or a depression like that which came with its vanishing. For a moment one became aware that other human beings were abroad on the lonesome water. And for days thereafter one scanned the tumbling sea, empty once more from rim to rim, as if hoping for a repetition of the miracle.

The wind changed in the night . . . swung around without warning to the southwest . . . piling up surface water to meet a continuing swell from the northeast and producing a motion that threatened to tear the schooner's ribs apart. The rain ceased although water continued to sluice along the decks. The barometer started upon a steady descent.

On the tenth day out from the Gambier, the twenty-eighth from Tahiti, Louie shot the sun. For the first time since the stopping of the chronometer he seemed worried.

"We are away south of our latitude," he said. "That is not so bad because you must come south to get your easting. But the sun does not come out and unless he comes out maybe we don't get another chance to take the latitude and then we go north of Rapa Nui. Now we go east nor'east and there is going to be bad weather."

There was no comment to make on that. The weather already seemed as bad as anybody could ask. The sea in its motion and aspect looked more and more like the North Atlantic in midwinter. The sun, after one brief struggle with the cumulus clouds at noon, went out of sight again. The water was gray with long streaks of white. The sky was the color of a neglected corpse. The swell was choppier, waves were higher. And Easter, a difficult objective even in fair weather, was some five hundred miles away.

That afternoon the barometer came up a bit, then fell rapidly. The wind veered fitfully—shifting in four hours from port to starboard and back again. The swell seemed to have a volition of its own and the tides that broke over the bows were seldom from the same quarter as the wind. For most of the day Louie stood behind the man at the wheel, leaving his post only for hurried peeps at the glass. At nightfall the rain came again. But the thin hand of the barometer had begun to move to the left. Louie gazed at it unimpressed.

"You had better strap yourself tight in your bunk," he said as he turned away. "This looks like a hurricane. . . . First the wind it blows on one side and then on the other and the sea goes crazy. Yes, I think it is a hurricane."

"And then what?" inquired the passenger. "Do we get through it or don't we?"

Louie shrugged.

"Who can say?" he answered. "I think maybe we do. This ship is deep. It takes a lot to upset her. If we could close the hatches. . . ." He paused to consider the possibility.

"And can't you close the hatches?"

"Maybe the one forward. . . . But there is a loose cover on the hole in the floor of the cabin here and I think we can't do so much with the cabin hatches. We do what we can." He shouted some orders in Tahitian. Sailors started about the decks with ropes lashing down everything that was movable. The captain went forward and presently the foresail came down. Only a wisp of forestaysail remained to defy the rising gale.

The night came down, black and impenetrable. Now and again the ship's bell clanged and the helmsmen silently changed watches in the rain. No one slept.

With the morning came a lull in the wind though the rain was still a torrent. The barometer continued its nervous dance. The schooner was riding on a fairly even keel but pitching fearfully. The horizons were gone. Black shifting hills rose close at hand and thundering crevasses yawned ahead.

At noon the gale came again, this time out of the north. The cook had got his fire going again and some hot dishes were steaming on the little table in the cabin. The menu has been forgotten. The captain and Louie and Hippolyte the supercargo, and the passenger to Easter were standing where they could find a foothold balancing plates of soup when, without warning, the ship heeled. Dishes crashed, the table overturned, and most of the soup went into the passenger's bunk. Luncheon was over.

The shifting of the wind had brought the rain around into a new and uncomfortable quarter. The deluge began to break under the little awning that hung across the cabin and after deck and pour in cascades down the ladder. The berths on the starboard side were filled with water.

The passenger hung a raincoat at the end nearest the hatch and turned about so that he might meet the storm with his legs instead of his head. A gust of wind took the coat out on to the deck and overboard. Not that it made any difference. The bed was wet from end to end.

The air was filled with noises like the screaming of shells with a background of musketry and hissing steam. The wind from the north had a velocity of about seventy-five miles. It lifted the little deck awning like a balloon and had the effect of slewing the stern toward the south. Simultaneously the Pacific broke over the bows. The crew, still wrapped in the second-hand finery of Pitcairn, came scrambling aft with water streaming down their worried faces and trickling in blue-black rivulets from their coat tails, to bind the awning under the main boom where it could do no more damage.

After that there was no check to the cataracts that sluiced about the deck. One became dizzy in an attempt to see where the water was coming from. Probably half of it fell right out of the bottomless black overhead and the other half was picked up by the ship's plunging nose as she drove across the wind.

The air had turned as bitter as that of the Argonne in a well-remembered November, but on deck half of the crew were stripped naked and the other half tying *pareus* outside of their Pitcairn overcoats.

It was significant that two men were always at the wheel. Near by stood the captain, placid as a figure in a fountain and as wet. Occasionally the faces changed, but the grouping, dimly visible through the opalescence of the rain, never varied. Up forward the pump was clanging.

The wind veered again. Old Tomas, the dean of the crew, was standing behind the wheel-box, wedged between that and a mooring stanchion, and tying himself into a buttonless slicker with bits of fish-line. Something hit the ship . . . a solid crashing blow. She began to heel over to starboard.

One saw the hurricane reflected in Old Tomas's face which changed in an instant—brown to lead—lead to ashes. His eyes were points of black in rings of white. He looked unseeing over the helmsman's head at something coming across the deck-house. There was fear in his eyes . . . stark horror. He caught hold of a piece of rigging and then went out of sight as Niagara fell on him.

Steadily the schooner listed to starboard. Through the leaking port—three feet above deck-level—one saw the rail go down into a frothy cauldron and disappear. One waited for the alternate roll—the lift. But there was no lift. The water came higher over the rail. It rose level with the port-hole and blackened it. A trickle started down the wall through the poorly calked fastening.

One swung a leg over the edge of the bunk and tried

to get out. The ship was settling—settling. . . . Slowly, inevitably she was heeling still farther toward the starboard with the deliberation of an old man measuring the depth of his grave with a palsied leg. The waves were breaking over the deck-house. There was a crash as part of the forward hatch cover went overboard. The sea began to pour into the hold. Over . . . over . . . the careening toward the starboard was faster than one could move to get out of the berth. The signal cord to the little engine coop was broken and hung about one's neck like a thuggee's noose.

One minute—two minutes—the ship lay within two inches of a course to the bottom. The alarm clock by the binnacle light ticked off the seconds unheard in the din. Then the hulk shook herself and raised the starboard rail perhaps a foot.

Freed of the strangling cord one got out on deck, walking, somehow, on the side of the ladder. The deck was almost vertical—all of it, save the port side, under unplumbed depths of water. The wheel was almost submerged and the three men clinging to it disappeared time after time as the seas broke over them.

Canvas and rigging and smashed wood strewed the Pacific and the mainmast only a few feet over the waves seemed ready to snap in the squealing wind. A rope had been stretched between the rails. It gave a handhold whereby one might fight one's way upward to the port side and out of the clutching water. There one found dubious refuge in wind that tried to tear one's fingers from the rail or flail one's brains out with flying wreckage. Three or four of the crew were held by hasty lashings to the rail. The other sailors moved miraculously through the breakers up forward doing something to the forestaysail. Among them was Old Tomas who had won his way across the deck-house roof when it was already well under water.

A hawser snapped with the report of a howitzer and more canvas went into the sea. The crew up forward had finished its job and now clawed its way up the sloping well deck to the dubious safety of the port rail.

Over the side of the deck-house came Louie the Navigator. Most of his clothes were gone. Waves fell and flattened him. He raised his head, shook the water from his eyes, breathed deeply and crawled onward. The wind caught his body and twisted it. Still he fought his way aft, inch by inch. Water drove him toward death on the starboard. Water slammed him with bone-breaking force against the port rail. But always when the froth receded he was moving again. He came to a mooring stanchion and took a turn of rope about his bare chest, then sprawled limply in a tangle of gear to get his breath.

The battered passenger clung to the rail close beside him. Louie saw him and grinned.

"Bad weather," he shouted—and his voice seemed to be a whisper coming from a great distance. "I tell you she is rough."

The passenger nodded.

"How long do you think we'll last?" he inquired.

"I don't know," said the youth. "But I think it would take this tub an hour to get to the bottom steaming full speed."

Conversation was interrupted by another comber which rose on the port side and dropped on to the ship with force enough to break her back. When it had receded Louie raised his head again.

"If we live until morning we have fresh meat," he said philosophically. "The anchor chain fell on the cook's pet goat."

Again the ship listed to starboard. Louie released his

hold on the rope and dropped himself into the boiling whirlpool about the wheel. He disappeared and came up again like a diver—reached for the wheel and missed—emerged again from the cauldron aft of the wheel-box and came forward, swimming—caught at the wheel once more and held on.

The ocean floor at this point was ten thousand feet down. Only about six inches of that made any difference to the *Ramona.* Her list must have been less than forty degrees. It seemed ninety. One knew instinctively that the tilt which would start her for the bottom was a matter of minutes and seconds. And then the miracle happened. The wind which had driven her down, struck from a new quarter and picked her up. The starboard rail came back into sight with a jerk that flattened the crew on to the deck.

The men at the wheel had won. The schooner came up into the wind. The captain looked up at her bare sticks as if surprised to see them still standing. So began a drift that lasted until two o'clock the next morning when the wind went growling into the southwest.

It was still blowing with gale velocity but the odd behavior of the barometer had ceased and the swells were conforming to the direction of the wind. The hurricane center had passed on and a mere gale seemed like a matter of no moment. The passenger bound up his fractured ribs with adhesive tape from film cans, crawled into his bunk, wrung the water out of his blankets and went to sleep.

Death under certain circumstances may wear a welcome guise as in war or in a hot jungle or in the feverish mirage of a desert. But it is a singularly uninviting prospect, this vision of dying in the loneliest spot in the world's emptiest ocean with a chill sky overhead and sharks waiting in the black water.

Chapter Twelve

RAPA NUI

The Island of the Dead

THIRTY-ONE days out from Papeete; position uncertain. The hurricane had gone on leaving ears so stunned that ordinary noises of the sea were whispers in silence. The stiff breeze from the Antarctic seemed negligible. And battered bodies were no longer conscious of the mountainous rollers that would pile up for days in the wake of the storm. The sky had been black at eight bells on the previous day. It seemed to have been black for ever . . . two shots at the sun since Pitcairn.

Louie the Navigator had taken a reading from the taffrail log, studied his rough notes on wind direction and velocities and stuck a pin into the chart.

"We are somewhere near here," he had commented. "I mark it with a pin because it looks better. Actually I could make it as close as we know anything about with my thumb. If I guess the drift right maybe we do well. If I guess wrong then, *voilà,* the south pole."

In the morning at five o'clock there was conversation out on deck—an unexpected sound that broke into a sleep which had been undisturbed by the hammering of the pump. One crawled out to discover Louie giving instructions to Old Tomas who held the wheel.

"You ought to be in bed," remarked the passenger.

"I have tried that," said Louie. "I can not sleep. Ile de Pâques is not large. But the ocean is large, I can tell you. And soon I will know whether I am a good guesser."

So he stood for many minutes with his chin on the edge of the deck-house staring forward through a network of spars and rigging into the darkness. Then suddenly he straightened. Simultaneously Old Tomas gasped. Up forward the pump ceased to function with one quick bang and there was a sound of voices in the forecastle.

Dawn was just cracking over the eastern horizon dead ahead. The sky was filled with its customary bank of heavy clouds. A thin drizzling rain had come from the south and seemed to fill all the world save for one rift squarely in the schooner's track—a flat-arched opening like the front of a titanic theater. There the sun was shining, scintillant gold as it broke through the beads of the rain. And silhouetted against this background of light rose the square profile of a headland. . . .

Easter Island, outpost of the earth.

Louie the Navigator kept his bloodshot eyes fixed for a long time on this smudge across the sunrise. He nodded his head gravely.

"That is either Rapa Nui or South America," he said. "And I don't think we have come far enough for it to be South America. . . ." He turned abruptly, went down to his bunk, crawled in on top of his instrument cases and was instantly asleep.

The island grew importantly as one approached it. Details, readily identified from map data and pilot book notes, took shape in its profile and had the odd effect of making it seem like something one had seen many times before. The headland first seen climbed higher out of the water to be recognized as Rano Kao, the ancient crater on the southwest corner of the island.

For a time the saddle of land between Rano Kao and the northern craters lay below the horizon. The northern peaks themselves were hidden in the rain-clouds.

Then, little by little, these elements of Rapa Nui's strange topography came out of the haze—at first in the form of two plateaus with three little islands between them, then gradually lifting above the rim of the sea as integral parts of one high rock wall.

Whatever the explanation for it, one looked at last on Easter, a vision denied to countless questing mariners—and out of one's own experience was able to draw a hint of how it might have been reached by the prehistoric wanderers who populated it. For nearly two weeks out of Manga Reva the schooner had been running through storms in which the sun had been hidden and instruments useless. The fate of the chronometer had been forgotten in contemplation of the greater evil of black skies. Twice since Pitcairn there had been severe tempests—one a hurricane. And this morning when the sun broke its little crevice in the cloud bank, the *Ramona* was headed not only toward the land but in a direct line for the charted anchorage at Cook's Bay. The ancient instincts of Louie the Navigator had succeeded where his sextant and logarithms had failed.

Without ever having set foot on the island one could quarrel successfully at this point with a cock-sure theory regarding the original settlement of Easter. It had always been held that the Polynesian voyager could not have made any protracted boat trip from west to east in these latitudes because of the prevailing trade winds. At this season of the year—says the pilot book—the trades should be blowing continuously from the southeast. As a matter of fact there had not been a single southeast wind for two weeks. The hardy canoemen of Polynesia might well have started from Manga Reva, and barring gales which are by no means a daily occurrence, could have fought all the head winds encountered by the *Ramona* with no great effort. The currents in these waters seem to follow the winds and are of small consequence.

As a person feels his bruises and recalls how the decks looked with the Pacific cascading over them he is willing enough to concede that the pioneers did not come from Rapa Iti (Little Rapa) two thousand miles to the westward. To start on such a trek would be asking much of luck. And a person suspects that the name Rapa Nui (Big Rapa) came, as has been said, from a misunderstanding of terms when so many Easter Islanders were taken as slaves to Peru. Te-Pito-Te-Henua, the old inhabitants called it—the navel of the earth—and that name, a weary voyager might hazard, seems apropos.

Easter Island as one approaches it from the west presents a long, dazzling panorama of blue-gray hills splashed with gold, a vision that seems, after thirty-one days of rolling on an empty ocean, to be as uncanny and ephemeral as a mirage. But as one comes nearer the coast and colors begin to show themselves through the morning mists, one becomes aware that the pastel quality of the other South Sea Islands is manifestly lacking here. There is none of the softness about these peaks that jungle growth has given to the mountains of Tahiti and Raiatea. They stick up on the horizon, harsh and bare, shaded by varying tints of sere green until they step back into the dim violet of the distance.

The coast-line rises from a high-plumed surf in cliffs which in places are a thousand feet high. Nowhere in the thirty-five-mile circuit of the island is there a real harbor. Nowhere is there a sign of water coming down out of the heights to the sea. Landing must be effected by means of small surf-boats guided with skill over spiky barriers of volcanic rock. Spongy masses stick out at right angles from the shore all across the western side of the island and from many sections of the south and east . . . black piles with fantastic and forbidding shapes—a prodigious slag-heap.

Behind these little promontories rise the cliffs, sheer planes slashed by the ocean and colored with bands of red and gray and black depending on the class of rock that the numerous volcanoes dumped there before the sea began its carving. Still farther inland the hills reach up to the sky-line—a series of cones flattened at the top and slightly rounded at the sides but as symmetrical as if they, too, had been constructed by some forgotten race of engineers. The headlands at the three corners of the island reach unbelievable heights. The altitude of Rano Aroi on the north cape is 1767 feet; Rano Kao on the southwest corner 1327 feet. The eastern cape is well over a thousand feet high.

The seacoast between these mountains is comparatively low but the ground in the middle of the island rises again and is covered with the button-like erections of dead craters.

Over the hills ride continuous veils of mist—clouds that are born in the steaming spray of the surf and carried by the constant winds across the land, to sprinkle salt on a soil already doomed to barrenness.

All of these things give a clue to the character of Rapa Nui long before one sets foot on shore. It is a dead land . . . dead as the craters that guard the corners of its triangular coast-line. One does not need to stare into the vaults of the burial terraces or disturb the endless caches of human bones to know that Easter is one with Karkemish and Nineveh and Angkor—a land whose struggle is over and whose history, though scratched in ciphers, is none the less completed.

The schooner, cautiously testing the washes and currents, came to anchor a few yards from the wreck of the French bark *Jean,* sunk by the German Pacific squadron early in the war. One goes ashore in the long-boat and steps to land over a mole constructed of stones that were once a part of a prehistoric tomb. And there one faces the native population to whom a visitation from the outer world is as important as one might expect it to be on the mountains of the moon. They press down to the water's edge, gazing wide-eyed and silent at these newcomers to their weird little world—curiosity but not too much friendliness in their glances. It is traditional that visitors have brought no good to Easter Island.

They are people of a peculiar strain. Despite the fact that their costuming consists mostly of the cast-off clothes of Valparaiso some of them are neat and good to look at. Many of the men are handsome. Their women—some of them—come closer to the romantic descriptions of the belles of the South Seas than one may find in the weary thousands of miles to the west. But they are a mongrel race. Only their brown eyes and skins and their black hair give them classification as Polynesian. Their features bear the national characteristics of the crew of every ship that ever was wrecked on the island. A long history of tragedy is stamped on their sullen faces.

And in looking at them one remembers the puzzles of Babylon and Angkor whose people vanished with the collapse of their culture although the blood of the builders flowed on unchecked through the heritors of their ruins. This race could not have built the great works of Easter. It is undoubtedly of the same flesh as the engineers and artizans. Spiritually and culturally it is not even distantly related.

The people cluster about the visitors, some of them afoot,

scores of them mounted on scrawny horses with saddles made of sheep's wool pads and bridles made of thongs. And in a dense press one moves forward toward the village of Hanga Roa, the last remaining settlement on the island.

It is purely curiosity that brings them into the procession. The strangers from the boat, of course, may be possible customers for spurious wooden gods and imitation tablets of script. Aside from that they have no great significance in the social life of Easter. They are considered by the populace merely as a species of fauna that comes seldom and soon departs.

A person senses this as he plods along in the red dust, jostled by the villagers at his elbows, pushed by their scrub horses at his heels. He feels annoyance at the crowding, the heat, the clouds of flies, the smells and the attitude of the throng with which he walks. Then suddenly they break silence and speak with one another in a language somehow familiar.

The stranger experiences a sense of shock. He knows now that, mongrels as they are, he can not dissociate these people from the mystery of Easter. They are as much a part of it as the grim gods that lie prostrate on the seacoast or stand sentinel on the crater of Rano Raraku. This dialect which they are chattering is spoken in one form or another as far west as Madagascar, as far north as Honolulu and as far south as the islands of New Zealand. The puzzle of one small island, however baffling and important, momentarily becomes a mere detail in the greater puzzle of Polynesia itself.

Hanga Roa village is a cluster of clapboard and sheet-iron huts set among a straggling grove of trees which, save for a similar grove at Mataveri on the slope toward Rano Kao, are the only trees on the island. One is surprised to discover that the village has ideas of importance, a sense of dignity and all the properties and machinery of law which permit it to play at being a seaport.

One is met by a prefect of police, a youthful Chilean in gaudy uniform, who wishes to examine one's passports and other bona fides. But he does not press this demand without due respect for official etiquette. He lets it be known that he is only the law-enforcing functionary of the island. The administrative officer is the sub-delegal, the governor, who, of course, will have business with the ship's papers. It is suggested that one go first to pay a visit of courtesy to the governor after which the prefect of police will be found awaiting in his headquarters behind the church. So one plods along through the dust to the house of the governor.

It is only in recent years that the Chilean Government which controls the destinies of Easter has gone to the trouble of providing all these legal tokens of its existence. From the time that France conveniently turned its head and permitted the sale of the island until long after the war, governors and prefects of police were institutions concerning which Rapa Nui had never heard. One finds it hard to believe the evidence of one's own vision when one sees a flag flying from a pole in front of an unpainted shack and discerns the official sign over a swinging gate: "Isla de Pascua" and with it the Chilean coat of arms.

The governor proved to be a kindly old gentleman with the profile and manners of a Spanish grandee. His office consisted of a rough desk in an unplastered and time-stained room. Clouds of insects swept through the unscreened windows and steaming heat dripped from the bare board walls.

The natives seemed to hold him in the utmost respect but it was apparent that they understood nothing of official privacy. They followed the visitors not only to the door but, in so far as they were able, right into the room. They packed themselves about the wall adding to the stifling atmosphere the heat and reek of massed bodies.

"You are welcome," said the sub-delegal after a perfunctory glance at the papers. "It is not often we have visitors here. You can see for yourself that our accommodations are not of the best." He smiled as he turned his head to include his quarters and his self-appointed staff.

"I wish I might invite you to stay for dinner," he went on. "But there are times when true hospitality is best served by failure to offer any hospitality at all."

The passenger promptly suggested that the governor dine aboard the schooner. But he shook his head sadly.

"It is better that I stay ashore," he said. "I must warn your captain that this coast is treacherous. If the wind changes he will not be able to stay in Cook's Bay. It will be safest for him to sail about the island continuously. If you want him you can hang out a flag at Hanga Roa landing. As for me, this is my post and if I went aboard the schooner and the wind changed I might be a long time getting back."

There was further small talk, translated from Spanish to Tahitian and thence to French . . . comment on the opening of air-mail lines between North and South America, a word or two about recent naval conferences—or rather naval conferences that had been recent when the governor last heard from the outer world—polite inquiry as to the possible hardships of the trip from Tahiti, the wish that there might some day be another meeting in some more civilized place, such as Valparaiso. For the moment one forgot the crowding natives, the dense atmosphere, the flies and the grim desolation that spread out

Eat-Man Cave
A scene of cannibal rites near Hanga Roa

Mataveri Ranch
Save for the grove here and another at Hanga Roa the island is treeless

From the Ranch House
Looking out through cool greenery toward the bare slopes of the volcanic blisters

The Ascent of Raraku
The crew of the *Ramona* carrying the motion-picture equipment to the image mountain from Tongariki inlet

to the horizon beyond the windows. One became aware that charm is independent of environment. The grim chamber might have been a drawing-room in a home of culture and all because of one man's magnetism.

It seemed scarcely proper, when one was once more in the meandering road, to speculate on the political vicissitudes that might have sent a man like this to such a post. His affairs seemed to be particularly his own. One suspected that he had taken his assignment to exile unquestioningly and would finish his service without complaint. Which, after all, is not the least of Easter's puzzles.

The office and living quarters of the prefect of police were found in what had been the sacristy of the now deserted church. The room was no better—certainly no worse—than that of the governor. And like the house of the sub-delegal was jammed to capacity with natives.

The voice of the law was loudly sonorous and the person of the law was dazzling with red piping and gold braid. There was much more formality in the examination of passports than had attended the stamping of the ship's papers. Ears only imperfectly sensitive must have caught the rumbling of the ponderous wheels of government as they revolved endlessly in this important cabinet.

"Leave the passports with us," commanded the prefect. "We shall study them to-morrow and acquaint you with our findings in due time." After which he conversed for some time on the status of pugilism in the United States and closed the interview by extending temporary permission to walk about the island. One emerged from his office aware that whatever had been the status of Rapa Nui before his coming a new era was well on its way.

The only industry of Easter Island is a sheep ranch covering most of the south coast, operated by Balfour

Williams & Co. of Valparaiso under concession from the Chilean Government. It is because of the ranch, established half a century ago when the whaling ships made the island a port of call, that the annual ship comes out from Chile. Only for the few pounds of wool that it produces does civilization remember that Easter exists.

To-day, despite flagpoles in front of the administration house and gold frogs on the breast of a prefect of police, government, authority and retribution are symbolized in the native mind by that deity of the new culture: The Company. The governor may sit importantly at his desk and receive deferential visits from the officers of infrequent gunboats, and the prefect may insure observance of his orders by force of arms. But such things are innovations of no consequence. Up there on the hill where Rano Kao lifts up out of the sea is the ranch-house of Mataveri where it has been since the earliest memory of the oldest inhabitant. Men have come and gone. Some have ruled. Some have been murdered. But always The Company has persisted, its power unshaken by criticism or revolt, its hold upon the land seemingly more eternal than that of the old stone gods.

Of recent years the natives have come to resent The Company. The revelations of local prophets, the arguments of returning wanderers have fostered the theory that the acres of Easter belong to the people and that the ranch and its people and its silly sheep should be eliminated for the good of the community. But little has come of this feeling.

Fear, always the principal ingredient in the atmosphere of the island, has seized upon the ranch where two white men stand face to face with a sullen hatred. But on the other hand it has enveloped Hanga Roa. For the subdeities of The Company control the food supply.

Once, when Easter was Te-Pito-Te-Henua, the people got along very well without any ranch. It was possible to keep body and soul together with such yams and plantain and poultry and fish as native industry was able to provide for itself. But the old plantations have dwindled more rapidly than the population. Easy work for The Company has provided a diet of fresh meat and condiments and wheat flour and things that come in tins from Chile. And whatever may have been Rapa Nui's plight before the coming of the white man and immediately after, it seems certain that quick starvation would follow any attempt to reestablish the ancient régime.

Quite possibly the people are little concerned with this remote contingency. Like all Polynesians they find that to speculate on the future produces nothing but headaches. Once when they had vineyards they burned the vines for firewood. Fruit trees have suffered the same fate. They killed off an important supply of wild fowl by improvident gathering of eggs. Bred in a tradition of immediate need they have never considered it good policy to go hungry to-day in order to stave off hunger to-morrow. And so it is no fear of what might happen if there were no Company that prevents a racial uprising.

Rather it is a form of tabu, surviving from the days when The Company impressed its will on the land and exercised a godlike power over life and death. Resentment may lead to violence—even to murder—but it never quite destroys the habit of submitting to authority.

Easter Island learned as other corners of the globe learned of the white man in a succession of tragedies.

One may pass over the eighty years that followed Roggeween's landing in 1722. The Dutch navigator was followed by others like him—explorers, land-seekers, pioneers of empire who were concerned only with the making of charts and the hoisting of national flags. Gonzalez, Cook and La Pérouse came and went, paying scant attention to the culture of the island, agreeing that it was too poor and unproductive to warrant any argument over its sovereignty.

Early in the nineteenth century, however, came visitors of another type, American ship captains on sealing expeditions in need of crews. And repeatedly the Kanakas of Easter were seized and taken away for duty on the white men's ships.

These raids were sporadic and made no great inroads on the population though they served to convince the natives that white people never came to Easter for any good purpose. A new feature was introduced into the island's scheme of life—distrust of those who came from the sea. As a more poignant and more tangible consideration than the ancient tabus it probably did much to undermine the influence of the old gods and to obliterate the remnants of the ancient culture.

In 1862 the old order was definitely overthrown. New guano fields were being worked by Peru and labor was scarce. Attempts to find workers among the Indians of Chile had failed and the cost of transporting coolies from China proved prohibitive. In this emergency slave ships were sent out to raid near-by islands in the Pacific and Easter was not too far away.

The raiders came ashore with gifts which they strewed about the shore at Hanga Roa. The skeptical populace kept for a time in the hills, but in the end curiosity and cupidity overcame caution. A few hardy spirits ventured down to the coast and gathered armloads of trinkets. Others followed them and eventually most of the three thousand men and women on the island came hurrying over the hills to see what the kindly visitors had brought.

More trinkets were tossed to them and they threw away their war clubs and spears in a mad scramble for the spoils. The raiders closed in on them.

The Peruvians attacked simultaneously from several points along the shore and so were able to knock down and tie scores of the islanders before a general alarm could be given. When the people at last were aware of the trick and fled back to the hills, a thousand of them lay trussed on the rocks.

Among the men thus captured were numerous savants or *maoris,* scores of the royal line and the last of the *ariki*—the great chiefs. It was this fact, rather than the wholesale removal of a third of the population, that finished the Rapa Nui culture. The long line of kings was broken and attempts to reestablish the hereditary leadership were beyond hope of success.

The captured natives were taken to the guano fields and put to work. Most of them never came back. While their seizure had been more or less secret, their arrival at Lima could not be concealed and wide-spread diplomatic protest resulted. The French minister called upon the Peruvian Government to repudiate the raiders and repatriate the slaves, and eventually his plea was heard. The Rapa Nuis were assembled at Lima to be shipped home, but of the thousand taken by the raiders nine hundred were dead—victims of smallpox, tuberculosis and other diseases of civilization.

Before the remaining hundred could be put aboard a ship, they too fell victims to smallpox and only fifteen lived to see Hanga Roa. Even then there was no end to the tragedy. Smallpox followed them to Easter and spread across the island almost overnight. Perhaps another thousand died before the scourge was ended.

Here begins what has been called the Christian era of

Easter. Whaling ships had brought word of the island to Valparaiso, stirring the missionary zeal of the "Congregation of the Sacred Heart" a Roman Catholic order, and in 1864 Brother Eugenio Eyraud came by schooner to Cook's Bay.

His arrival was inopportune. The memory of the slave raid was still vivid and the natives were suspicious of his motives and hostile toward his white skin. They stole his clothes and his food, forced him to work for them and subjected him to all the cruelties they might have reserved for the Peruvians. Eyraud, whose letters show him to have been a man of much deeper faith and determination than many missionaries who followed him, bore all these indignities without complaint. But when, in 1866, he returned from a visit to Chile, he brought with him Father Roussel who if no more devout was certainly a hardier spirit.

The natives resumed their persecutions and for a time forced the missionaries to remain barricaded in their house. But persistence, even in missionary-baiting, is beyond the talents of the Polynesian. Eyraud and Roussel eventually went abroad about the island and, after one encounter in which Roussel beat a man about to stone him, were unmolested. Brother Eugenio died in 1868 of tuberculosis which was completing the work of the smallpox in the depopulation of the island.

By that time Father Roussel had become a power in the community. He had convinced his charges of a disinterested spirit and had won their confidence. In a way he gave them the leadership of which they had been in need since the kidnaping of their chiefs, and soon after Brother Eugenio's death he was temporal as well as spiritual director of the island. In one person he combined the *ariki* or hereditary chief, the *maori* or savant, and the *ivi atua* or soothsayer. He was at once the figure of law and justice and a protector against malign spirits and evil visitors. And then came Dutrou Bornier.

Bornier, a veteran of the Crimean War, held a trade commission from Alexander Salmon of Tahiti and on behalf of his patron had been touring many of the lesser South Sea Islands. He landed at Hanga Roa from a ship that had brought two missionaries to assist Father Roussel and straightway looked over the island to determine its commercial possibilities.

The whalers were still coming into the Pacific through the Strait of Magellan at that time and Easter Island, far from being an isolated spot, was well located on their course toward Tahiti. Bornier found that there was plenty of land aside from the yam plantations that could be used for grazing purposes and he envisioned a ranch on which sheep, horses and cattle might be raised for the Society Island trade.

He conferred with the head men of the remaining families—all of which had been gathered together at Hanga Roa—and offered to give them calico for the miles of waste acres along the south coast. They agreed and, for a few bolts of red cloth, fixed their marks to deeds by which Bornier became the legal possessor of more than two-thirds of the island. The missionaries protested without result and dropped the argument. Bornier put up a house at Mataveri on the foundations of some prehistoric erection, took a native wife and for a time consented to peace.

At this time Easter's population had been reduced to less than a thousand. Slave raids, smallpox and tuberculosis had taken it well along the road to extermination. Virulent disease seemed to have been checked temporarily at least but the birth- and death-rates very nearly balanced each other. It was doubtful whether the next generation would see one person alive on the island. In which situation Bornier announced his intention to send three hundred natives to the sugar plantations on Tahiti.

The missionaries rebelled and precipitated a bitter struggle. Bornier, who had shown considerable sympathy toward their work, publicly denounced them. He set up two ship's cannon on hills overlooking Hanga Roa and sent occasional shots into the village to indicate his command of the island. He established at Mataveri a church of his own for the express purpose of undoing all that the priests had done. There with mock ceremonial he unmarried couples who had found the sacramental contract of the missionaries tiresome. He released young native nuns from their vows, took away their veils and added them to his harem. And finally he achieved what he had set out to achieve when he put three hundred men and women forcibly aboard a schooner and dispatched them to Tahiti.

So ended the war. Father Roussel obtained permission from his superiors to move to Manga Reva and a ship was sent for him. When he went aboard virtually the entire population of the island followed and would have sailed with him save for the refusal of the skipper to carry so many. One hundred and seventy-five were sent back to shore, which number constituted the entire population of the island in 1871. Bornier was murdered shortly afterward while stepping from a ladder in front of his house. The news of his finish occasioned no surprise.

The Salmon interests inherited the ranch from Bornier and on the death of Salmon the land passed to the Brander brothers of Tahiti. The Branders disposed of their interests to the Chilean Government in 1888. And so began the current chapter in the history of Easter.

To-day the census shows a population of nearly four hundred and this despite the devastating effect of indigenous and cultivated diseases including syphilis and leprosy.

The spark of Hotu Matua, the great founder, may be half smothered in ailing, miserable, mongrel flesh, but it is still alight. All of the virtues of the image-makers and their empire-building kings may have vanished save their tenacity. Beaten down, scourged, all but stamped out, the race still carries on, surviving not only its own heritage of evil but its acquired blessing of civilization. There is something pathetic about it, and something admirable.

Chapter Thirteen

THE PADRE'S COFFIN

The Strange Resurrection of Father Rivero

The rain stumbled on the tin roof; a whistling wind drove streamers of water across the porch and spattered the screening which covered the open door. There were eery noises in the orange grove and the cannonade of the surf had become a continuous roar.

"Nice night," commented the manager as he arose, walked around the end of the table and adjusted the kerosene pressure lamp. "If the captain of your tub knows his business he'll run her about ten miles out to sea and pray."

"She's been through worse weather than this," answered the Man from out Yonder.

"But not in this neighborhood. This coast was just made for ships to pile themselves up on it." He opened another tin of cigarettes, then sat down once more, not to smoke but to cock his head at an angle as if listening for the crash that would mark the finish of the *Ramona.* The uncanny noises, the throbbing of the island, the drive of the rain through the light beyond the threshold and the state of nerves harassed for more than a month made all of this seem like an act from the Grand Guignol.

He sighed presently and put a light to a cigarette.

"When you write the story of this island," he said, "save a place for the man who brought his coffin here from Chile."

On the face of it, that seemed like a good idea.

"Easter has gone back to the ways of the heathen now," he observed. "It didn't have far to go, for all its outward show of Catholicism. But few of the natives now alive will forget this hardy spirit. He was Father Rivero of Valparaiso, a splendid humanitarian and a man of great doctrinal attainments. He taught these birds at Hanga Roa that it was wrong to steal sheep. And that's what did for him. His ideas of reform were too far ahead of the times. Everybody in his congregation figured that sheep-stealing was one of the ends for which man had been created and the elders of the people wouldn't stand for any such subversion of the old traditions."

"But the coffin?" mentioned the inquisitive Man from out Yonder.

"Oh, yes, the coffin," he remembered. "Well, I suppose I might as well tell you the whole business as it occurred. History is always the better for a few facts." And he was silent for a moment as he marshaled the details in their proper order.

The rain continued. The roar of the surf struck a new crescendo.

Father Rivero was one of the favorites of the diocese of Valparaiso—he said.

He had served long and faithfully in a parish. And as far as parochial work is concerned, he was what most ecclesiastics would consider well off. He had a good church, a comfortable house, willing and intelligent curates and a congregation that caused him little loss of sleep.

It worried him. Whenever opportunity offered he would call on the bishop and explain to him the danger of stagnation that attends the routine of a city pastor.

"I live in nice surroundings," he would mention. "And I have three meals a day, and my parishioners are all good people who could easily be cared for by some young man who needs experience in caring for good people. As for me, I feel that I should be out somewhere in the wilderness carrying on a work against odds, suffering a few privations for the good of my soul. In other words I should like to be sent to Easter Island."

"I wonder if that's far enough," commented the bishop who had heard this same story regularly for a number of months. "I suppose it will have to be. . . . You can't get much farther and still be in Chile. . . . All right. You may consider the post as yours. You are now the spiritual adviser of Isla de Pascua, and you may get out to your new position as soon as you can, and when you come back your old parish will be waiting for you."

"I don't think I shall come back," sighed the newly made missionary. "I shall probably stay there indefinitely. Easter Island is a savage place."

The friends of Father Rivcro held a great banquet for him. Many of the notables of Valparaiso were present. There were speeches and testimonials and tearful farewells. And at the end of the proceedings a gift which, it had been announced, was useful as well as ornamental was brought in for solemn presentation. It turned out to be a fine oak coffin.

"This is one of the few things we might give you which is certain to be useful on Easter Island," said Don Enrico who spoke in behalf of the donors. And Father Rivero was visibly touched as he accepted it.

"This is just what I shall need to remind me of my purpose in going to Easter Island," he said. "I shall keep it always with me—or just as close at hand as it is possible to keep so large and obtrusive a gift."

The annual ship sailed for Easter three days later and with it went Father Rivero and his coffin.

The new pastor landed to discover most of the population on the beach and he was surprised to discover that his overtures of friendship evoked only a sullen response. The natives had been their own spiritual advisers for some time and they felt that a pastor must certainly interfere with some of their best theological decisions. However, they refrained from any violence at the moment. There would be time enough for that.

They stole Father Rivero's hat and five of his shirts while escorting him ashore. And he smiled bravely.

"A simple kindly people with no idea of property rights," he diagnosed. "It is clearly time that some one came here and informed them of their duties to society."

Percy Edmunds, at that time manager of the Easter ranch, suggested that the new pastor take up his residence at Mataveri. But the priest declined.

"My place is with my people," he said. "I can do so much for them. I can point out the error of their ways and comfort them and join in their simple pastimes."

"I think not," said Mr. Edmunds who was a great deal of a realist. "The simple pastimes of these charming people are murder, mayhem, robbery and arson."

The pastor smiled at this quaint conceit. He proceeded to the village and installed himself in a lean-to at the rear of the church—the shack later dedicated to the functions of the police. There, until the boat which had brought him sailed back to Chile, he was unmolested.

The ship left on a Tuesday. On the following Wednesday he was aroused by the sound of pounding on the roof over his head. He went out and discovered one Teodoro, usually a calm, not to say lifeless, parishioner, perched on the ridge-pole swinging a hammer.

"What on earth are you doing?" inquired the priest.

"Getting nails. What did you think I was doing?"

"But that's my roof."

"So it is. . . . But you are our brother and we are your brothers and so everything you have is ours. . . ."

Father Rivero sighed.

"I don't want to take any undue credit as a prophet but something is going to happen to you, my brother," he said.

"Not while I have the hammer, most honored of our family," replied Teodoro, and he went on pulling nails.

That night it rained and the roof leaked. In the morning Father Rivero brought his complaint to Mr. Edmunds as the only representative of Chile on the island.

"I understand," said the manager. "But I don't see what you are going to do to correct the situation. These people have developed the highest kind of socialism. They believe in common ownership of property—that is to say anybody else's property. They steal our sheep and they steal our horses and every now and then they raid our store."

"I think I see the way of it," said the priest. "They are misinformed. An educational program seems to be indicated."

On the following Sunday he preached his first great sermon. His text is of no great moment except that it had to do with property rights. Inasmuch as he spoke in Spanish, which few of the congregation understood, he was not assassinated immediately, and by the time a suitable translation got around he was safely locked up in an old stone cistern.

"We can't submit to anything like this," declared Teodoro indignantly. "What right has any man to come here and tell us that it is wrong to do the things our fathers and our grandfathers did? If we listen to him we dishonor our ancestry. It is plain that steps should be taken."

"What do you think we ought to do with him?" inquired the one-time sacristan of the church.

"Killing him would be about as effective as anything,"

observed Teodoro. "And that plan has the added merit of being about the quickest thing we could do."

There was enthusiastic acclaim. The idea was universally accepted but it could not be worked, chiefly because of the dispiriting lack of cooperation on the part of Father Rivero. He dodged five rocks, a hatchet, a knife and three bullets and that took him well over into the fall of the year. He was still on the alert when a gunboat showed up in the harbor. Through the agency of a little girl too young to recognize him as an enemy to the community, he sent a letter to Mataveri and after a while six men under arms came into the village. They entered the house of the priest and carried out his coffin.

The populace stood by indignantly.

"He is sending away his beautiful coffin," observed Teodoro. "That means he intends to defy us and live. As soon as the boat leaves we can burn his house down and smoke him out. I wonder why we didn't think of that before."

But why go on with a story when everybody knows the end of it? When the gunboat was well past the eastern headland breasting the rollers of the two-thousand-mile ocean track to Valparaiso, Father Rivero stuck his head out of his coffin and asked for a glass of water.

"Do you wish to alight?" inquired the solicitous commandant.

"Ah, no," replied the ex-missionary. "I wish to lie here and meditate on the fact that I can get out of this thing whenever I want to."

Chapter Fourteen

SCORNFUL GODS

The Weird Puzzle of the Pacific . . .

THE ship drops anchor well out from the eastern headland, a long-boat picks its way through snarling currents, lava barriers and mountainous surf, and one goes ashore presently in the shadow of a burial vault to experience all the sensations of landing on another world.

No other graveyard of man's hopes and works is like this either in its aspect or its atmosphere. In Egypt and Syria and Mesopotamia we see beyond the crumbling pyramids and columns and ziggurats of forgotten cities into a period definitely past and definitely dead. We know the builders of Angkor only through their ghosts—ghosts that have become thin and wan with the passage of the centuries. We may concede that these makers and destroyers of empire were quite like ourselves but there is no doubting as we stir the lizards in their crumbled palaces that they have gone from us. Time has not paused for them and automobile tires are leaving tread-marks in their chariot ruts. Whereas on Easter . . .

It is difficult to describe the weird spell of this barren island. One is instantly conscious of the difference between it and other human reliquaries. Chiefly it seems to lie in the fact that there is no dividing line between prehistoric past and the present. The old order has never given way to a new. Antiquity here is not something that one can study only across a chasm of centuries. It persists.

At the gates of Damascus a person thrills at the thought that he has turned back the calendar two thousand years. Here he does not need to turn back a calendar. In the ruined cities of the Khmers, of an evening when the moon is full and the loose-headed drums are sounding, the wanderer feels that the clock has stopped. On Easter he has the uncanny certainty that there never was any clock.

It may be the permanence of the great stone figures—a permanence suggested by the air of disdainful superiority that envelopes them. It may be their background of legend; but surely something about them gives one the impression that the grandiose carvers and the swashbuckling engineers are not yet dead. For the moment they have laid down their tools, these immortals. They are asleep perhaps in their canoe-shaped huts or squatting about the tribal fires in one of the craters. But they will be back. Such energy as theirs can never die.

One skirts the great burial platform of Tongariki and journeys over a boulder-strewn flat where yellowing tundra grass snares one's feet. Ahead rises the cone of Rano Raraku, cleft by some convulsion so that its seaside face is a perpendicular precipice nearly a thousand feet high, formidable and menacing. The spectacle of this great wall is in itself an awesome thing to travelers who have known the endless flatness of the Pacific. But one speedily forgets it as one comes closer to the west slope and sees the sphinx-like images rank on rank, carrying on, as they have carried on for hundreds of years, their inspection of the empty landscape and the interminable sea.

At first sight their vertical black lines against the yellow green of the grass-covered slope suggest an irregular and badly broken barrier zoning the crater. From closer at hand when their size becomes more evident, they seem like the ruined columns of some vast work like the temple of justice at Palmyra. Then one comes squarely under the hill and sees faces peering at one from a hundred angles—faces that express plainly an annoyance at one's past and a lack of hope in one's future. And one realizes that these massive images are individuals—a part of no great building scheme save perhaps the fostering of a religion or the aggrandizement of a monarch.

That an experienced modern should feel something of awe at these seemingly purposeless erections of a lost race is in itself significant of the power expended in their production and expressed in their carving. And one does feel awed. One stands by a statue thirty-five feet high, unable to reach the chin with one's outstretched hand, and is conscious not of the stone god's size but of one's own littleness. The proud upturn of the face, the thin sneering line of the lips, the inscrutable depth given by shadows to the uncarved eyes, are all at once understandable. These ancient sphinxes are quite right: man has never amounted to much and never will.

A secondary impression that grows too slowly to be immediately noted, is that all of these images are alike. Some are large, some are larger, some are weathered and old enough to have been indigenous to the island when some three-fingered Polynesian god fished it up out of the sea, some are as smooth as if the carvers quit work on them only yesterday; some show a glint of humor about their hard mouths, some are pensive. But this variety seems to be no variety at all. One model might have served for all of them and quite likely did.

The observer is aware almost instantly that much of the effect of these weird faces lies in the fact that they are like nothing else under the sun. The foreheads are high and receding. The brows protrude and cast deep shadows into the recesses that serve to represent the eyes. The nose is long, narrow and slightly upturned. The lips are thin and thrust slightly outward. The lower jaw is long, massive and square. If any such creatures ever went about the world in the flesh they have long since vanished from the ken of the ethnologist.

Many things about these faces suggest a Melanesian influence. The peaked head, for instance, is still to be observable in tribes which shape the brows of their infants between boards. The long, Simian cast of countenance is similar in many respects to the figures carved by Solomon Islanders for canoe prows. Moreover the ears of the statues are long—reaching almost to the lower curve of the jaw—portraying an artificial distension of the lobe seldom found in Polynesian islands but not at all uncommon in the cannibal zone north of Australia.

It is only after a long study of the faces that one notes these details. The ensemble effect is too overpowering to permit of analysis. Long before one discovers that the statues have long ears one is aware of the brooding silence that envelopes them and of the fear that radiates from them. A civilization that holds no commerce with stone idols is thousands of miles away beyond the rim of an unfriendly ocean and seems never to have existed. The images are here and their dead environment is a tangible, though unpleasant, reality.

When training and logic have come to function a bit tardily and a person has conquered an urge to get away from these frowning faces he forgets his first surprise at their evil effect in his astonishment at their existence. How did they come here? What engineering genius worked out a plan for their transportation? What great organizer massed the man-power that put his plan into execution?

The carving of the statues is in itself enough of a puzzle but after all a matter whose details may be worked out by those who understand sculpture. The engineering problems are far removed from a world of power machines and derricks and winches. The largest of these great monoliths weighs something more than forty tons—the smallest of them twenty tons—and in this treeless land must have been moved without rollers by the crude strength of bare brown arms.

Wherever one turns on Easter—from Rano Kao on the southwest corner to the eastern headland and from there to the tall peak of Rano Aroi on the north—one finds these images. But the quarries from which they were taken is right here in the crater of Rano Raraku. When one finds a statue face downward near Mataveri on the west coast one knows that by some unaccountable process it was taken from this mountainside and borne across hill and dale for a distance of ten miles. That dominant fact, even more than the purpose of the statues and the weird culture that they represent, has puzzled science for two hundred years.

Early voyagers to Easter brought back reports that the stone giants were composed of some sort of plaster and advanced the theory that they had been molded instead of carved. Other investigators spread the news—generally accepted until a few years ago—that the images were made of stone, but a sort of stone that could not be found anywhere on the island. And one who looks at the empty niches of Rano Raraku can not but wonder what the hardy explorers did with their time.

The plaster theory is not difficult to explain. The stone out of which the monuments were carved is volcanic tufa, a soft porous substance, whose chief ingredient is lava ash. It is found all about the rim of Rano Raraku in strata whose position shows how it was formed. For a long period after Raraku ceased to erupt it continued to simmer and sent out great quantities of ashes the bulk of which

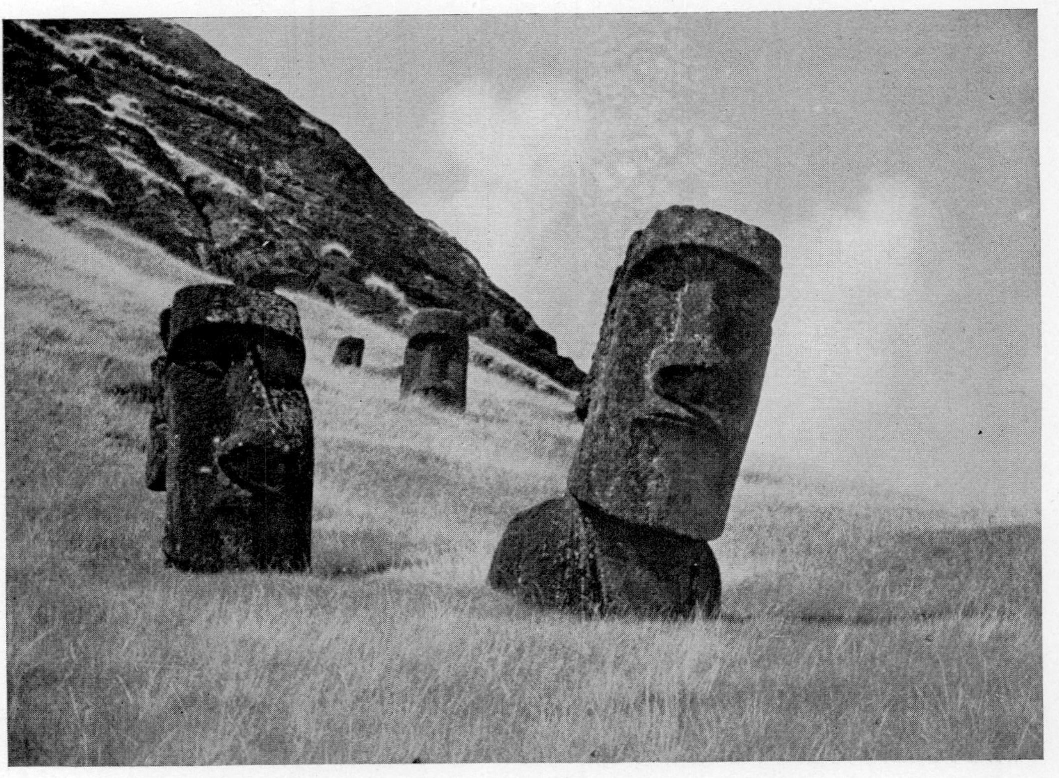

THE GODS OF EASTER
Whose massive, square and disdainful faces gaze out upon the sea

The Last of the Race of Image-Builders of Easter Island

fell on top of the crater. Rains moistened this deposit. More ashes fell, and with them splinters of igneous rock. And so in time was built up a layer of conglomerate, soft and brittle but closely bound. Sculptors compelled to work with tools of diorite or obsidian could have found no better material.

Not only was the tufa of Raraku easily worked with stone chisels but it had the quality of withstanding weather—a fact which becomes immediately evident when one looks on images that have stood on the open plains of Easter for two hundred years and possibly for centuries before that. So the image-makers, questing a source of supply, set up their workshop on Rano Raraku and ringed its base with the signs of tabu.

To-day the whole front of the hill is scarred with the niches from which statues were taken. Toward the sea on the west slope the terraces rise above one another like the steps of some vast open-cut mining operation and isolated cuttings farther north show where new beds of tufa were being opened up at the time when the sculptors dropped their tools.

It is not hard to trace the method by which the images were produced. Top soil—where any existed—was removed to expose the tufa and the rock leveled off inside a rectangle slightly longer and slightly wider than the statue to be carved. Then the sculptors blocked out a figure lying on its back and generally, though not always, with its feet toward the base of the hill. In this position the statue was completely carved save for a keel along the back attaching it to the mother rock. When all details had been finished stone wedges were placed beneath the image to hold it in place while the artizans cut away the keel. Then the work was launched down the hillside probably on mud slides.

The statues as one sees them to-day are merely gigantic busts rising from the tundra grass. But that is because the loose soil of the hillside has shifted and buried them. In their original state they represented a body from the hips upward. Thin arms hung down from the shoulders, terminating in hands with slim fingers crossed over the abdomen. For legs a peg-shaped extension was substituted and the statue was placed in an erect position through the burial of this peg in the ground.

In this respect the images standing about Rano Raraku differed from those which were carried out to the seacoasts and mounted on burial platforms. The great statues mentioned by Roggeween, La Pérouse, Cook and other early explorers were carved without the peg and were set up on bases of stone. The mortuary images also wore huge cylindrical hats of red tufa cut from a little crater near the west coast and were generally smaller than those which remain near the quarries.

Archeologists of two recent expeditions to the island advanced the theory that the west slope of Rano Raraku was used as a sort of show-window for the display of the sculptors' wares. And it was suggested that eventually all of the images would have found their way to burial platforms. But as one toils up the slippery grade to the lip of the crater one sees much to upset this idea.

Here in its niche, complete and ready for launching save for the keel that still binds it to its rocky bed, is the master work of the image-makers—a statue measuring fifty feet in length and representing a weight of something like sixty tons. No such mass of rock as this was ever placed on a burial platform. That it could have been slid down the hill is conceivable but that it could have been transported any distance over uneven ground is wholly incredible.

Then one comes to the top of the slope and looks down

to the crater lake across a Ragnarök of these same stone giants—scores of them—just as supercilious, just as aloof as those which gaze out over the landward side. Some of them are ranged near the top edge of the bowl. Some are hundreds of feet farther down, near the shore of the lake. And it is obvious that when these figures were set in place they were meant to stay. It is asking too much to suggest that they too were on display for the benefit of vault-makers. Images on the outside of the crater might have been uprooted and carried away, but imagination balks at the picture of these inside the volcano being hoisted back up the slope and across the stony barriers around the rim.

There are one hundred and sixteen images scattered about this interior slope—some of them standing, some thrown like ninepins in a wide zone extending from quarries at the lip of the bowl to the rushes that border the water. Earthquakes or slides have carried on the work of burial here as on the landward hillside.

One clambers up over the rocks to the quarry. Inside the crater, despite the leering images, is peace. The slopes are covered with green grass and descend gently to a lake no more romantic than an Iowa mill-pond. On the opposite side the gradient mounts again, a strip of green moving up toward fleecy clouds and a sky of robin's egg blue. Then one scrambles along a ledge of black rock and emerges under the roof tree of the world to look out once more on chaos and desolation. On the south side the broken cone falls sheer five hundred feet to the narrow zone that serves here for a coastal plane. On the west the slope cascades over the steps of the old quarries tumbling past the fifty or more images that still keep the watch over the land. And beyond the slope one sees the bare hills roll on and on, scarred by fragmentary roads, spotted by the broad-backed carcasses of fallen gods.

Burial cairns follow one another in monotonous succession along the white line of the surf until haze envelopes them under the distant blackness of Rano Kao. Alone and shivering in a spray-filled wind from the wintry reaches of the South Pacific one feels that at the worst one has been snatched up to the surface of some strange planet—at best one has stumbled into a madhouse of the Titans.

Chapter Fifteen

THE KING

Hotu Matua and His Dream of Empire

Hotu Matua, the king, whom an admiring populace was later to revere as "the prolific father," wrapped himself in the red-feather cloak which marked his rank and gazed down from a protected cliff into the jungled valleys of Marae Renga. Where the pandanus growth was not too thick and the flaming sun struck down through the coco-palms his quick eye caught the glint of obsidian spearheads and the satin sheen of polished war clubs. A tide was flowing in the valleys—a tide of brown-bodied men that presently would cast up a flotsam of dead at the foot of the cliff.

Hotu Matua sighed. Things had gone amiss down there in the valley. He thanked the gods for the masses of acacia and fern trees that hid most of the tragedy from his sight. Yet he stared fascinated and spoke without turning his kingly head to Haumaka the Skilful Tattooer.

"Our warriors seem to be having a bad time of it," he said. "I have been bitterly deceived by the people of Marae Renga. I thought that they would have intelligence enough to make me king without all this palaver."

"Your brother Ko has a smooth tongue," commented Haumaka the Skilful Tattooer.

"A smooth tongue is always softer than a war club," returned Hotu. "But we can't get much consolation out of that because he seems to have more war clubs than we have. I thought that his bent was oratory but he seems also to be able to fight."

"He is a scoundrel. Your father would have cooked him over a slow fire for this."

"My father, unfortunately, is dead. And there seems to be an excellent chance that I shall presently join him. We can only hope that our fighters are doing a better job over on Marae Tohio."

Haumaka turned nervously about and stared across the sea toward a misty gray uplift that he knew to be the island of Marae Tohio. Two things came instantly before his tired eyes—a dense black cloud rolling up on the far horizon, and a number of dark specks on the flat and coppery surface of the ocean. In spite of himself he cursed aloud and his curse broke the spell that had held Hotu Matua's attention to the rout of his army.

The king turned about with slow dignity and gazed unperturbed toward Marae Tohio.

"You're right, of course," he observed to Haumaka. "Our canoemen have run into difficulties. We have lost Marae Renga and we have lost Marae Tohio. This just doesn't seem to be our day."

"What can we do now?" inquired Haumaka. "We can't recruit any more fighting men. . . . Your brother . . ."

Hotu Matua took off his feather cloak and laid it carefully across a stone. From the ground at his feet he picked up a spear tipped with volcanic glass.

"I am going down to get into the fight. Perhaps I may meet my brother . . . Little Ko whom I taught to fish for pearl-shells. It will be a touching encounter."

Haumaka seemed horrified.

"But you mustn't," he objected. "The soothsayers have told that you are to remain here until sunset."

"The soothsayers haven't done me much good up to this point," was Hotu's comment. "Had I been down there things might have been different."

Haumaka shook his head.

"It would have been all the same," he argued. "You couldn't have fought here and at Marae Tohio at the same time. Something is going to happen. I feel it. I have with me the talisman that Tohu gave to your father, the pearl ornament that kept the divers from being eaten by the big fish."

"It would be very useful if we had only big fish to worry about," conceded Hotu Matua. "But without wishing to discount the great wonders connected with your talisman I'd like to point out that it isn't quite good enough." He started toward the rocky path that would have taken him down into the valley and its shambles, then halted suddenly, threw himself on his face and fought to keep from being blown into the sea.

The cloud that had been a black smudge on the horizon was now covering the whole sky. Of a sudden the sun had disappeared and the tall palms of the valley were cracking to pieces. A hurricane had struck the island.

That night, in a cave half-way down the cliff wall, Hotu Matua the king, Haumaka the Skilful Tattooer, Vaikai-a-Hiva, the wife of Hotu, Hinelilu, the warrior, and Ava-repua, the wife of Hinelilu, sat about a small fire and listened to the frenzied wind, the broken-bone crackling of uprooted forests and the din of an ocean gone mad. After a while they fell asleep.

In the morning the storm had passed though the surf still ran high at the foot of the rocks and tossed up tragic relics of the war fleet. Bedraggled fighting men huddled together in recesses in the cliff or came staggering into the cave to fall exhausted at the feet of the chief. Haumaka, the last to rise, smiled benignly.

"I was right," he announced. "There is still some virtue in the old talisman. I have had a dream."

"Good," conceded Hotu Matua. "I had one once myself. I dreamed I was an emperor ruling over Marae Renga and Marae Tohio, the islands of my father."

"You have a larger destiny than that," said Haumaka. "There is a land to the east where you will rule unmolested and make a name for yourself that the world will never forget. It is a place where there are three islets and a big hole which is the gateway to the spirit land below the earth."

"I wonder what happened to my brother's army," commented Hotu Matua, and he went out to see.

The great island of Marae Renga spread before him broken and desolate. Lakes of water tossed up from the sea by the hurricane swirled in the valleys where the cocopalms and pandanus had grown. Brown bodies, vividly tattooed, floated among the shattered logs.

Hinelilu came and stood by the king.

"We may be able to take the island yet," said Hotu Matua. "If my brother's warriors are drowned we shan't need many men to take the villages beyond the valleys."

Hinelilu shook his head.

"Ko still has a force in the hills," he said. "We have about three hundred men left and he has a thousand. Our luck lies in the fact that while the water stays on the land he can't get at us."

Hotu Matua shrugged his broad shoulders and the birds with which he was so beautifully tattooed seemed suddenly animate. "I wonder," he commented, "if, after all, there might be something in this business of the talisman."

When the surf had calmed a bit three canoes that had been kept in a cave and so had escaped the storm were brought down to the beach. One of the canoes was small and into it Hotu Matua placed six warriors famed for their skill in paddling.

"You will go at once," he ordered. "You will take with you yams and fig seeds and slips of cane and ti. And you will plant them in this land where the big hole is supposed to be."

So the small canoe set out in the direction of the sunrise and Hotu Matua embarked with his wife, his attendants, his soothsayers and the remnants of his people in the two remaining canoes. These were large boats, each long enough to carry one hundred and fifty persons with food and water supplies, plants and seeds and fowl. When the waters subsided and Ko, the victorious, marched his warriors across the swamp-land he found no trace of Hotu Matua. The king had gone and the people of Marae Renga and Marae Tohio never heard of him again.

For many days the six men in the small boat paddled toward the rising sun. Day and night they drove onward against wind and rain until their arms were tired and their food and water all but gone. Then one morning they made a landfall—a high island along the south shore of which clustered three smaller islands and they knew that destiny had guided them correctly.

The high island was Rapa Nui, one day to be known as Easter, and the islets were Motu Nui, Motu Iti and Motu Kao-Kao. On the southwest corner of Rapa Nui they discovered the crater of Rano Kao and they needed no talisman to tell them that this was the great hole which Haumaka had seen in his dream.

The six men went ashore and planted the seeds and shoots they had brought with them. They slept in caves and drank from fresh-water springs under the salt of the surf. And they did what might be done toward raising a crop of yams and sugar cane to feed the people of the king who presently would be approaching in the two large canoes. But fortune was unkind to them. Tall grass sprouted in the bowl of Rano Kao and smothered the gardens they had planted there. And one of them named Kuku was fatally injured in an attempt to capture a sea turtle. The surviving pioneers built cairns outside the cave in which he died and sat down in deep despondency to await the coming of Hotu Matua.

The ships of the king were great war canoes—eighty feet long, deep keeled and broad of beam. Outriggers gave them stability in heavy seas. Masts of hardwood and sails of fiber gave them motivation and speed independent of the power supplied by the paddlemen. In addition to that they had the *mana,* the supernatural aid, of Haumaka's talisman. So, as might have been expected, they came one day to their destination.

Hotu Matua stood in the prow of his canoe under the black face of Rano Kao and shouted. But only echoes answered him. He cast an apprehensive eye along the coast for some sign of the garden plots that his emissaries should have planted. Instead he saw rocky uplifts and volcanic blisters and slopes of boulder-strewn earth covered with grass which no man had ever disturbed.

"Something has happened here," he told Hinelilu. "This is a bad land. Nothing grows on it. No birds nest on it. The talisman has tricked us."

"It may look better on the other side," advised Hinelilu. "But the sun is going down behind us and it will soon be dark. We had better tie up our boats to this islet (Motu Nui) and wait for daylight."

Hotu Matua agreed. The canoes were moored in a rocky cove and the voyagers slept. With the dawn the king went ashore and discovered, close to his hawse lines, the recumbent forms of two of his advance party. He awakened them.

"What have you been doing here?" he inquired.

One who was called Ira answered him.

"We have been sleeping," he said. "There is nothing else to do here. The land will not bear. The things we planted failed to take root. Nothing grows here but grass. So we sleep and gain strength and to-morrow we shall start back to Marae Renga."

"You would be no better off on Marae Renga now than you were when you started," said Hotu Matua. "The sea has ruined everything. We shall stay here and make the best of it. Is all the coast like this?"

"There is an inlet on the side to the north," said Ira. "It is called Anakena and has a little beach of shell sand. That would be a good place for the landing of the canoes."

"I seem to remember having seen a place like that in a dream," stated Hotu Matua. "We shall go in search of it."

So, once more, the boats set sail. This time they separated at the base of the Rano Kao, one traveling to the east, the other following the coast to the north. And they met at the cove of Anakena and landed. Thus came the first men and women to Rapa Nui.

Despite the ornament which this legend has received in its modernization it is substantially the same as told to early investigators by natives who were still carrying on the island's ancient culture. There was a king named Hotu Matua and he came from a far island where he had suffered a defeat in a contest for a throne. And whatever embellishments a story-teller might see fit to add, that basic element of the tale seems true. In little it is the whole history of Polynesia. . . . A leader was defeated. He went away into the blue with his wives and his warriors and his chattels. If the natives of Easter had never had such a legend, students of migrations in the South Pacific could have provided it with no effort.

Balboa had not yet looked upon his great and nameless ocean when Hotu Matua set out to the west. It is scarcely likely that Columbus had sailed from Spain. Europe's hardy mariners were still worried about journeying to the edge of a flat earth where, conceivably, one might fall quite a distance. The Atlantic, save for some unreported findings by diligent Norsemen, was still a region of perilous mystery.

At this time, as we looked back at it across our school geographies, the Pacific Ocean stretched between the empty continent of America and the unredeemed civilization of China—an undiscovered sea waiting since the creation of the world to thrill at the coming of Magellan. As one takes a second look at the matter from a crater hard by the little cove in which Hotu Matua grounded his boats one blushes a little for the immodesty of one's ancestors.

Long before the Atlantic was crossed, the Pacific was cluttered up with the weird craft of its own Magellans . . . nagivators who peopled a zone four thousand miles across. They made charts of woven reeds and sighted the stars through holes drilled in coconuts. They knew the currents of the great ocean as no white cartographer has ever known them. They had never heard of a compass or a sextant or a chronometer or a table of logarithms. But they journeyed continuously from Tahiti to Hawaii and from the Marquesas to New Zealand. They knew the constellations and the positions of the sun and the holes on the rim of the world whence the three-fingered gods released the winds. And they drove their boats across hundreds of miles of open water as if in a groove.

Hotu Matua who made the long journey to Easter with his chieftains and his people may or may not have existed as a man. But as the Spirit of Polynesia he is a figure easily understood and easily credited.

Chapter Sixteen

THE PIONEERS

The Skilful Removal of Oroi the Killer

Given a bit more territory Hotu Matua might have built an empire. He had a knack for it, a vigorous brain, a tireless body and a compelling energy. In the Europe of his day he might have made history and altered considerable geography. But of course one is hampered in such pursuits on a barren island thirty-five miles in circumference.

The recent king of Marae Renga and Marae Tohio discovered even before he set foot on the beach at Anakena that he was to have no peace in this land to which the talisman had directed him. He had merely substituted one enemy for another. In the far country from which he had come there was no great danger save from tidal wave and hurricane and the spears of Ko, his brother. Here, as he looked inland across the bare slag-dump of the dead fires, he saw without the need of soothsayers or amulets the leering face of starvation.

Hotu Matua made this evil land produce and it is for that rather than for his other manifest qualities that his name was revered by his descendants. He planted yams where his emissaries had planted them, in the wide craters and he tended them and kept down the grasses. He showed his people where to place the shoots of sugar cane and how to set out the arrowroot. He found patches of soil that would support the wild banana. And about the cove of Anakena he planted shrubs of the toromiro and sandalwood tree. Under his care agriculture prospered and his little kingdom was saved from extinction.

Numerous circumstantial stories of Hotu Matua's early days on the island once figured in the native lore. They have been preserved in reports of voyagers who listened to them about the fires of Hanga Roa generations ago—and that is fortunate inasmuch as the present-day Easter Islander knows little of the past save for the heritage of wretchedness that it has handed down to him. The old tales are forgotten or distorted and Hotu Matua himself—once the hero of a saga so complete that he seemed almost historical—to-day is the ghost of a myth, an unnamed menace who sits on some distant cairn and contributes his bit to the eternal Fear.

The legend has it that with Hotu Matua on his long trek from Marae Renga came one Oroi, a stowaway and a scoundrel. Oroi had been in the councils of Ko and had led a conspiracy in which were killed Hotu's sons.

Oroi's identity was discovered when the party came ashore at Anakena but he slid from the grasp of the warriors who were ready to kill him and he fled into the hills. Why he had come is not made clear unless, as some have pointed out, he might have been in ignorance of Hotu's destination when the great boats set sail. At any rate he landed and became what in another civilization might be classed as "the criminal element" of the population.

He foraged for his food and managed to keep himself alive for many years—which speaks well for his ingenuity. He ate yams when he could steal them and human flesh when occasion offered.

The people put up with Oroi for a long time in patience. The community, marveling at his longevity, endowed him with many of the attributes of a demigod and became afraid to mention his name. He seems to have been classed as an evil such as hunger, disease and death. Nobody seems to have thought about hunting him down, and this apathy is probably ascribable to two good reasons: in the first place, he was dangerous; in the second, it takes a lot of energy to chase murderers over blistered hills in a hot sun.

Then one day came one Aorka of Owaihi to lay a complaint before Hotu Matua.

"I had five children," he said. "I moved from Anakena to the cove of Owaihi to protect them from Oroi the Killer and they grew very well there. But yesterday they went out to swim and after they had come out of the water they lay down on a rock near our house to sun themselves. While they were lying there Oroi crept up behind them and killed them all. I think something ought to be done about it and I have no relatives who would join me in catching this murderer."

"He killed five of them," repeated Hotu. "That's very interesting. One ought to have been enough for him. The other four represent a downright waste. We'll have to put Oroi out of the way or he'll be depopulating the island."

So Hotu Matua announced to the people that he would undertake the task of disposing of Oroi the Killer himself. And the word got to Oroi as such things will.

A short time afterward Hotu went along the coast to visit his daughter who was married and living in a house of her own. He wore his cloak of red feather so that he could be seen and recognized from a great distance. And he kept a wary eye on the rocks which lined the path.

Not far from his daughter's house he saw a noose of grass rope lying on the ground squarely in front of him. He pretended not to see it and walked down to the shore where he examined some of the sandalwood saplings that he had planted years before. But he was not deceived. He knew that behind the rocks lurked Oroi.

He proceeded along the water's edge and so escaped the noose.

Late in the afternoon he brought his visit to a close and started back to Anakena. But not alone.

"I am just about to kill this Oroi," he told his daughter and son-in-law as he was leaving. "If you have nothing else to do you might follow along behind me and see what happens."

They followed.

Hotu Matua, instead of following the shore-line, took the path in which he had seen Oroi's snare and presently he came to the noose still lying where he had left it. This time the king seemed to be paying no attention to his surroundings. He stepped slowly into the loop and allowed himself to be tripped. He lay as if stunned on the rocks.

Oroi the Killer rushed forward from his hiding-place with a stone upraised to brain him. But the stone was never thrown. The wily Hotua seized Oroi about the legs, lifted him from the ground and broke his back across a lava dike.

To this day there are old men on Easter Island who will point out to you the place where Oroi came to his end. The dike is still there and that proves everything.

Hotu and his daughter and her husband then built an oven of loose stones and put the late stowaway inside it for cooking. But Oroi seems to have been a perverse character even in death. He came to life, crawled out of the oven and had to be killed all over again.

Hotu considered the matter with much thought.

"The juju is wrong on this side of the island," he said. "I dare say that is why this reprobate has been able to operate all these years. We'll take him over to the other side."

So they carried Oroi to the other side and built a cairn

which still bears the name of the killer. On this cairn they started another fire over which they roasted Oroi according to the best traditions of Marae Renga cuisine. They ate him and did not complain later about the feast although, probably, he was a bit tough.

One can always while away an afternoon, or for that matter two or three weeks, on the island arguing with the local savants over the personal appearance of Hotu Matua, particularly with regard to his ears. The legends are definite in stating that a long-eared clan and a short-eared clan were closely inter-mingled in Hotu's pioneer community. But there seems to be considerable disagreement concerning their origins.

One version of the story makes Hotu himself one of the short-ears and holds that the king's canoe carried none but people of his own kind. The long-ears, according to this account, were in the boat of Hinelilu.

Another story has it that the two tribes were mixed up before the arrival of Hotu Matua and a third ascribes the long-eared strain to the emissaries who preceded Hotu.

One might attach no significance to any of these yarns were it not for the fact that a study of the Pacific Peoples has revealed an essential difference between the culture of races whose ears were normal and that of more primitive tribes whose ear-lobes were artificially distended.

The Polynesian as a rule paid no attention to the shape of his ears. On the other hand it has always been a practise in Melanesia to pierce the lobe and by filling the hole with wooden plugs or bits of shell to force its growth in a long, rope-like ring. Of all the Polynesian Islands only the Marquesas show any evidence of this ear-stretching process. The Melanesian influence noticeable in all the islands seems to have been stronger in the Marquesas.

So, in the light of what is known about racial characteristics in the South Seas, the stories of long-ears and short-ears in Hotu Matua's community give a clue to the mystery of Easter and provide a pretty puzzle. It becomes manifest at once that Hotu's Marae Renga may have been somewhere near the Marquesas. As against that we have nothing to prove that he did not stop at some Melanesian Island on his way to Easter and pick up a contingent of long-ears, or, for that matter, that he himself did not come from some island in Melanesia.

The legend-builders of Easter Island presumably had no idea that scientists would one day be concerned about the origins of these short-ears and long-ears. With one grand gesture the story-tellers had settled the matter of origins for all time: hadn't it been said that all of these people came with Hotu Matua from Marae Renga? Very well then.

But the continuing activities of the rival cultures after their transplantation made history of a sort for Rapa Nui. One has only to glance at the stone images to realize that when Easter came to its moment of glory the long-ears were in the ascendancy. All of these images show the distended ear-lobe, and whether one considers them the portraits of some maniac despot with delusions of grandeur or an artistic striving or man's expression to forgotten gods one knows that they were carved by men who considered this characteristic feature a mark of superiority.

It is more than likely that the carvers themselves—undoubtedly the great cultural class of the island—were of the long-eared clan. And as one stirs up visions in the flying salt-mists of Rano Raraku and recreates the sweating hordes dragging these gigantic blocks to their places on the burial cairns one does not need to strain one's second sight to discover that the laborers had normal ears.

With this evidence in the background one can not but find significance in the tale of the great war between the long-ears and the short-ears. It is told that after a time the long-ears became clannish and established settlements of their own at Orongo—on top of Rano Kao—and at Vinapu, on the seashore just east of the crater. In addition to these two communities there must have been a larger one about Rano Raraku where the images were made.

As in the case of Oroi of lamented memory the short-eared populace concealed any resentment it might have felt toward the long-eared element until cultural differences came to a climax in the matter of dietetics.

There lived at Orongo a short-eared man named Ko Pepi who had seven sons. He appears to have been an ordinary citizen whose effect on the destinies of the people would never have been forecast by the most enthusiastic soothsayer. He was a neighborly soul who never quarreled. He fished a little, grew a few yams and did his bit in the hauling of stone images. The uneventful tenor of his life was never upset until one rainy afternoon when he came home to his little cave-like house on the top of the crater and discovered that one of his sons was missing.

He might have passed this over as a mysterious but scarcely terrifying event had not another son disappeared almost immediately . . . and then another . . . and another. In a week all seven of the sons had vanished and the distracted father set out to make an investigation.

It is not related how he came to suspect Ko Ita, a long-ear who occupied a large house at Orongo. But he did suspect him. Ko Pepi hid himself in the spongy rocks at the rim of the volcano and kept watch for many hours until

Ko Ita and the women of the house had gone down into the crater to gather yams. He stole into Ko Ita's home and found there the remains of thirty young men who had been killed and eaten, among them the still recognizable body of one of his own sons.

Ko Pepi, crazed by grief, ran down the long slope to Hanga Roa, screaming his hatred for the long-ears and demanding vengeance. He fell at length frothing at the mouth and his brothers came to him and heard his story. They took up war clubs and assembled their relatives.

Distaste for the aristocracy of long-ears seems to have been fairly prevalent at the time among the short-eared caste. For many who were in no way related to Ko Pepi demanded an opportunity to take up his quarrel. The indignation spread and by nightfall a general uprising was in progress.

A savage mob swept up the mountainside to Orongo. The surprised long-ears found themselves surrounded before they had any chance to resist. In a few minutes they were all dead. The short-ears poured down the east slope to Vinapu and completed the massacre.

By this time word of the trouble had spread all across the island. The long-ears of the coast villages fled to Rano Raraku and thence to the eastern headland. The short-ears from north and south and west gathered at Hanga Roa for a war of extermination.

The long-ears displaying to the last the intelligence which had made them masters of Rapa Nui, dug a ditch across the corner of the island where rises the eastern volcano and they filled it with brushwood and grass that could be set afire in the event of a concerted attack.

The ditch stopped the short-ears temporarily. The massed warriors camped on the west side of it awed by the threat of fire. But Destiny was no longer favoring the

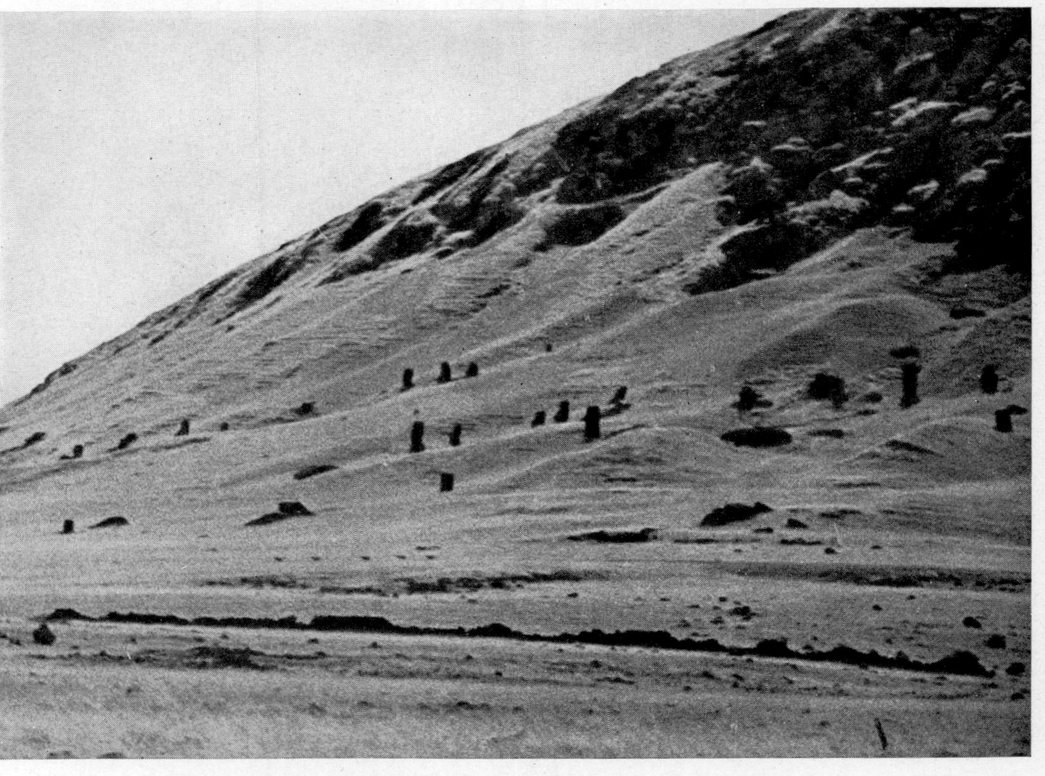

An Olympian Conclave
The Titans in close formation on the west slope of Rano Raraku

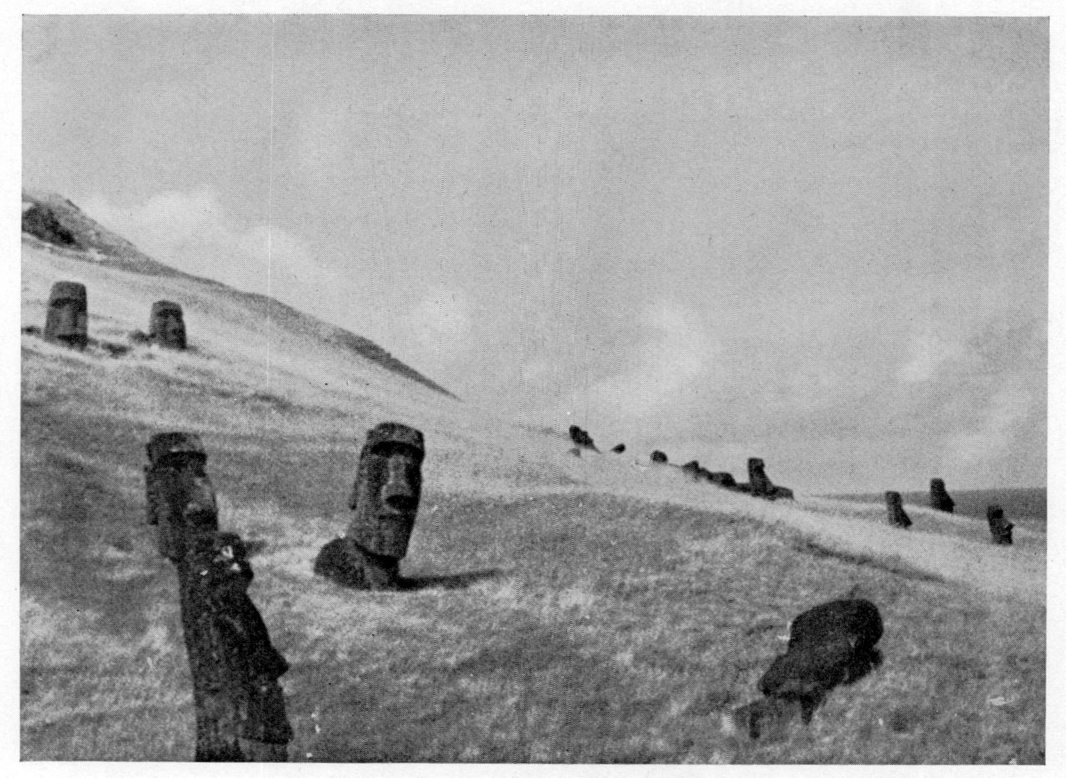

PLAYGROUND OF THE GIANTS

Nearly a hundred figures remain standing—and sneering—at the foot of Rano Raraku's western slope

long-ears. An old woman came by night to the camp of the attackers and pointed out a rocky bridge by which the ditch could be flanked.

One body of short-ears moved silently along the coast and up the slope of the volcano from the east. Simultaneously other warriors threw torches into the great ditch. The long-ears, attacked from the rear and on both flanks, fled in panic down the hillside and were driven into their own ditch where they died in the fire-trap that they themselves had set.

Whether or not this tale is true one feels that it ought to be. The journey of civilizations from and back to the dust is marked by numerous parallel incidents. Standing by the ditch of the long-ears near Rano Raraku one sees again the slaves of Angkor rising to destroy their masters and to commit cultural suicide. Whether a man is hauling fifty-ton gods whose utility is highly questionable or fifty-ton rocks for the most beautiful temples in the world his reactions are quite likely to be the same. Here as elsewhere in the world despotism has come to its logical end.

On Easter, of course, no evidence is very positive. The great ditch appears to be a natural depression. But there are signs of man-made embankments at its ends. Perhaps instead of digging a trench the wily long-ears made use of one that a volcanic uplift had left ready for use. Or, possibly, this saga of battle and blood has no basis in fact whatever. One can never be sure of such things.

It would be a help to one puzzling over the remains on the island if one could accept the tale in its entirety. Granting that the long-ears were the custodians of learning and that the short-eared commoners rebelled against them and killed them off we have an explanation of why the vast and futile work of image-building came to so abrupt an end.

But, unfortunately, the problem can not be reduced to such simple terms.

Roggeween, La Pérouse and Cook tell of having seen men with distended ear-lobes at Hanga Roa and elsewhere on the island. And natives still alive have been quoted as describing long-ears who were in the census only a few decades ago. Where legend competes with fact one would always prefer to accept the legend. . . . It is generally more colorful, more logical and certainly more easily believed. But there are always practical souls who prefer facts and on their account one hesitates to destroy or conceal the evidence—especially when destruction and concealment might so easily be detected. The reported extermination of the long-ears seems to have been a little incomplete.

Hotu Matua, says the legend, abdicated his kingship before his death. He is something of a tragic figure, this Hotu Matua, despite his approach to deity in the traditions of his people. On Marae Renga his march to empire was checked by his own brother, and his sons were slain. On Easter he fought a weary and uncertain war against starvation and set his followers on the road to civilization only to find in the end that his wife, Vaikai, and his eldest son, Tuumaheki, were plotting against him. He left Tuumaheki to rule in his stead and went to live a hermit's life, on the south slope of Rano Kao.

There, one morning, he heard the cock crow on Marae Renga far across the sea and he sighed contentedly and died.

Hotu's children were with him at the end and to one of them he made a prophecy:

"You are Kotuu," he said. "And you shall have many sons. And their descendants shall be as numerous as the sea-shells and little stones that are strewn on the beach at Anakena. But in the end their bones shall pave the land and your line shall disappear."

And here, at least, fact and legend are unanimous. The prophecy of Hotu Matua is near its fulfillment.

Chapter Seventeen

TREK

The Tide of Peoples

Asshur had not yet gone forth from Sinar to build Nineveh. Sumer and Akkad were as deeply imbedded in the mists of the future as they are now in the mists of the past. The Aurignacian man was making chalk portraits of red bulls on the walls of caves in what was one day to be France. Straggling clusters of huts along a red river were laying the foundations for a nation that was to be called Egypt. And on the slopes of the Caucasus and in the dusty white hot land of the two rivers, and amid the close-woven bush of India, the peoples were astir. Life was elemental. Humanity's urge to art, science, social service, politics and civic uplift were expressed in one single compelling instinct—the desire for food. All else—even the propagation of the species itself—was secondary to that.

For many generations the problem had been of no great importance. If one was hungry one had only to wander a few feet from the hole in which one lived and pick berries or fruits, or, with a little more effort, trap some stronger and handsomer but less intelligent animal. But of late humankind seemed to be outgrowing its environment. There came a day when the berry supply wasn't sufficient to go around. The world for all its vast—and empty—continents, seemed suddenly overcrowded. Man's social status was changing while his appetite remained as it had always been, and in the circumstance there seemed to be only one thing for him to do. He moved.

The peoples spread out across the plains of Europe and down through the fecund valleys of Africa . . . into the far northland to bore holes in the ice and match their dim intellects against the strength of Arctic animals and the greater forces of the cold . . . into endless deserts to cling as parasites to a beast called the camel, and to know the misery of blinding days and bitter nights and the thirst that began at birth and was assuaged only by death. By the banks of broad rivers, where soil was fertile, they halted till the pressure of other peoples behind them became too strong, and thus they learned to live in groups that became cities. They ceased to rely on the food plants that accident had set in their paths and discovered means for growing a supply of their own. They tired of wandering and would have rested in gentle downlands to tend their animals or watch the growing of their crops.

But always behind them, in the never-ending flight from starvation, came other peoples, driving forward as they had driven—a mass relentless as the creeping glaciers on the top of the world and like the glaciers growing as it moved. History repeated itself world without end. Man found a brief respite from his wayfaring in some spot where nature was generous with food—and he stayed there until the mouths of his children became too numerous. Over the centuries humanity flowed in streams as constant—and as erratic—as rivers, sometimes at full flood, sometimes narrowed to a thin trickle, but always moving. It is still moving.

Out of Ur in Chaldea, in the land of the two rivers, came a people questing a food called *ari* which the Western World names rice. Up out of the plain they came—at first in hundreds, then in countless thousands—to scale the ragged hills of Iran. They struck the hills like a surf, rising against a barrier, breaking on its crest, receding in defeat and rising again. Only a portion of the wave won over the mountains. What had been a tide at the rocky base was a spray at the top. But always behind them came the great tidal force of a people in motion. New waves came on. The surf grew stronger and mounted higher. The streams of marching men took on volume in the passes, and torrents of humanity cascaded down the east slope to merge once more at the bottom and spread out in a rimless lake on the plains beyond.

The vultures rode with the men of Chaldea. The old and the very young died on the steep ascents to fill the crevasses with their bones. Exhaustion struck down the strong . . . and the stronger went on across their prostrate bodies.

Hunger marched unnoticed at their elbows. To-morrow, perhaps, in that far land where the *ari* grew, there would be no more hunger. But they had known him in the land of the two rivers and it was not surprising to find him here. The trek went on. And so, eventually, these wanderers came to Irihia or Vrihia, the land of plenty.

They rested for a time. Food was plentiful, winds were not too harsh. The days were pleasant and the nights were filled with the bright stars they had known in the homeland. Other men of Chaldea came unceasingly over the mountains to join them. Up in the north was a race of strangers—people who had come earlier into Vrihia from some source that is of no consequence. They had retreated before the tide coming out of Ur, ready, since resistance would have been of no avail, to abandon their fields and rivers and seek new dwelling-places in the region where the stars came down so close to the earth. But their quest was not favored by the high gods. They should have gone east. Instead they went north and came to a wall of mountains, sheer and desolate and topped with snow. They stopped on a plateau swept constantly by icy winds from the distant peaks, parched by one season and flooded by the next.

In such a climate *ari*, the food plant, would not grow. But they could not go forward, they dared not go back. They built dwellings of stone and lived as best they could on what sustenance this barren land provided. Miraculously, they prospered. Their children grew straight and lean and hard, skilled in the use of weapons necessary for the killing of wild animals, inured to hardships, almost, though not quite able to live without eating. Their tribe increased in numbers and in power.

Then one day the old drama was reenacted. There were too many people for the plateau. They must move or starve. And they recalled the tradition of the lowlands of Vrihia whence they had come. They poured down out of the hills and into the plain, this time not as a wave but an avalanche.

All these years the people of Ur had sat by the rivers of Vrihia growing rice. They, too, had prospered in their fashion. Then had softened a little, but not much. The rewards of agriculture were still far from certain. One had to work now for what one ate. And the rear-guard of the great movement was still coming up out of Chaldea and each year found more people on the plain who had to be fed. The people of Ur were still as hard as they had been when they came over the mountains of Iran. The trouble was that they were not so hard as the hillmen who came pouring out of the north.

Once more the people of Ur resumed their long trek. It was a disheartening quest. Other surges of men and women from the land of the two rivers or from lands that had no name had come into the forests of Vrihia ahead of them. And the wanderers from Chaldea, stricken by hardship and fatigue and disease and hunger, were beaten again and again in their struggles for land. The whirling vultures plotted their wake for hundreds of miles.

For long dispiriting years the march went on. . . . Across plains as hot as the flats of the Euphrates, over mountains higher and craggier and colder than the hills of Iran. They forded rivers and hacked their way through jungles. And the last of them came on over the bodies of those who had gone before.

At last when the land of the two rivers was little more than a hazy tradition, the descendants of the men who had set out across the hills of Iran broke down through the north wall of a deep peninsula and forced their way to the sea. They had come—although they had no way of knowing it—to the last outpost of Asia, the doorstep of a new world.

They were of the same race as the men who had come out of Ur and yet different. Their language was tempered by the tongues of men with whom they had fought or bartered in the lands across which they had come. They were straighter and stronger and leaner and more purposeful.

The long peninsula was quite obviously their last hope for a home in all the continent. But it gave them only brief consolation. Behind them, on the trail marked by ever-increasing piles of bones, other tribes were pressing forward, driven by still other hungry men. And the peninsula was already filled with half-hostile folk who had been there first and showed every intent to hold what they had.

There remained the sea and the men of Ur took to it. They learned from the tribes of the coast the art of making and operating boats. They learned the names of strange gods who governed the winds and the currents. They learned of the tides that salute the moon. And they saw new uses for the lore of stars that they had brought with them through the years from Chaldea.

They stayed for a long time on the peninsula, wresting a living from the established tribes and standing valiantly against the horde that massed against them from the north and west. Old leaders died. New ones came to take their places and presently not even the gods of Ur would have recognized in these people any trace of their origin. They were still children of the sun with the nomad's nervous feet and eyes that remained fixed on far horizons. But the traditions of the desert had vanished and with them the fear of the open water. They had become a breed of fishermen with questing minds; sailormen with a sailorman's urge to find out what might lie beyond the rim of the world.

Always the tide of peoples came on and on over the course that they had taken. And then one day the land for which they had fought seemed no longer worth the struggle. They shoved their boats into the sea and set out along a chain of islands that they had often visited, seeking the homeland that the gods of the blue water had promised them.

The rolling ocean was roofed with their boats—hundreds of them—thousands . . . long gaunt craft steadied by outriggers and fitted with sails of tapa. They hid the blue of the sea under their own gaudy coloring—coloring which flowed and merged and parted as waves and wind changed their position in a vast patternless movement. The black paddles rose and fell and threw back the sun in a glitter that spanned the horizons. The great trek had begun once more. A nation was driving onward as its ancestors back in a dim and almost forgotten age had dashed themselves against the cliffs of Iran.

The boats carried not only an army of paddlemen but the old men and the women and children of the people . . .

and supplies of food and water, and seeds and growing shoots and pairs of domestic animals. The race from the land of the two rivers was bidding good-by to the continent of Asia for ever.

The trek went on along the coasts of the familiar islands toward the sunrise. The smoke-plumed mountains that had guided them in lesser ventures fell at last below the horizon to be succeeded by blue peaks that they had never seen before—ridges that burned red against the sky at night and veiled themselves with black clouds by day.

They touched at these islands but stayed only a little while. Other migrants had come before them . . . a people whom they felt to be somehow related to themselves yet different in stature and color and culture . . . a black-skinned race with kinky hair and spreading nostrils. They moved on again.

There were other islands. For months on end the paddlemen drove the canoes to the east from archipelago to archipelago and from island to island. Always these men with the kinky hair and dark skins had been before them.

They heard vaguely of lands to the north and east—empty paradises that the gods had built for them. It was a tradition among the dark-skinned people that venturesome canoemen had seen them. But no one had gone to investigate the reports. There was room enough for the kinky-haired ones in the islands they now occupied. They had ceased to care about the rewards that might come to those who dared seek them in long voyages—they remembered only that the sea was wide and treacherous. The sons of the men of Ur came at last to regions where there were no more islands. What lay before them not even the most talented soothsayer could determine. They swept onward across an ocean that had neither beginning nor end.

Not all the brave boats survived the journey. There came storms that scattered the fleet, engulfed half of it and piled new miseries on the backs of the weary paddlemen. For days the canoes rode up and down on shifting mountains of water and the half-drowned women remembered vaguely the stories they had heard of a warm dry land in a zone of eternal sunshine. The storm abated and they found what it meant to die of thirst. The story of these wanderers was near its finish. And then, one day, a gray peak broke out of the sea ahead of them.

They landed there and beached their canoes. A great fertile island rose up to heights beyond the clouds. A deep cool valley was before them. They did not need the soothsayers to tell them what they had found. This was Hawaiki . . . the promised homeland. And it was theirs to do with as they pleased for no one lived in its high distances save the twin gods of the echo and the silence.

So, in its essentials, reads the legend of the Maoris explaining the origins of the Polynesian race. And right or wrong the story has some startling features. The Maori name for the land whence the migrants came on their quest for rice is Uru which may or may not be the same as Ur of the Chaldees. The name *ari* in a Polynesian tradition is in itself an amazing thing inasmuch as it applies to a foodstuff not to be found in the South Pacific. In the identification of Irihia or Vrihia, so called by the Maoris, one comes to more recognizable clues for Vrihia is a name which in the old Sanskrit tongue meant India.

It is not difficult to believe that the voyagers in setting out from some point in Malaysia should have traveled for a long time among populated islands. The Melanesian—the dark-skinned man with the kinky hair—was in the Pacific before the Polynesian. He held the land and forced the newcomers to set out once more into the blue, but not before he had given them some of his features and gods and words and culture.

Hawaiki, the homeland, is closely associated in Maori legend with Tahiti and quite likely they were one and the same. At any rate some movement such as the long trek of the people from the land of the two rivers brought the Polynesian to Tahiti just as it brought the Malayan type of cultivated breadfruit tree to these eastern islands.

In Chaldea a nation called Babylon had fallen. . . . A nation called Rome was rising. . . . The dust was already beginning to settle upon a nation called Egypt. Peoples were stirring in the forests of a river called the Rhine and another great movement of peoples was about to begin.

The mystery of a thousand years pressed down once more upon the Pacific. But no one recognized it as a mystery because no one had ever heard of the Pacific.

Chapter Eighteen

THE CARVER OF THE TITANS

A Culture Died When He Listened to a Woman

When, as the departed missionaries have promised, a spirit called Gabriel sounds his trumpet over the waters and the dead rise up among the burial *ahus* to assemble their scattered bones, then all mankind will know how great a sculptor was Rapu the carver of images. Alone on the topmost crest of Rano Raraku, decked in a crown of scarlet feathers and a cloak of painted tapa-cloth, his body etched most delicately in the finest blue spirals of Hotu's best tattooing, his ear-lobes distended and hung with strangely wrought ornaments of nacre, he will answer the summons grim and proud as the gods of his own making. He will receive the homage of all the skilful carvers that the world has ever known. Then at last his scornful soul will be at peace.

He has been dead these countless centuries—or rather the body of him has rested in an unmarked vault by the dike of Tongariki. But unlike so many of his contemporaries he has never gone completely from the life of the island. Something of his own intolerant spirit lingers about the disdainful giants he contrived. Even the pride of the gods might be shaken after hundreds of years in the rain and wind and salty spray. When one is forgotten it seems so useless to be arrogant. But always Rapu walked among them in the howling night, whispering in their stony ears the language that only they can understand, encouraging them to remember their divine origins, counseling them lest they cease from their eternal scorn to laugh at the comic antics of the race whose history they share.

They have seen "towns burned and murder done." They have seen great kings borne in solemn procession to the *ahus*—which was a matter of no moment—and they have been stolid witnesses to the collapse and burial of ideas—which was real tragedy. They looked across the hills of Easter when the grass was green and a people had begun to lift themselves out of the dust. They watched the building of a vast society and saw the rise of a strange culture. They listened to the chants of the soothsayers and the *ariki* and the chieftains who walked with the high gods. They learned the secrets of the mysterious world beyond the sky and the dreadful lands that lie beneath the earth. By night they stood near as weird and bloodstained figures danced past them in the light of smoking flares. They learned all that man had to teach them. They remembered the ancient mysteries when man forgot. And still they never found any cause to regret their facial inflexibility. They were able to sneer and they never found need for any other expression.

Dawn had come. Rapu the Carver stirred himself out of his bed of dried banana leaves and rush matting and walked along the lip of Rano Raraku to see the sun tear the misty purple shadows from the eastern headland. Below him the crater lake steamed through its border of green shrubs, still holding on its broad bosom a little something of the night. Men were astir on the slope inside the bowl. At the foot of the hill to the west flames were leaping up in the villages of the Hotu Iti. From a distance came a chant in a strange and forgotten tongue. The soothsayers of the Miru were making their prayer to the gods they had left behind on Marae Renga.

Rapu turned from the vision of sky and hill and ocean and sat by a gravelike opening in a bank of gray tufa. He picked up a chisel of diorite and began to rub its edge on a whetstone. Other carvers with the sleep still in their eyes came past him with reluctant steps. Food and water awaited them at the end of the path. They reminded him sleepily of breakfast as they stumbled onward. But the scrape of Rapu's chisel went on in rhythmic cadence as they walked. Food could not interest him so long as the edge of his chisel remained dull. The last man was well down the slope before he arose to follow. Rapu was that sort of workman.

There came to him as he devoured his hot yams a stripling of the Marama clan whose head-dress showed his origins and whose eyes displayed that reverential fear which the inartistic people always felt in the presence of the image-makers. He stood inarticulate for many minutes before Rapu deigned to look at him.

"Well," said the sculptor at length, "what do you want?"

"I am a great admirer of your wonderful talents," answered the boy. "I have sat for days at a time looking into the faces of the stones to which you have given life. And as I looked at them I have heard the voices of the gods whispering to me. I have felt that I am not the same as the others of my clan. They do not understand art. They spend their time swimming or fishing or sleeping or growing yams or hunting rats. And when they go down to the burial platforms they hardly notice the tall and beautiful *moai* with their lovely red hats."

"That is all very true," admitted Rapu. "But what of it? Art is the expression of the elect to the chosen few. It will always be like that. Even the gods can't change it."

"That is why I wish to get away from the Marama

clan," sighed the boy. "I have had the misfortune to be born in the wrong locality. I belong here with you. I wish to become a great artist. I know I have it in me. I feel something inside of me that drives me to do such work as you are doing. . . ."

Rapu smiled and looked for a moment like one of his own statues.

"You have come too late," he said. "Where would you serve your apprenticeship? Who would teach you the secrets of our guild?"

"I have made some chisels and I have done some work in small stones that my friends have thought very good," said the boy. "I was in hopes that you might let me serve you until at last I learned how to do these things for myself."

Rapu shook his head.

"It won't do," he objected. "The adepts of our guild learned their art in the land whence Hotu Matua brought us. We worked for many years with blocks of wood until we had discovered just what words to say when lifting the chisel and what ones to say when striking it with the mallet. We created many strange gods and left them to edify the populace in the temple groves of Marae Renga.

"Perhaps, if we were back in the homeland with only such minor products to occupy our time, it might be possible to teach you something. But here there is no wood. We have to do the best we can with soft stone and it is not good material. One who has learned the rudiments of his trade can handle it. But life is too short to spend it in showing an amateur how it can be tooled without breaking. Go back to the villages of the Marama, son, and forget about art."

The youth seemed close to tears.

"I can not forget about art," he protested. "And I am a very good engineer. I have discovered how you may move a big rock with a stick of wood and I know a method for hauling large blocks."

Rapu seemed impatient.

"I can do nothing for you," he declared. "I can not quit my work to instruct you. I have sworn to the gods that I shall go on carving the beautiful images come rain, come storm and that nothing shall stop me. So long as I live I shall give the example to the other men of my guild. My art is my love and my life, and my great stone statues are my children."

The youth arose and walked with shambling steps toward the coast. Rapu finished his yams and mounted once more to the rim of Rano Raraku.

In a moment he had forgotten about the ambitious youth of the Marama. There was a great work to be done to-day. All of the carvers were assembling at a point on the steep south wall of the crater where a pole of toromiro wood had been erected in a hole in the rock. Guys made of braided grass stretched from this mast to anchorages among the big boulders. Another grass rope thicker than a chiselman's arm swung down from the top of the pole in a graceful curve into space and was lost beyond the rim of the volcano.

The plain below the hill, beyond the quarries of tufa—beyond the rank of gods who kept their scornful vigil over the pass to the north and the flat country to the west—was quivering with life. From over the ridge had come the *ariki* of the Miru, the dignified magicians, in all the regalia of their station. Behind them—scarcely identifiable from the misty heights—were men and women of the lesser clans, Marama, Haumoana, Ngatimo, Ngaure, and Raa. . . . Thousands of them. Their tattooing made their bodies a luminous blue in the morning light, and the color of them blended in a strange cloak-like mass that blotted out the green of the grass and filled the black shadows of the distance.

The chief of the Miru had called and these men had come. They bore no spears. They came down through the passes like the rivers one remembered having seen in Marae Renga, their quarrels forgotten. To-morrow perhaps they would be at one another's throats again. Today they stood in the truce of god, carrying out the will of the magicians.

Rapu stood for a moment watching the men at the guy-ropes but made no comment. These workers were of the Hotu Iti—the clans of the artizans and they needed no direction. Many a time before they had done this. The mast rose straighter as if of its own volition and the thick line that stretched over the brow of the hill came up taut with a curious spinning motion. Rapu moved to the west rim and waved a flaming banana stalk in an arc above his head.

The men in the plain came forward, a brown tide that presently split into numerous formless blots. It might have seemed to a stranger that chaos had come into the movement. But Rapu knew better. The men of the plain still came forward no longer as a mass but as a group of coordinated units, each unit assigned to its own task and performing it with speed and precision. The tide struck at the base of the slope and came onward—straight up the mountainside without thought of grades or rocky obstructions. . . . And behind each clambering unit trailed a line of woven fiber only slightly less cumbersome than the one attached to the mast.

Presently the hill was covered with men—vertical ranks of men clinging to their ropes at intervals of three or four feet. Near the mast their leaders were winding loops about a stone figure prostrate on the rim and precariously balanced over the dizzy void where the south cliff sweeps down to the sea. Rapu inspected this work and tested the knots, for these men were not of the guild. One could never be sure of them. This statue, now, represented weeks of labor—weeks of labor that would be wiped out in an instant if these occasional craftsmen were slipshod. That a considerable portion of the populace might be wiped out at the same time was a minor detail to which Rapu gave no consideration.

He approved the knots. The men on the hillside and in the crater moved once more and presently the lines of grass rope radiated from the mast like the tentacles of a squid. Once more Rapu waved the smoking brand above his head.

Men at the edge of Rano Raraku thrust levers under the image and pried up the end of it while other men removed wedges of stone. The mast bent and creaked. The great hawser sagged. The statue swung outward from the cliff and hung suspended in air five hundred feet above the plain, a mile from Tongariki platform where the other end of the grass cable was anchored.

A troop of men skilled in such work swung themselves on to the rope and worked their way foot by foot down the swaying catenary. As they went they smeared the surface with yams by way of lubrication, for this was their particular job.

Then, at another signal, the men on the hillside began a march toward the southeast, straining their bodies against their tightening lines. They walked and the huge image began its slow descent, the loops which bound it sliding freely over the yam-greased cable, the lines in the hands of the laborers restraining it from disastrous flight toward Tongariki.

In twenty minutes the image lay on the platform.

Workers with poles and tackle were setting up a crude derrick by which the rope crews would presently hoist it into an upright position. From the edge of Rano Raraku, Rapu the Sculptor gazed on the scene with no show of emotion. Another task had been decreed and as usual it had been carried out. He descended the west slope and stood among his stone gods.

"I have consecrated myself to a worthy work," he said in a voice that made his words a prayer. "And here once more, in the moment of great achievement, I repeat my vow that nothing shall ever lure me from my service to the gods."

The boy of the Marama clan went home and sat for a long time on top of the rocky arch of Eat Man Cave staring moodily at the sea. There, as the sun was setting, came Hautere, his sister, to sit by his side. He told her his story, not because he had any hope that she might understand, but because it is not a good thing to keep such sorrow to one's self. Hautere seemed only slightly affected.

"I think this Rapu is highly overrated," she said. "I never did think much of his statues anyway."

"He is a great artist," moaned her brother. "He has an intense, passionate nature and he is entirely wrapped up in his work. It consumes him. It leaves no place in his life for anything else. No wonder he refused to listen to me. I might as well have talked to a flame."

The girl looked at him oddly.

"I wonder if, after all, I could have been mistaken in this man," she commented. "An intense, passionate nature. . . . And like a flame. . . . You should have been an artist yourself. You make a much more interesting picture than those stone *moai*. I could very easily be indifferent to a *moai* even if it weighed fifty tons and stood sixty feet

The Start of a Statue

Still clinging to the mother rock it remains to-day as it was when the carvers dropped their tools for the last time

Maori Carvings

In other climes the artistic talents of the Polynesians were expressed in other forms

A GIANT THIRTY-FIVE FEET TALL

The weight of this one has been estimated at forty tons. Larger images were being carved when this phase of Easter's culture passed

high. . . . Whereas a man with the right sort of disposition . . ."

"Think nothing of it," advised the brother wearily. "He wouldn't look at you. What is a woman to a man who is almost a god. . . . Besides I have an idea he is one of the Miru clan."

"I think I shall go down to Rano Raraku," said Hautere irrelevantly. "I'm beginning to realize that art hasn't meant as much to me as it should have."

Once more the clans assembled on the west slope of the image mountain. On a platform of stone well above the throng stood Rapu. The hum of voices came up to him like the echoing of a high surf—eagerly, excitedly. There was expectancy and admiration in this noise of a thousand tongues if Rapu had noticed it. But the eager clansmen might have been in Marae Renga and Rapu himself on the silver plains of the moon for all the impression that they made upon him.

He stood detached in body and spirit while he surveyed the grim face of the image that peered up at him from out of its new-cut grave. And modest though he was Rapu knew that he had wrought a masterpiece. No finer specimen than this had ever come from the tufa beds of Rano Raraku. He doubted seriously if one as fine could ever be carved again. He whetted his chisel and stood for a long time lost in thought.

When at last he gave the signal four chieftains clambered up the slope and stood beside him. He knew at once that his judgment had not been at fault. For these men, leaders of their people, shrank back amazed at the power of that silent stone face. It was as if he had imprisoned in his statue some animate principle. As if for the moment he had been a god.

The rope bearers made the steep ascent but not in the formation that had been required for the transport of the figure to the Tongariki platform. No wooden beam or hawser made slippery with yams was erected over Rapu's masterpiece. Mud-carriers had been at work all morning bearing water from the crater lake and mixing slime on the slope below the quarry. Now, at Rapu's command, an army pulled at ropes below and another army slacked off on ropes above, and the statue slid feet first from the open end of its grave, descending the hill with all the slow dignity that one would deem proper in so well made a god. At the bottom of the mud skid the base of the image went squarely into a hole. The rope men below bent their shining bodies in one final effort, the giant came erect, shivered a moment and stood still. The deep mysterious eyes peered out over land and sea. Engineers filled up the hole about the base. The rope men unfastened their nooses.

The awed multitude, suddenly hushed, looked for a moment at the newest of the gods, then turned suddenly for home as if glad to get away. Rapu grinned with satisfaction at the implied compliment. He picked up his mallet and chisel and began to chip away the keel from the statue's back.

Up in the crater other chisels were sounding and over the throb of the surf there came now and then the low echoes of voices in the distance. Otherwise deep silence had settled over the mountain. A pebble fell on a dry leaf and Rapu turned suddenly to discover a girl swinging her bare legs from a rock on the slope above him.

His artistic eye noticed that as women went she was a pretty little thing, lithe and muscular. Her straight black hair was rippling over her shoulders to frame a face which, though it lacked the stern dignity of the stone gods, had noticeable qualities. Her eyes were half closed and smoldering. Her mouth was small and sensuous. And her beautiful body was wrapped in a cloak of tapa-cloth. This final fact Rapu noted impatiently. There was something not quite right about this fad for clothing, he felt. It tended to reveal too well the things it was supposed to hide. . . .

"Who are you?" he demanded.

"Hautere of the Marama," answered the girl with a deep sigh that irritated him.

"What do you want?"

"I have walked many a long mile from Hanga Roa just to look at your beautiful statue. . . . You must be Rapu the skilful one. No one else could have made so lovely a thing."

Rapu sniffed unconvincingly.

"You can start walking right home again," he told her. "The miles are longer going back and the sun doesn't stay up for ever."

She sighed again.

"I am in no hurry," she said. "I'd rather sit here and talk to you among these excellent gods."

"I have no desire to talk to you," he declared gruffly. "You distract me from my work."

"The boys of the Marama say that I am very desirable," remarked Hautere modestly. "Why shouldn't you talk to me?"

"I can't be bothered with women."

"Neither can I. I much prefer men."

"Go on home."

"I don't want to. . . . And you're very impolite."

"I didn't ask you to come here."

"Of course you did. You made the beautiful images and

then I just had to come. I guess it's because I have an artistic nature."

"Such things are not for women."

"I know that . . . I feel that the gods put a curse on us when they gave us an appreciation of art without the brains and muscle to express ourselves. That's why woman asks the companionship of great souls such as yourself. You reach up to heaven and she feels that you are doing it for her . . . that without you she would be compelled to stay for ever in the dust."

"But suppose some of us have sense enough to refuse this companionship. What then?"

"You don't know what you're missing. Great men like you shouldn't be lonely. You are entitled to worship such as the pious people give to the old gods. But you don't get it. You sit in loneliness all the day long. And when some one comes who adores you, you say 'Go on home, little girl; you annoy me.' "

Rapu considered this for a long time while his mallet and chisel hung motionless at his side.

As he gave the matter thought for the first time since he had begun to carve statues on Rano Raraku it occurred to him that the work had been lonely and poorly recompensed. And this chatterbox of a girl was not like other girls. She had sympathy and intelligence and a gift of expressing herself. And also she was very pretty.

"Just the same," he said after a while, "I think you had better run along home." And he added irrelevantly: "Another statue will be ready for launching day after tomorrow."

Once more the clans assembled and once more a stone god came sliding down the hill. This giant, smaller and artistically inferior to Rapu's masterpiece, was destined to occupy a pedestal on the *ahu* of Vinapu, so it was not upended in a hole at the bottom of the slope. Instead it was carefully bound with pads of woven reeds and rolled on to a carpet of split banana stalks six inches thick. The mud-carriers came up from the sea and over the lip of the crater like a procession of ants, preparing a path of slime to the seacoast and along the shore-line westward for many a long mile.

When the preliminary work had been completed Rapu gave his quiet signal and two thousand men stuck their shoulders into the yokes of matting. . . . Four thousand legs moved in unison. The image on its raft of reed work slid smoothly in its trough of mud and at a rate of a mile an hour started on its journey to Vinapu.

Rapu stood for a few minutes watching it, then turned back to the rock where he had seen Hautere. Oddly enough she was there waiting for him.

"You are the most surprising man I ever saw," she told him. "You raise your hand and the whole island works for you. You are a bigger man than a king . . . something like a god."

Rapu tried to seem indifferent.

"Did you get very tired walking over here?" he inquired.

"I never get tired coming here because I know I am going to see you . . . and of course all the beautiful statues. I find it very weary going home. I have a brother at home who is quite artistic. He has made some excellent little figures. And I know he'll be waiting there in the village, eager to hear about you—wanting to know what you have said—and this and that. . . ."

"Let's not talk about your brother," suggested Rapu. She had a nice manner, this girl, and inviting eyes. He remembered the long empty nights when he had lain in his stone house on the lip of the crater alone save for the cold stars and the misty spirits of the gods. It came to him that one who sacrificed all for the slavery of an art might be rated something of a hero. He hadn't thought of himself in that light before. . . . And as for the beauty of women—well he was one of the old school that favored the strong line and the rough angle in a face. Nothing would ever swerve him very much from that standard. No woman had yet been born whose face could radiate strength as the images radiated it. But on the other hand there was something very close to beauty in a woman's delicacy of figure—in her helplessness, her touching trust in man's strength, her worship of his skill.

"You should tell your brother that the life of the image-carver is very sad," he told her. And he felt as he said it that he was listening to the speech of a total—and misinformed—stranger. "There is no room for a woman in an art that requires all of a man's time and energy and thought. Your true artist is born to loneliness. He must warm himself on the fire that is in him."

"Why?" inquired Hautere as she slid down from her rock to the grassy slope by his side.

On days when the northern ridge danced and shivered and seemed to float under a hot sun, and on days when the rain blotted out the south coast and filled the crater with the tails of its ragged cloak, and on days when the spray-filled winds came howling out of the Antarctic, the carvers plied their busy chisels. In fair weather or foul a fire signal on the hill brought the army of workers down through the passes. Stone gods passed down the cable to Tongariki or through the mud slides on the west slope. Energy never relaxed. . . . Discipline never faltered.

And in the concourse of the people few could have noticed the child Hautere, daughter of the Marama, who came often to look upon the work of Rapu the greatest of the image-makers.

At Hanga Roa her brother practised his crude art and seemed close to despair. There were times when he was impatient with her.

"It seems to me," he said repeatedly, "that if Rapu tolerates you, you should be able to get him to do something for me."

"He is still wrapped up in his art." The girl's answer was always the same. "Sometimes I feel that he doesn't even see me."

"It's surprising that he lets you talk to him at all. . . . He hasn't any use for women. . . ."

"I know that. . . ."

"Then why do you keep running back to Rano Raraku?"

"It may be because he doesn't like women. It may be that I like him. But mostly I think it is because I am interested in his work. I can't tell what it is but something about those tremendous images makes me tingle all over."

In his house on the rim of Rano Raraku night after night Rapu the Carver considered his loneliness. And night after night he arose to peer down the mountainside and look upon his works in the moonlight. Thus he reassured himself of the importance of the task he had assigned to himself and the logic of his course in renouncing the world.

A wailing cry was echoing from the distances along the seacoast. The hills picked it up and threw it back. And in the passes it swelled to a terrible roar. Rapu, preoccupied, went on with his wielding of mallet and chisel. Then presently the blue hills were aquiver as from every crevasse and over every crest an avalanche of men and women coursed down to the plain. Rapu looked up in surprise.

No signal had been given for such an assemblage. It would be a day, perhaps two, before another image should be ready for transport. And yet they came . . . not only the rope men and the mud-carriers and the engineers of the Tongariki cable, but their women and children, and the old men who never took part in the launching of the statues.

He hurried to the top of the crater and skirted the rim to the north. There he stood motionless, listening for the relayed shouts of village headmen. And presently he knew. . . . The king was dead. On Rano Kao he had lifted himself up from his bed of rushes and had looked out over the sea toward a vision of Marae Renga, the homeland. And he had died. The great intelligence that had conquered starvation and made a close-knit people of the ten clans had gone out into the emptiness where the dead fires go. Rapu sighed and shrugged.

After all, what did it matter? Already another king sat among the magicians of the Miru at Anakena. . . . Another all-powerful will was abroad in the land, compelling the yams to grow and the fowl to multiply and enforcing the discipline of the image-bearers. Man must die even though he be one of the demigods of the Miru. And his successors after him must die. . . . Only art was permanent. He moved slowly down the hillside to act as spokesman for the guild of carvers in the assembly of the people. At the rock, beside his finest statue, he found Hautere huddled in a pathetic little ball to protect her thin shoulders against the crisp wind.

"You are early," he said. "Did you run all the way?"

"I didn't go home yesterday," she told him simply. "I slept here all night. And it was cold. And now I'm hungry." She seemed suddenly conscious of the onrushing people.

"What's the matter?" she asked.

He told her and she stared at him as if only half comprehending what he said.

"But what will it mean to you? You have always carved these images in the likeness of the king. Will you start now to make new images—portraits of our new king?"

He did not answer at once. When he spoke it was as if he had forgotten her and was talking to himself:

"I have spent the best years of my life reproducing that face. In cold and heat and hunger I have never thought of anything else. I have covered the island with the likeness of one man. I have made it possible for him to sneer at the sea from hundreds of platforms and pedestals and hillsides. . . . And now he is dead and I can live with a new face. That is what we pay for our craft: we live like dead men to make some one else immortal. And we grow hard in spirit and at last we forget what it is like to be men."

For the first time since she had known him she sensed defeat. Here in this field of the Titans—now the graveyard of one man's multiplied vanity—she realized that something more powerful than the lure of woman had directed this odd guild of the image-makers. In a little they had been gods—creators. What had she—what had any one—to offer in competition with so glorious an urge.

"I understand," she said in a low voice. "I can see now what it means to have power over life and death. Kings can never die when you are here to make them eternal in stone. I said that I could worship you. I think that I do worship you. But I am going home now and I shall never come back here again. . . . Your craft is all that matters. . . . It makes everything else seem trivial. . . ."

"That subject is highly debatable," he said. "I am going to Hanga Roa with you."

And he threw away his chisels.

Chapter Nineteen

THE ENGINEERS

An Epic in Black Basalt

The most glib of Easter Island's traditions stutters a little at the story of Rapu and Hautere. Oddly enough (or perhaps not at all oddly) one finds no mention of them in the tatters of myth and legend on the island itself. Only in the remnants of the old Rapa Nui Colony on Tahiti does one hear the stories from which one may piece together the record of their strange meeting and stranger wooing. The hint of the modern in the psychology of the greatest of all the carvers is too obvious to be ignored, and the lady's violation of certain definitely established tabus gives her an air of unreality.

But one who would turn an inquisitive ear to the echoes that come from burial platforms and the mustering places of forgotten gods hesitates to quarrel with pretty stories. All legend, back on the fringes of time, has had some association with fact and in this chronicle of Rano Raraku one finds many things which ought to be true even if they are not.

Hautere, the beautiful daughter of the Marama, who wanted a man merely because he was denied her, is not wholly incredible even as an individual. As the personification of tribal rebellion against the restraint of a domineering intelligence she seems quite real and understandable. So, too, with Rapu the Greatest of the Carvers. He may have had an existence as a fanatical artist. He may be merely a fiction in whom all the sculptors of Rano

Raraku find an expression. No matter. There certainly were carvers and they certainly threw away their chisels, whether through love or ennui makes little difference after all these hundreds of years.

There is something startling in the detailed accounts of the image-making and in the pictures of a whole people putting their necks into the yoke to drag the stone giants for miles across the island. The story of the fiber cable that stretched for a mile from Rano Raraku to the platform of Tongariki seems wildly imaginative. And yet one must pause to reflect that none of the stone giants traveled far of their own volition. There is nothing in the present-day folk-lore of Rapa Nui to suggest the existence of Hautere or her talented lover, but there is plenty to show that tradition had accepted without question those portions of the tale that would explain the engineering.

On Rano Raraku one finds the carefully drilled round holes which legend identifies as receptacles for the timbers of the overhead tram-line. And there, high above the gallery of the gods, the project does not seem so fantastic.

It is probable that there never were large trees on the island. All early voyagers seem agreed on that point. But the legend of Hotu Matua, so demonstrably accurate in a number of details, mentions that the great chief of Marae Renga brought with him to Te-Pito-Te-Henua, the sandalwood and other trees. None of these trees ever grew to a great height or had a trunk larger than eighteen inches in diameter. But it is not at all impossible that a number of these small logs could have been bound together with ropes of woven fiber into a timber capable of supporting tremendous weights. And there one leaves the story of the aerial transportation. The imagination required for the construction of such a device is scarcely greater than that necessary for the manufacture of a legend about it.

As for the movement of the images across the land the traditional account seems to be as good an explanation as any. Mud slides, grass ropes, a vast concentration of human effort—these are all simple elements in the puzzling picture of Easter Island. The principal engine at the command of the genius who built the amazing social structure of the island, was human muscle. That he used it seems fairly obvious.

In the affairs of Rapu and Hautere one finds another hint of truth where the sculptor considers the task of carving a new set of gods with new faces. There are two possible interpretations to this phase of the legend: that the carving and transportation of the images began and ended in one generation; and that one man—the great chief who brought the people under his discipline—was the model for all of them.

Even without the story one might guess at something of the sort. The similarity of the scornful faces makes them seem at once to be the product of some short constructional period. That the art which produced them had been long in developing and had reached a stage of conventional design is fairly obvious. That it was brought to the island from some point where the carvers served their apprenticeship is also a reasonable supposition, for all of the statues on Easter have been produced by men of approximately the same skill. Nowhere does one find the fumbling efforts of the beginner—or for that matter samples of the stages by which the art of one generation rises beyond that of another. The sameness of the sculptures is sufficiently pronounced to make one class them as portraits of a single model. But even were they of widely varying models their uniformity of treatment would tend to place them all within the lifetime of one guild of carvers. Art—even a standardized art—does not remain static over a long period of years, especially when it is the expression of a people as new as the remodeled Polynesians of Easter.

The first and outstanding enigma of Easter is the distribution of the images. The barrenness of the island, its constant suggestion of starvation and death, led many years ago to the propounding of a thesis which has been repeated glibly ever since: that these rocky valleys and sere hills could never have supported a population large enough to haul monoliths of from ten to forty tons. Acceptance of this idea has led to a search for a sunken archipelago or the remnants of the fabled lost continent of the Pacific from which came food supplies for the army of workers who lived on the island.

It seems senseless to argue with a theory which can be neither proved nor disproved but one can arrive at a basis for discussion, at least, when one considers the agricultural possibilities of Rapa Nui as one finds it to-day. Residents best qualified to speak on the subject have pointed out that if available fields were cultivated, and garden products augmented by a supply of fish and fowl, the island could provide a living for seven thousand people. Even if this seems to be a radical estimate one may recall that the early voyagers reported a population of from three thousand to five thousand and it is historical that there were more than two thousand inhabitants on the land at the time of the Peruvian slave raid.

If one presupposes a population of five thousand, subsisting on yams, bananas and fish, one has to deal with a condition not much different from that to be seen to-day in many of the Polynesian islands. Agriculture requires little time—fishing, little more. The populace under such conditions, while living primitively, none the less must have had considerable leisure. The detachment of a thousand men—a fifth of the population for two or three days' labor each week would seem to involve no great difficulty.

There are more than four hundred images still to be seen on the island, most of them within a few hundred yards of the crater of Rano Raraku where they were quarried. Less than a hundred and fifty found places on the burial platforms, and of these not to exceed fifty were carried distances of more than five miles. The statues on the *ahus* are the smallest on the island. Few of them are more than twenty tons in weight; most of them are less than ten.

The soft tufa from which they were carved was easily worked even with primitive tools. If one places the total of the images at five hundred the entire display could have been carved in fifty years at a rate of ten a year. As a matter of fact ten skilled chiselmen must have been able to rough out a thirty-ton monolith in fifteen days and finish it in another fifteen. Even if one considers that the carvers comprised a sacred guild and admitted no neophytes to the study of their art it is conservative to say that twelve statues could have been produced in one year, or in round numbers, a hundred in eight years. Thus the total period necessary to the production of five hundred statues is fixed at approximately forty years or a little more than a generation.

There is abundant evidence in the traditions of the island to show that the image-makers were not one small, select group, but a clan whose membership went well into the hundreds. If one grants that there were forty of them, one arrives at the conclusion that Easter's gods, the puzzle of centuries, could have sprung from the rock in ten years.

Not so many years ago the islanders undertook to obtain an image for a museum in Chile. The entire male population, totaling less than two hundred, marched to Rano Raraku and dug up a specimen fifteen feet high. With ropes, rollers and man-power they loaded it on to a bullock dray which carried it nine miles to Hanga Roa landing. There, in removing it from the cart, they dropped it, breaking off the tip of the nose.

There was wailing throughout the village. A Kanaka, especially a modern Rapa Nui, is averse to hard work in a hot sun. Moreover the annual ship was due to sail for Valparaiso in thirty-six hours.

At this juncture there came Juan Tepano, a lad whose intelligence has identified him with at least two expeditions to Easter. He borrowed a cold chisel from the ranch house at Mataveri, worked all night, and in fifteen hours had carved a new image out of the old one. The result stands to-day in a Valparaiso collection, similar in every detail to the works which strew the slopes of Rano Raraku.

Even more significant than the handiwork of Juan Tepano, last of the carvers' guild, is the feat of the men who helped to dig up and transport the image he rebuilt. While the bullock dray accounts for much of their success it does not eliminate the fact that they accomplished the loading with materials and instruments hardly less primitive than those of Hotu Matua's time. And less than two hundred men furnished the power.

If one estimates the weight of an average image on the burial platforms at twenty tons and its maximum distance from Rano Raraku at ten miles, one arrives at some mathematical facts: If a thousand men were available to lift a twenty-ton weight, each individual would have to raise forty pounds. If only five hundred men were engaged in the task the burden of each would be eighty pounds—in neither case anything to tax the energies of a normal Polynesian. At a rate of one mile an hour five hundred men might well have carried such a statue the entire length of the island in a single day.

If, in addition to sheer man-power as applied by woven grass ropes, these carriers had had the assistance of a few rollers or a simple wooden sled, one could see the accomplishment of all the transportation on Easter in the hands of two hundred men. . . . And without further evidence one would hesitate to state flatly that they had no such equipment.

The transportation of the red hats which once crowned the images on the platforms has never been a mystery. The hats were cylinders of red tufa and could easily have been rolled from the hill near Hanga Roa where they were quarried to any of the coastal *ahus*. They could have been moved into place along a temporary runway of earth.

Probably a greater mass effort went into the building of the burial platforms than was required for the production and transport of the stone gods. One investigator has pointed out that these terraces—some one hundred and twenty in number—are made of squared matched stones and represent an amount of labor equivalent to that which went into the building of Westminster Abbey. The puzzle becomes more stupendous the longer one looks at it, but it is not entirely without an answer.

There are acres and acres of squared stone on Easter. One side of the seaward wall at Tongariki is as long as the elephant terrace at Angkor, and in its way as remarkable. The terrace at Vinapu has a finish that would have done credit to the masons of Egypt and looks more like a Peruvian wall than anything else on the island. But it should be noted that these are only two of the platforms—and the best ones on the island.

The squaring of most of the stone that went into the seaward piers of the terraces was done by Nature when Rapa Nui first began to cool. Most of this rock is columnar basalt which breaks off into rectangular shapes neatly adapted to wall building, and the supply along the rocky coast was always fairly close to the building sites.

Masonry of this type is by no means unknown among other Neolithic peoples. There are Cyclopean fortifications and irrigation terraces on the island of Rapa, due south of Tahiti; a stone portal with mortised joints is one of the exhibitions of native handiwork in the Tongan Islands; large stone structures have been discovered in the Carolines. This phase of building is something that the numerous races of the South Sea Islands discovered simultaneously or else preserved traditionally as a heritage from Babylon or India or Uru, or wherever they came from originally.

It is because of the wall of Vinapu that the theory has been advanced which would connect the people of Rapa Nui with the temple-builders of Peru. But, save that both races knew how to square rock and make close joints in their masonry, there seems to be no real resemblance.

There are no markings of any sort on the Vinapu terrace. None of the figures with which the Inca-builders loved to ornament their handiwork have ever been found on Easter. . . . Nor have any of the Rapa Nui symbols ever been found in Peru. There would seem to be as much justice in connecting the Easter Islanders with the Angkoreans or the Egyptians or any other master masons as in classifying their terraces with any similar group on the South American continent.

Thus, when one studies the massive erections of Easter out of the disconcerting vision of the scornful gods, one feels that one has come close to the heart of the island's mystery. One discards the simple native explanation that the *moai* and platforms were built in the forgotten long-ago by supernatural beings, and one supplies more prosaic, and possibly less believable theories.

But always a person is faced by one puzzle that can not be reduced to terms of human perspiration and elementary arithmetic: the collapse of a culture whose beginnings were so brave, whose day was so brief and whose end was so sudden. It is a little like the enigma of Angkor, this unanswered question of Easter. It wasn't the departure of the Khmers from Angkor that wiped them from the face of the earth . . . it was the departure of something from the Khmers themselves. And here in the thrones of desolation one reads a parallel case.

Chapter Twenty

WHITE SPOT

A Melodrama of Pride

Hard by the abandoned church in Hanga Roa village is an unkempt cemetery from which rises a large wooden cross at whose base is a tablet with a Latin inscription conveying a message of hope. One might write a new elegy here or verse of splendid irony: Hope proclaiming itself from a shrine of tragedy and fear . . . Hope struggling with weeds and tundra grass and decay and human apathy and housed in a cemetery while the spirit of Despair walks abroad in the land.

The cairns of the ancient dead which spread like links in a vast chain about the island—the acres of bleaching skeletons that mark the passing of a strange and powerful people—the whistling ghosts that the night wind stirs in the abandoned villages—are awesome things that link one uncomfortably with the desolate past. But there is nothing poignant about them—nothing to arouse in the beholder any sense of personal concern. . . . These people lived a long time ago and must certainly have died before now no matter how kindly Nature had treated them. . . . In the little graveyard of Hanga Roa one comes into close contact with the sorrows of human beings whom one can see and understand. . . . Men and women who seem eons removed from the demigods who made the images, creatures of clay and poverty and sin who have known the sufferings of the flesh. There are not many graves here. It has been the lot of the islanders since the advent of civilization to die in far places—in the guano diggings of Peru, the cane fields of Tahiti or the pearl harbors of Manga Reva. But small and poorly tended as it is, probably no other burying-ground in the world contains so many evidences of stark tragedy.

Here is a new mound. . . . So new that the grass has not yet hidden it. Its marker is a simple cross of wood. There lies beneath it a Chilean ensign who came ashore last month from the *Baquedano,* a naval training ship. He shot himself by accident and will rest here until a coffin is sent out from Valparaiso. . . .

Not far away is another hillock less neglected than the rest. In this grave is buried a murdered ranch foreman.

And there is a third grave sufficiently new to show that Death, so manifestly reverenced by Hotu Matua's pioneers, is still plodding along undiscouraged. The Easter stock, despite its degradation through additions of Caucasian scum from seven seas, is virile. It has the habit of resisting the end. . . . A will to live, for what reason no man can say. It carries on shivering in the daylight through dread of the dark. And it has survived, miraculously, the catastrophes that threatened to give the island back to the stone gods and the infrequent birds. In the end, however, all this struggle ends as it does everywhere else in the world. Famine may be temporarily halted but disease has come to take its place. . . . This third grave . . .

When, at some distant date, the men of science cease to argue over the purpose which activated the ridiculous empire of Easter it is scarcely likely that they will find any record of the story of Estepan and his father Totaro. The little dramas of people like these are of no moment to the world. They are too common to attract attention even on their own stage.

Estepan was an assistant policeman, hired by the ranch company and equipped with a blue uniform and a rifle and a clip of five actual bullets. Estepan rode the range fences on a fast horse with a saddle of genuine yellow leather much superior to the rawhide with which less fortunate islanders had to be content. Estepan had the authority to shoot people whom he might catch stealing sheep. And though he never quite got around to exercising this prerogative, the village was conscious of it. The civilian populace looked upon him with an awe just slightly removed from terror.

Totaro was fond of this talented youth. He displayed a paternal pride which, while not entirely foreign to the nature of the Rapa Nui, was sufficiently unusual to attract attention. He became noted as a poor conversationalist in a district overpopulated with poor conversationalists because he could not discuss fish or yams or the overlords of Mataveri's ranch-house without bringing in some comment concerning "my son Estepan who is the assistant prefect of police."

People grew tired of hearing about Estepan and his dignity and his duties and as a consequence they tired of the company of Totaro. Totaro presently found himself shunned and lonely . . . not that he cared much about the company of the sullen people of Hanga Roa but because they had constituted his only possible audience. It is difficult to boast about one's children if no one will listen to the boasting.

Even so Totaro could have borne this sorrow readily enough had it not been for the strange attitude of Estepan himself. Estepan from his tall horse could look upon the heads of his Hanga Roa neighbors in proud disdain. What cared he if they loved or if they feared him? He could always make them talk to him should he feel a craving for society. They knew better than to rise and walk away when he came near. For his position was superior to their whims and his rifle was always ready at his saddle for purposes whose nature the crowd could readily imagine.

But Estepan was a bit annoyed at Totaro's attempt to make himself unpopular. He spoke to the old man—not roughly, understand, but in tones of great firmness.

"Old man," he said, "you are making a fool of yourself and of me. You talk too much. And it has got to the point where the girls will speak to me only when I make them speak. They do not realize that I am the assistant prefect of police. They realize only that you are my father and a blabbing old fool."

Totaro seemed greatly moved and naturally a bit ashamed.

"It is only my pride and my love for you that have made me boastful," he said. "I never wished to do you any harm. But I shall be silent. I know a little place where I can plant a yam patch over on the other side of the island and I have been thinking of moving there. I shall not stand in your way."

"That, old man, is a good idea," remarked Estepan, ready, as always, to concede parental wisdom in cases where it was fairly obvious.

But there was difficulty in the accomplishment of this plan. On the following day, at the complaint of one of the overseers of the ranch, Estepan was called before the subdelegal.

He was not surprised at the order. In his capacity as assistant prefect of police he had frequently been summoned to the presence of the tired old man who represented the august government of Chile. But he was surprised at the abrupt manner in which the message was delivered. The prefect of police himself stood at the door of Estepan's hut and commanded that he come out at once. The prefect would not permit him to get his rifle or horse and walked at his side in hostile silence all the way to the governor's house.

Estepan was thoroughly frightened when at length he stood in a hot room, swarming with hungry flies, and faced the desk at which sat the sub-delegal.

"Why have I been brought here?" he demanded in sudden panic. "Why has my chief come after me? I have not committed any crime. I swear that to you. I can prove that all night I have been in my own home. Totaro my father will tell you that. If a crime has been committed somebody else has done it."

"Be quiet," suggested the governor in a tired voice. "Nobody is accusing you of any crime. Take off your coat and let me see your hands and arms."

For a moment the none too nimble wit of Estepan failed to note any significance in the order. In puzzlement he fumbled with his brass buttons and stripped off his blouse. Then, just as he was extending his forearms for inspection, he realized what the procedure might mean.

"This is an outrage," he said hoarsely. And he drew back. The old man looked up at him kindly but paid no attention to his protest.

"Your arms," the governor said. "Show them to me."

Estepan turned pale and looked at the door which was crowded with villagers. But there was no chance for escape in that direction. As if in a daze he extended his arms before him and stood staring at the white splotches extending from his wrists to his elbows.

"A clear case of leprosy," diagnosed the governor. "You will go to the colony, of course. And you will stay there."

There was a commotion at the door and a shriek. The crowd drew back suddenly and Totaro hurled himself into the room.

"He is not a leper," moaned the old man. "I am the only leper in our family. I have tried to hide it. But now I see that I have failed. Take me to the colony and leave Estepan here. My son Estepan is a strong healthy boy. The prefect of police needs him."

The sub-delegal looked at him oddly.

"Take off your clothes," he ordered. "All of them."

"It is not necessary," mumbled the old man. "I admit that I am a leper. I'll go to the colony without any trouble."

"All of them," repeated the governor monotonously. "Off. . . ."

Totaro's feeble hands reluctantly loosened his grass belt and clutched the collar of his shirt and presently he stood naked before the village.

There was not a spot on him.

"This is not a case of leprosy," came the unemotional voice of the governor. "Take him out."

"He is my son," shrieked Totaro. "You can't take him away from me. I have been so proud of him. He has been such a good boy . . . such a fine son to me."

"Take Estepan to the colony," directed the governor. "And do what you can for this father. . . . There are times when I would rather be dead than the sub-delegal of this island."

So another assistant gendarme with a blue uniform and a rifle motioned Estepan toward the door and thence up the long hill to the unpainted shack where Easter's lepers are entombed before death.

"He is my son," Totaro kept repeating. "You can't take him away from me. . . . You can't take him away from me."

He followed up the long slope away from the village and when Estepan staggered across the threshold into the company of the lepers, Totaro, still naked and still spotless, reeled out of the sunlight behind him.

The new assistant prefect of police closed the door.

And that is the reason for the third new grave in the little cemetery. Totaro, who had been spotless, was dead in six months. Estepan, according to reports from the colony, will continue in this life, such as it is, for some time to come.

That, as the villagers will point out to you, is because Estepan's vigorous routine as assistant prefect of police gave him a sturdy constitution.

Chapter Twenty-One

CRYPTOGRAM

"The Moving Finger Writes—and Having Writ——"

EASTER even without its Titanic statues would still be the great puzzle of the South Sea Islands in that it gave to the world the only written language ever evolved in Polynesia. Numerous copies of its queer script are extant to-day, rescued just in time from the general debacle of the island culture that followed the Peruvian slave raids. Tablets of wood and bark, incised with the semi-pictorial representations of sea-gods and fish and animals and phallic symbols that made up this ideography are to be seen in the museums of Valparaiso, the British Museum and Smithsonian Institution, a tantalizing cryptogram in which if one had the key, one might read the solution to the entire ethnographic mystery of the Pacific.

But there is no key. No Rosetta stone by which the hieroglyphs of Easter might be translated has ever been found. One needs to be little of a prophet to forecast that none ever will be found. Even at a period close to our own when there were *maoris*—wise men—on the island whose lives were closely associated with the scripts, the meanings had been forgotten. Translations obtained from native scholars were speedily proved to be no translations at all and the tablets went back to their glass cases with their hidden message interpreted by one all-embracing modern character—a question mark.

Kohau-rongo-rongo, the natives called the tablets, roughly things to be recited or sung. And Professor Mac-

Millan Brown logically deduces from the name that within recent years at least they had ceased to be read as books are read. Long ago when sweating laborers were dragging Easter's massive art works from Rano Raraku to the distant burial *ahus* they had come to occupy an important place in the social and religious life of the island. Tabus encompassed them and the men who guarded them or copied them or recited their contents at feasts were shrouded in an atmosphere of holiness and awe. But it seems unlikely now that the art of writing which originally produced them survived the general decline of culture. At the end, most likely, they were the Pacific counterparts of the sibylline books—volumes whose secret contents might have been generally known to the cult who had their custody—but whose ideographs had become meaningless and whose component words were no longer recognizable.

Legend has it that the writing was brought to Easter from Marae Renga by Hotu Matua in sixty-seven tablets and that the original scripts comprised a group of songs, a genealogy of chiefs, and a compendium of racial traditions. The spurious translations obtained from modern Rapa Nuis always fell into one of these three classifications, sufficient evidence of what the populace supposed the *rongo-rongo* to be though useless as proof of what they actually were.

It is fairly certain that Hotu Matua, or the pioneering intelligence that Hotu Matua is supposed to represent, made of the tablets the bible of Easter's culture. *Maoris*—special scholars—were designated to learn their meanings and to copy them and to become, somewhat in the fashion of the keepers of oracles, important figures in all religious functions.

Professor Brown holds that the original meanings of the characters had been lost before Hotu Matua came to

Easter—that they were not and could not have been used as a means of communication in the new settlement. And this contention seems to be upheld by the fact that the script was found by white men only in the conventionalized groups on the tablets and never in a form which might be taken as a message from one person to another.

He sets forth the theory that the *rongo-rongo* men were taught to recognize each tablet as a whole and made to memorize its traditional subject matter. Thus the characters ceased to represent syllables or words and served merely as stimulants to memory. In view of what happened to white investigators who attempted to obtain translations, this theory seems well supported.

According to the tradition, the first writings were on paper—probably a species of bark cloth. When these scripts began to wear out they were copied on slabs of banana stem. Afterward they were recorded more permanently on wooden boards. The styles with which they were copied were made of sharks' teeth or points of obsidian.

No one is now alive on the island who has any comprehensive knowledge of the *rongo-rongo* and their preparation. The Routledge expedition in 1914 obtained some general information from a few old people who had survived the slave raids. From such sources it was learned that the *rongo-rongo* men were cultural leaders in all clans—the teachers and philosophers and learned ones. They instructed favored youths in the science of copying and reciting the scripts and as the island's only educated class were much revered.

In each clan settlement these scriveners lived by themselves in special houses which they did not share even with their wives and families. At regular intervals they assembled their pupils in the banana groves and there super-

The Easter Script
(From copy in Chilean Museum)

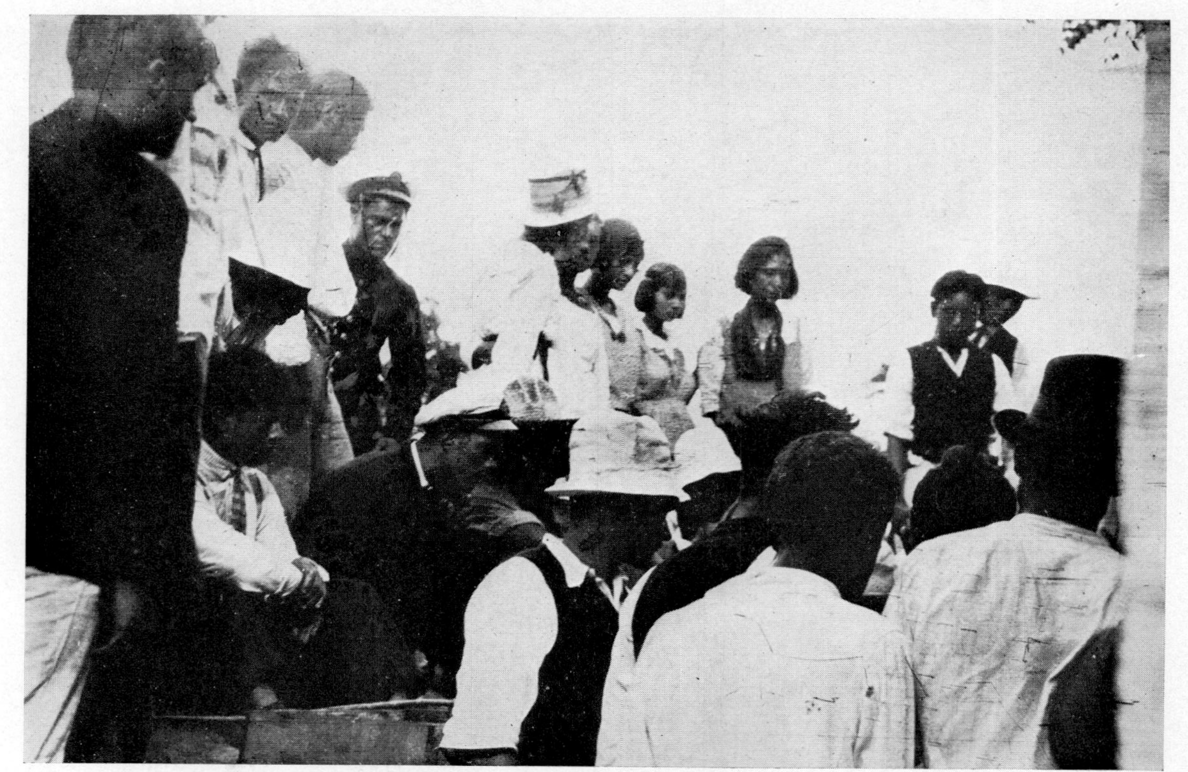

Sad Heritors of the Image-Makers

The last of the Easter Islanders dress themselves in Valparaiso's old clothes and apparently see no great hope for the world

vised a study of the scripts character by character. Practise copies of the tablets were made by the pupils on banana stems and the beginner was schooled in this work until he could be trusted to try his hand at better material.

It appears that in the early days on the island the tablets were considered tabu to all but the *rongo-rongo* men and certain other classes. But at the time of the coming of the missionaries they were widely circulated and had come to be considered valuable domestic possessions in every family. Mrs. Routledge's informant told her that they were highly rated as war prizes.

The religious significance of the script is made evident by the frequent repetition of the Makemake figure—the combination of bird, man and fish which in the art of Easter symbolized the spirit of the sea. Makemake was the traditional purveyor of food—the local equivalent of Vishnu the preserver—and possibly, as Professor Brown believes, the apotheosis of the great genius who founded the island's culture. He dominates the script just as he dominates the carvings on the bird rocks at Orongo, sometimes unaccompanied, sometimes clutching a fish and frequently associated with characters that seem to be merely emphatic of his component elements.

Some of the other symbols seem familiar enough. Their meaning will never be known but their derivations are evident—the fish, the bird, the crab, the sun, the female emblem of fertility. One stands amazed to discover that many of the glyphs might have been taken bodily from inscriptions recently unearthed in the palace of Midas in Crete. How voyagers from the Mediterranean could have carried their writings to a point of rock in the South Pacific seems to be the ultimate enigma until one realizes that it is no enigma at all. The Cretan script and the Easter script probably have nothing in common save the basic imitative instinct of man. The glyph makers in both cases have begun by making their written characters picture the things they saw about them in Nature. Perhaps they arrived at the form of their characters through independent effort. Perhaps they carried them half-way about the globe from some point of common origin. Where the word *raa* means sun from Egypt to the coast of South America one finds it difficult to deny that written symbols might have had a similar distribution. There were probably plenty of tablets in existence on the island when Roggeween discovered it but they were given little attention by Europeans until 1864 when Brother Eyraud, the missionary, wrote a report about them. He said that they were being used for firewood and was instructed by Bishop Tepano Jaussen of Tahiti to obtain some specimens before the supply should be completely destroyed.

At that time there was a considerable colony of Rapa Nui natives in Tahiti—men and women brought there to work in the Brander and Salmon sugar plantations. Bishop Jaussen canvassed the colony until he found a man who professed to know the secrets of the script and volunteered to make a translation.

This man Metoro stated that he had himself been one of the *maoris* or *rongo-rongo* men and that from his youth he had been familiar with the making and reading of the characters. Frequently, he said, he had recited them at the great feasts. He recognized the bishop's specimens and set out to read them rapidly.

But the bishop was suspicious. He said frankly that Metoro seemed to be reciting something that was in his memory rather than deciphering what was before his eyes. So he insisted upon a transcription, character by character.

Metoro was baffled.

"I know what the whole thing—the ensemble—means," he said. "What difference does it make what each of these marks may mean by itself?" He pointed hesitantly to the Makemake and one or two other symbols and gave each of them a number of meanings so widely divergent that Bishop Jaussen abandoned his attempted translation.

In the introduction to the monograph which he wrote for the Paris Académie on the subject of the Easter scripts he says definitely: "We must give it up. . . . There is nothing in it." And that, indeed, is the conclusion reached by every other scholar who took up the work after him.

Ten years later J. Croft, an American living in Papeete, read what Bishop Jaussen had written and became interested in the tablets. He felt that the bishop had been too easily discouraged so he obtained copies of the tablets and made a personal search through the Rapa Nui colony for an interpreter.

This *rongo-rongo* man, whose name is not revealed, came one Sunday to Mr. Croft's home and translated one of the tablets with ease. The American wrote down the translation as it was given him, intending to use it later as a basis for the study of the individual glyphs. On the following Sunday his interpreter came again. Mr. Croft failed to find his notes.

"We have wasted that much work," he said. "But fortunately we are just at the beginning. We can translate the first tablet all over again." Which was done.

Mr. Croft, on reading over his transcription after the interpreter had gone, found much to convince him that the second reading differed materially from the first. He ransacked the house for his notes, discovered them and compared the two translations. They were entirely dissimilar.

He said nothing to the interpreter about the matter and

when the man arrived on the third Sunday put out the first tablet for another reading.

A third reading was given just as glibly as the earlier ones had been given and investigation showed that it resembled neither of its predecessors. So ended Mr. Croft's experiment.

The experience of Paymaster Thompson of the U.S.S. *Mohican* repeated that of the bishop and the American amateur. Ure Vaeiko, said to be learned in the science of the scripts, was called from the Salmon plantation in 1886 to examine photographs of the Jaussen tablets. At first he declined to attempt a translation on the ground that he had become a Christian and had foresworn all such heathen contrivances. But later, under the influence of Tahiti rum, he abandoned this pious attitude and chanted the *rongo-rongo* with speed and zeal.

Mr. Thompson in the meantime had learned something of the scripts. He knew for example that only alternate lines are right side up and that, in reading, a tablet would have to be reversed at the end of each group of characters. Thus he became aware speedily that his interpreter was not following the symbols. His turning of the tablet did not correspond to the arrangement of the characters although otherwise the reading was convincingly given.

At the end of the performance Ure Vaeiko was dismissed and told to return the next day. When he appeared again he was shown an entirely different tablet from which he read word for word the same story he had professed to find in his previous reading.

"He could not give," reported Mr. Thompson, "the significance of hieroglyphs copied indiscriminately from tablets already marked. He explained that the actual value and significance of the symbols had been forgotten but that the tablets were recognized by unmistakable features...

just as a person might recognize a book in a foreign language and be perfectly sure of the contents without being able to actually read it. An old man, Kaitae, who claims relationship to the last king Maurata, afterward recognized several of the tablets from the photographs and related the same story exactly as that given previously by Ure Vaeiko."

In 1895 a more interesting, though scarcely more successful, attempt was made to discover the secret of the individual characters. Monsieur C. de Harlez of Louvain made a careful study of the Rapa Nui language and the tablets from texts brought to Europe by Brother Tavel. It is apparent from the monograph that he later published on the subject that he made his work an amplification of that undertaken by Bishop Jaussen. He reached the conclusion that each character may represent not only one word or phrase but even two or three and he applied his theory to the translation of several lines of the tablets. He achieved the same results in his various attempts, which is more than was done by native experts, but of the results themselves Professor Brown says: "It can not be said that he has made anything very intelligible out of them, though some of his phrases have evidently some connection with the figures they are supposed to translate."

Brother Eyraud seems to have hit upon the status of the script in his first report concerning it, a letter to the superior of his order in 1864.

"In all the houses are found tablets of wood or sticks covered with hieroglyphs," he said. "These are figures of animals unknown in the island which the aborigines form with sharp stones. Each figure has its name; but the little esteem they show for these tablets makes me think that the characters are relics of a primitive writing and that they are now preserved without any inquiry into the sense of them."

Ngaara, the great *ariki* who died before the Peruvian raid, showed considerable interest in the scripts. He exercised a control which might be compared with that of a minister of education over the *rongo-rongo* men of the island. Frequently he called upon them to produce their pupils for examination. He had learned the secrets of the writing from his own grandfather and was highly esteemed as a teacher though feared as an examiner.

Recently men were alive on the island who had witnessed his assemblies of the sub-professors and their pupils. He would sit before his own house and gravely examine the copies they had brought with them. If these were satisfactory he would call upon each pupil to read his own tablet.

In a way these examinations were graduation exercises, for, if a pupil had made a fair copy and read well, Ngaara clapped his hands as an indication that the pupil had passed the test. He congratulated the teacher and presented him one of his own tablets. If the pupil failed he was sent back for more instruction and the professor was roundly reprimanded.

One of the great social events of Easter was the annual conclave of the *rongo-rongo* men at Anakena. The *ariki* sat on a pile of tablets near the great burial platform, like a king at a tourney, and watched the assembling of hundreds of the elect together with most of the less-favored members of the populace. Sticks with clusters of feathers tied to them—Easter's substitute for floral ornament—were stuck in the ground on all sides of the chieftain. Great quantities of food were brought for cooking in a stone oven fifteen feet long.

The *rongo-rongo* men arranged themselves in two rows

on the beach of the cove along a pathway leading from the *ariki's* throne to the sea. Ngaara, his son Kaimokoi, and all the learned ones wore feather hats. All carried tablets.

At a signal from the *ariki* the older men arose in order of birth or intellectual importance and read their tablets where they stood. There was no inspection of their writings as in the case of the examination of pupils, but if an old man failed to satisfy the chief with his reading, Te Haha, Ngaara's young son, was dispatched to seize the ancient and pull his ears.

The younger men, whose turn came next, were not subjected to this indignity. If one of them made a bad translation he was called up to the throne of the *ariki* and told of his mistakes. So the performance went on throughout the day.

When Ngaara died the whole island turned out to do him honor despite the fact that his clan was no longer in the ascendency. Thousands of feather sticks were made by the natives and planted about his house, his tomb at Tahai and on the tops of the bare hills. He was borne to his last resting-place in the *ahu* on a litter made of *rongo-rongo* tablets. Some of his remaining tablets were distributed to the older members of the *rongo-rongo* fraternity and the remainder passed through the hands of his servant, Pito, to Maurata, the chief, who was taken away to Peru. It is said that they were subsequently hidden in a cave and lost.

Despite a close watch over the body of the dead Ngaara some admirer contrived to steal his head which, like his tablets, has never since been located.

The Routledge investigators reached the conclusion that the glyphs contained portions of ceremonials, genealogies and a list of murdered men. But, like others who attempted to find some basis for understanding the symbols, they confessed their ultimate defeat.

To-day no copy of the tablets that Hotu Matua brought to Easter remains on the island and few of the natives now alive ever heard of the glyphs. This chapter of Rapa Nui's mysterious history is finished. The book is closed and locked with no chance for the reading of the dénouement.

Chapter Twenty-Two

THE CLANS

Of Such Was Babel

It was no race of supermen that Hotu Matua brought with him from Marae Renga to Easter. The culture of the island is indigenous and elusive, but the language, physical characteristics and traditions of the people link them at once to the other neolithic tribes of the Pacific. They were no more brilliant mentally, and bodily no more powerful, than their kinsmen in the homeland of Hawaiki. They were Polynesians who, had they stopped at Manga Reva, would shortly have seemed no different from the natives of the Gambier, or, in the environment of New Zealand, would have fitted at once into the great tribal scheme of the Maoris. And in this, perhaps, rests the greatest of Easter Island's puzzles.

To-day, as one looks across their tumbled fields of bones and stands beside their sardonic images to look upon the wretched state of their descendants, one sees in little the thing that makes civilization . . . one bright light . . . one flare of intellect and energy that presently is gone. And one can not but wonder whence it came. Explain that and the amazing engineering works of Easter—the burial *ahus* and the procession of stone gods—are no longer a mystery. Something more than a carver's apprenticeship and a convenient supply of stone went into these monuments. The basalt walls of the tombs and the ambitious distances traversed by the statues show a direction of energy far more startling than the art that developed on Rano Raraku. It is a tradition that three hundred sailors and two hundred natives were required to bring from the slope of Rano Kao to Hanga Roa—a distance of two or three miles—the four-ton image that now sneers at London from a portal in the British Museum. And remembering this one scarcely dares venture to guess what staggering mobilizations of man-power transported Titans of from twenty to forty tons all across the island.

There was organization here, an organization grounded in discipline such as that which tossed up the ziggurats of Babylon and the massive works of Egypt. Physical force was available when and where needed. Not one group of men but an entire community must have listened to the crack of the whip. Thousands of lean brown shoulders stood poised for the word of command . . . thousands of bodies thrust forward as a unit when the word was given . . . thousands of legs moved in unison . . . thousands of human wills submitted themselves to a directing intelligence. It is a picture that has no place in Polynesia.

No rolls of papyrus or translatable inscriptions on stone tablets give a picture of the frustrated emperor who brought all this about. The traditions of the island are hazy in the minds of natives who remember the old culture as something that had already become hearsay in the days of their youth. But the record of one man's power is manifest in its accomplishments. Thousands of stony facts augment legend in the reconstruction of an amazing history.

One turns from the tangible present to survey the ghost of Hotu Matua with new respect. Men of far less talent have filled our histories. Few if any of our own Titans could have done what he did in such an environment. He forced upon a savage people an idea of culture. He conquered their laziness and apathy and anarchy and made them stand to heel. When he spoke they obeyed. And his voice went echoing down the years still strong, still an influence in the life of the people until the Peruvians ravished the land and broke the line of the ancient kings.

It is scarcely likely that Hotu Matua landed on Easter with the intention of staying there. He had come from a fecund land where there were running rivers and green forests and fields where yams and sugar cane grew almost without care. He must have seen little hope for the imperial idea in the rocky shore-line and the volcanic blisters of Rapa Nui. One may hazard the guess that he sent out other canoemen as he sent the six from Marae Renga to drive on once more toward the sunrise and search for a better dwelling-place. But the scouts—if indeed he sent them—were doomed in advance to failure. Ahead of them, save for the stony reef of Sala-y-Gomez, there was no land for more than a thousand miles and even had they reached the South American coast they could scarcely have returned to tell about it. Not even the Polynesian instinct for navigation could have guided men indefinitely to a tiny island in a region of shifting winds and currents.

In the end Hotu Matua submitted to destiny. The gods had brought him to this outpost at world's end. It would be useless for him to start back to his sunken homeland. In the parts of Marae Renga still above water Ko his brother ruled by a superior force and Hotu's wanderers had grown no stronger in the hegira to Easter. Here they had come and here they must stay until they were fit to travel again.

It is probable that the nostalgia for more kindly islands never left Hotua till the day when, an old man, he looked out from Rano Kao toward the west and died. Something of his intention to go back some day and wrest from his enemies the kingdom he had lost is manifested in his very first efforts to train his followers. He gathered the children at Anakena and taught them the elemental principles of war. He showed them how an army of spearmen should form in a line for battle. He staged sham battles in which ranks of little boys opposed one another with lances of supple reeds. Skill in these fights led to participation in other encounters in which the weapons were stalks of sugar cane. And in young manhood the boys were armed with spears whose shafts were wood and whose tips were volcanic glass.

He fortified the steep hill at Anakena Bay presumably as a further exemplification in the art of war since he had little to fear from questing war canoes. He supervised maneuvers of attack and defense about the forts he had built and prepared his growing army for campaigns that were never to exist except in his dreams.

As an army Easter Island's military force would seem to be a retinue for the stone images—the gods of lost motion. But the psychology that brought it into being had a far-reaching effect. One recalls the British general who made his weary troops polish the backs of their brass buttons . . . and the endless squad drill that followed the armistice in the World War is too poignantly recent a memory to need mention. In such rountine is born discipline.

How many years were spent in Hotu Matua's military experiment is not known. But it is certain that in the early decades of the colony on Rapa Nui while a prolific race was multiplying rapidly the males of the community were being subjected almost from birth to the king's will.

In his sham battles he fostered that spirit of competition which goes hand in hand with esprit de corps. And as the population increased he carried the idea still farther

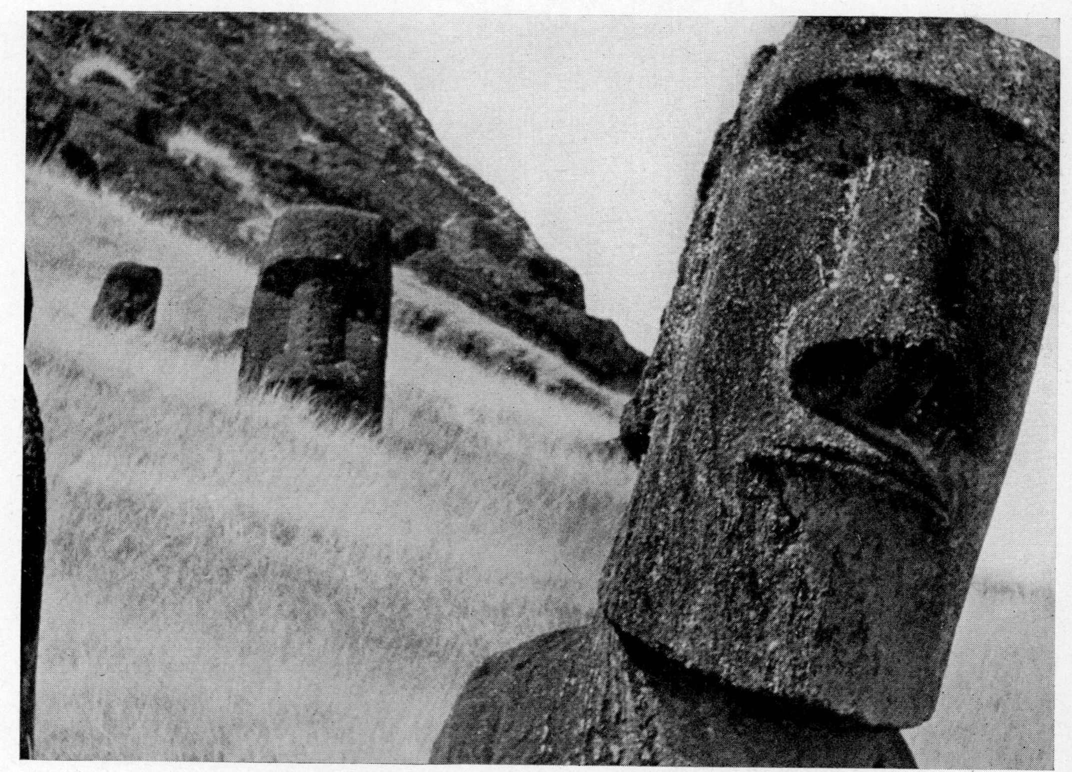

THE PRINCE OF DISDAIN

All of the images seem to be copies of the same model and carry on his message of contempt for the slaves he drove

KING OF THE ISLAND
One need not ask this sphinx what he thinks of the human race

THE SQUARE BACK
The general contour of the gods was canoe-shaped, and they stood out of the ground from the hips before buried by slides

with the creation of clans in each of which he encouraged a pride of caste. These groups appear to have been selected arbitrarily and assigned to new villages about the coast when the facilities of Anakena became overcrowded. At first they were distinct from one another only through their differences in location. Only one of them, the Miru clan, to which belonged the king, laid any claim to cultural superiority.

There were ten clans in all divided into two main sectional groups, the Hitiuira, Tupahotu and Koro Orongo of the Hotu Iti or eastern federation; and the Miru, Marama, Haumoana, Hamea Miru, Ngatimo, Ngaure, and Raa, comprising the Kotuu or western alliance.

The Hotu Iti group occupied the territory about Rano Raraku including Tongariki and La Pérouse Bay. The Miru and associated clans were found on the north and west coasts. The Haumoana lived on Rano Kao and the Marama took in a territory from Hanga Roa along the foot of Rano Kao to a point midway between the eastern and western headlands on the south coast.

It is difficult to see what functions these divisions had in later years save to provide excuses for war. The clans were not subject to the tribal rules and tabus which exist between barbaric peoples who live in separate communities in other lands. Membership in one clan was not a barrier to marriage with a member of another clan. Nor was the line of residence closely drawn. Many people of neighboring groups might cross the boundaries and live in each other's territory without exciting comment. It is noticeable even to-day, however, that one feels a sort of family pride in his clan. He may marry into another just as a king might smile at a beggar maid but he never forgets his noble origin.

When dissensions came to trouble the land, they were between groups rather than individual clans. Thus tradition tells of several fights between the Kotuu and the Hotu Iti. But dissensions did not come until after Hotu Matua had died and the tremendous energy that he had built up and stored in his people was spilled out aimlessly over the bare hills.

Under Hotu the clans were probably small administrative units each of which he was able to control with less difficulty than he might have experienced in dealing with a massed population. He discouraged illusions of grandeur among the petty chiefs of his creation by making them all of equal importance. And he established himself and his line for ever by endowing the Miru clan—his own—with the attributes of godhead.

Wisely he made the Miru a small association. Its members were *ariki*—the great ones—and noble people upon whom the gods have smiled lose their importance if they are too numerous. He filled their daily lives with ritual and cloaked them with superstitious signs and legends and cut them off from the commoners by means of rigorous tabu.

While it was permitted for one clan to mingle with another in marriage it was a crime savoring of sacrilege for any one of the lower groups to mate with a Miru. The dire punishment that followed such a sin was not postponed until after death. The angry gods were certain to act quickly and the offending commoner was certain to be seized with a lasting and painful intestinal disease.

Sorcery was the gift of the Miru. These clansmen knew the mysterious incantations that caused plants to grow and hens to lay. They could slay at a distance and work other wonders. So, as objects of universal awe and fear, they did not need force of numbers to protect themselves. As Hotu Matua had foreseen, the Miru at first walked with the gods and then became gods themselves. Until the coming of the white man destroyed the social fabric of the island, their superiority persisted and no man dared to oppose them.

If the Miru were placed aloof from fighting, this pacifism established no precedent for the other clans. They were under no restrictions regarding family feuds and tribal wars.

The Miru—including Hotu Matua and his successors—were to take no part in such conflict. From the first they established their rights as neutrals, and one might be puzzled at this attitude toward bloodshed on the part of a chief who had spent so much time developing the military idea were it not for parallel cases in modern times. Hotu Matua, who had never heard of a place called Europe, was merely putting into practise a simple course of strategy used by one Louis XI of France: rivals who wasted their strength fighting one another would be less likely to have traitorous designs upon the sacred person of their king.

Hotu's control over the clan system was further strengthened by his appointment of his sons to be the leaders of the lesser groups. And inasmuch as they partook of the sacred character of their father, their followers were bound to the central government by religious as well as political ties.

The chiefs of the Miru clan were, of course, the kings of the island and its high priests and its demigods. The roster of the royal line starting with Hotu Matua was memorized by wise men in each succeeding generation and the tradition of it was presumably accurate at the time when Dutrou Bornier began his exploitation of the ranch. Name lists obtained since then have varied. Thirty chiefs are entered on two of them—fifty-six on another. Whatever the number, it is significant that Hotu Matua had designed his government with a complete understanding of the psychology of his people. His dynasty endured.

There is a legend on Easter—oddly distorted and a bit inconsistent in its details—that the overlords of the Miru were white. Fragments of this tale, brought back to Europe by mariners, have aroused as much imaginative comment as ever greeted the theory of a lost continent. But when one analyzes it one finds little to cause astonishment.

The basic strain of the Polynesian is Caucasoid and varying hues of skin from blond to black occasion no surprise in the Pacific Islands. If Rapa Nui legend holds that a chief was white he may have been actually white as a European understands the word. On the other hand he may have had the slightly sallow complexion of the Mongolian.

Mrs. Scoresby Routledge interviewed numerous natives who had seen Ngaara, the last of the chiefs to carry out the functions of his ancient office.

"He died shortly before the Peruvian raid," she writes, "and becomes a very real personage to any one inquiring into the history of the island. He was short and very stout, with white skin as had all his family, but so heavily tattooed as to look black. He wore feather hats of various descriptions and was hung round both back and front with little wooden ornaments which jingled as he walked. . . . Ngaara held official position for the whole island but he was neither a leader in war nor the fount of justice, nor even a priest; he can best be described as the custodian of certain customs and traditions."

It is significant that when the Peruvians interrupted succession to the office of this man who was neither a leader in war nor even a priest, the old order of Rapa Nui came definitely to its finish. The force of Hotu Matua seems to have derived from its very intangibility, and so with his successors. This king who was no king said to one man "go" and he went, and to another "come" and he came; and apparently nobody ever stopped to think that he lacked the judicial and executive power to enforce his orders. His rule was based on something stronger than physical force. In it we have not far to seek for the abiding spirit of the island: the great fear.

Hotu Matua founded his little empire on reasoning whose soundness was proved by the testing of long centuries and he lived to see the accomplishment of what probably had never been possible before and has never been recorded since—the disciplining of a race of individualists whose only theory of political economy was anarchy, a wretched, hungry, agitated people whose appetites must have prodded them continuously to revolt against restraint. A mere king, however nobly descended or however strong in battle, could never have commanded obedience such as this. But when Hotu Matua spoke the ears of his subjects were prepared to hear the echoing of thunder. His commands were the voice of a god.

So when the king called, the populace rose up and stood mute; the carvers swung their stone mallets against their chisels of diorite; the sweating thousands picked up their tackle of woven grass and slipped their necks into yokes of basketry; and the stone gods rode ponderously across the hills to their distant thrones.

It is not new, this theory that one man, one indigenous Rameses, brought a people out of the stone age so close to civilization. It has been frequently suggested by visitors to the island who have been impressed by the patent similarity in the faces of the images. And it has been scoffingly dismissed by authorities who have denied the possibility of a close-woven social organization in a primitive people except under constant threat of physical force.

One pauses to gaze into the mists beyond Rano Kao and visualize the Gambier Archipelago which lies some sixteen hundred miles on the other side of the horizon. One recalls the spires of the cathedral vaulting above the coconut-palms, and the stone road that winds up the mountain-side, and the awesome ruins of shrine and monastery and school and palace—an imperial city of coral block falling to pieces almost unnoticed by an indifferent remnant of a doomed people. And one points out that the cathedral builders were not much different from the people of Rapa Nui—their cousins in blood and tradition and brain. They accomplished feats of engineering and architecture without equal in the South Seas because one man—a mad priest—willed that they should. His was the intellect, theirs the man-power.

One scarcely needs to point the parallel.

Chapter Twenty-Three

BIRD CULT

Conclave of the Egg-Seekers

It was the great day of festival and the chosen ones of the clans were gathering. They came in a troop over the hills from Anakena and up the sacred road from the field of the stone gods, their bodies a moving filigree of blue tattooing, their heads crowned with brilliant ornaments of feathers, their hips girt with little wooden bells that made a musical sound when they walked. Ahead of them marched the *ivi atua*—the soothsayers whose guild knew the secrets of a black magic more powerful even than that of the Miru clan's *ariki* . . . wrinkled men whose eyes were rheumy with the strain of peering too long and too intently into the clouded future . . . men whose dried muscles bulged like the tendons of mummies from their honored but emaciated arms and legs . . . men who carried staves topped with rooster feathers and decorated their persons with amulets of bone. Behind them plodded a procession of youths who wore no badge of rank save the symbols of the bird cult tattooed across their hips, eager young men whose duty it was to serve the chosen ones.

By the wayside stood envious thousands denied a part in the spectacle. They were not entirely cheerful in their attitude toward the chosen ones. It rankled that the gods should have displayed that foolish favoritism for which the deities of black magic have always been so notorious. Many a private clansman of Rapa Nui felt that he could have made a better selection without any recourse to chants and juju and auguries. But the gods had spoken again—after their fashion—and so the proceedings must go on for another year at least. . . .

From here and there among the spectators came sounds of chanting and even of gaiety as the members of the leading clan shouted encouragement to their own representatives. Wooden drums were making a clatter that now and then rose in thundering volume and smothered the noise of the surf. The earth shook and echoed hollowly to the beat of slowly moving feet.

The throngs poured out of the hills above Hanga Roa and through the pass at the foot of Rano Kao, and the landscape was brilliant with the coloring of feathers and tapa draperies and woven fiber ribbons and headbands. For the moment the bare landscape of Easter was blooming with patches of scarlet and blue as the fabled hills of Marae Renga, the homeland, had bloomed with the foliage of the more kindly tropics. But unlike the flower-tapestries of other islands, this blaze in the uplands was constantly shifting—intensifying as the clans came on from east and north, fading into the yellow of the tundra grass as the horde passed down to the seacoast at Hanga Roa.

There was to be a fine feast at Hanga Roa. True, it was an affair in which the favored ones of the gods got all the best of it, and chiefs and diviners and clansmen of high social rating came in for second choice. But there was certain to be enough yams and taro and plantain and fish for everybody. And there would also be dancing and a recital of passages from the *rongo-rongo,* the sacred script. The ancients would tell all the old stories of how Hotu Matua had come from far over the sea to establish his people in the fair fields of Rapa Nui and to make the edible plants grow in the craters. One really couldn't ask for much finer entertainment.

At Hanga Roa the stately march of the favored ones continued down the coast to a promontory of volcanic sponge where all the lesser personages were dismissed. The elect descended to the beach where, in the entrance of Eat Man Cave (Ana-Kai-Tangata), a huge fire had been lighted. The hunt had been successful and a man designated by the soothsayers had been killed. He would presently be placed in the oven of hot stones, later to be served to the chosen of the gods.

That night the west coast from Mataveri to the northern headland was ablaze with fires and the simple festivities went on and on till the dawn. The celebrants, tired but no longer hungry, greeted the sun and lay down to sleep in the wreckage of their feast.

In Eat Man Cave the soothsayers went on with their auguries and the favored ones went on with their eating. The huntsmen took to the hills again and brought back more provender for the hot stone ovens and so were passed many days in pleasant converse.

It was July—winter-time in the latitude of Easter. The sun was warm enough even when harsh winds came up out of the Antarctic. The feasting might have gone on indefinitely had not some of the prospective food supply developed fleetness of foot. Eventually the chosen ones remembered what had brought them to Hanga Roa and Mataveri. They adjusted their feather crowns, drew their cloaks of tapa about their shoulders and came out of Eat Man Cave. The procession formed once more. The soothsayers mumbled their sacred chants. The wooden drums resumed their din. The long column moved up the slope of Rano Kao toward the distant summit.

The vast assemblage of spectators stood for a long time on the seashore watching the rank of the elect, thin and black on the mountainside, rise at last to the crest and disappear behind the rocky outcrop at the lip of the crater. Then gradually the throng dispersed and took the paths past the burial platforms and hills of the images to homes at far scattered points about the island.

It was not yet finished, this social event. In two months the people would be back once more at Hanga Roa, feasting, cheering, rioting as they saluted a man whose name would take rank alongside the lists of the kings . . . a noble character after whom the year would be called in the calendars of tradition. But for the present this cultural giant was still in the making. One could serve no good purpose by staying at the foot of Rano Kao. So one went home to await the day of triumph.

At the top of Rano Kao, on the side of the crater where the cliff wall dives down to the sea, there were clustered the stone houses of the village of Orongo. Into these houses moved the chosen ones and their soothsayers and their vassals. The solemn air of a religious rite attended the occupation of the little town. The drum beaters and the *rongo-rongo* men, versed in the reading of the sacred script, moved slowly between the groups of houses to a dike of tumbled stone cubes where had been carved numerous intricate figures of the frigate bird, and Makemake, the sea-god, whose form is a composite of bird, human and fish.

A row of houses set aside for their personal use stood near these rocks and at the cave-like entrances the *rongo-rongo* men sat and chanted all day long with one brief pause for luncheon. Elsewhere in the village dancers performed in the sunlight by day and in the glow of the fires by night. Food was brought up daily by the women folk of the chosen ones. And what with the practises of sorcery, religious fervor and a full program of amusements the months must have passed pleasantly and rapidly.

At the end of the first month the young men who had come merely as *hopu* or servants of the elect bade a reluctant farewell to this scene of gaiety and picked their difficult way down the seaward slope of the volcano and the second act of the great national drama began.

Excitement began to pervade the conversation of the favored ones. A nervous tension seized upon the whole island. For a new moon was rising and a new hero was about to receive his accolade from the gods. The sooty tern, a highly respected sea-bird, was about to visit the island and lay an egg.

Long ago—almost a year ago to be precise—the soothsayers had retired to their dugouts and caverns all over the island and had done the magic necessary to reveal to them the circumstances attending this bird's projected arrival. When they had performed the secret rituals each of them foresaw the laying of the egg. Each envisioned the search of the chosen ones for that priceless trophy. Each, in his own way, received a revelation concerning the identity of the man who would succeed in the quest. Oddly enough, however, each soothsayer picked a different winner.

Lack of unanimity in the reading of the future did not deter the sorcerers. Each went to the man whom he had seen as the successful searcher and whispered to him the message from the gods. Thus it came about that when the great ones marched down to Rano Kao there were many of them—each walking proudly with the assurance that his competitors were the victims of poor advice.

Each year it was the same. And it had been the same since the days of the lamented Hotu Matua. Each spring came the favored ones to the stone houses of Orongo. Always the wise men who knew how to read the sacred script performed their chanting under the bird rocks. Always the dancers danced and the drummers beat their wooden drums. And the chosen of the gods sat at the edge of the cliff and waited for the sooty tern and the laying of the magic egg.

In the early days of the custom, perhaps, the competitors did their own searching. But efficiency comes with practise. The soothsayers agreed—and their agreement on any subject was sufficiently odd to be convincing—that inasmuch as fate had decreed in advance the winner of the contest, he was certain to succeed whether or not he made any personal effort. That being the case it seemed simpler for the elect to transfer the actual labor of the search to the *hopu*—the young men not yet marked for greatness—while they themselves lingered in their comfortable surroundings on Rano Kao.

It was a delightful thing, this contest by proxy. One's days were unbroken by worry inasmuch as his apotheosis had been revealed to him in advance. His surroundings were wildly beautiful—the magnificent bowl of the volcano on the one hand, with the rolling grandeur of the south coast stretching out to the horizon beyond it, and on the other hand the sea tossing up its garlands of white feathers about two rugged little islands.

The larger islet, Motu Nui, had acquired a character almost sacred in the affairs of the bird cult, for it was the favored nesting-place of the sooty tern. To Motu Nui, at the beginning of the second stage of the vigil, the *hopu* made their way. They dived through the breakers below Rano Kao and swam for half a mile in turbulent waters to the caves of the islet where they were to live for a month. Their food supplies consisted of what they could carry with them and their dwelling-places must have seemed cold and wet and miserable had it not been for the burning ardor that intoxicated them. So passed the month of August.

Bird Rocks
Carvings near the haunt of the cult on the summit of Rano Kao's dead crater

Stone House at Orango
Artificial caves of laminated rock were built to house the bird men

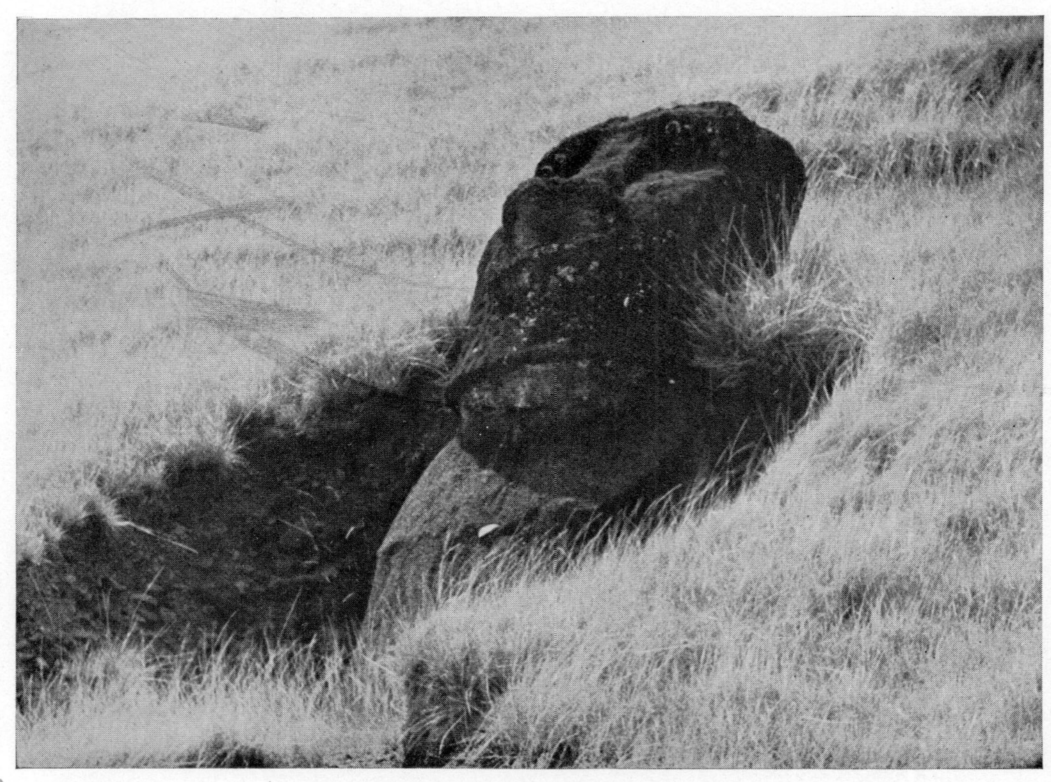

THE GRAVE OF A DEITY

This image was excavated by the Routledge Expedition and reburied

The air about Rano Kao was filled with chanting. The atmosphere of Motu Nui was vibrant with expectation.

At Hanga Roa the celebrants assembled once more. Again the fires were lighted and the feasts were spread. The huntsmen of the elect dashed about the island in pursuit of their reluctant prey. The old moon vanished. The new moon came. And shortly afterward was enacted the great climax.

The quick ears of the *hopu* caught the sound of rushing wings. The alert eyes of the watchers on Rano Kao saw the first bird of the season come riding through the mists above the spray. There ensued a moment of tense anxiety while the plenipotentiaries on Motu Iti stole silently from rock to rock and from aerie to aerie. Then one day some young man who, of course, represented the most actively favored one among the chosen of the gods came upon an egg. He picked it up and rushed with it to the shore facing Rano Kao. With trembling voice as befitted the solemnity of the occasion he shouted to his employer: "You are the successful one, the bird man. The egg is yours. Shave your head and rejoice." And he would sing out the name that his principal had selected in advance as his bird name.

One can only imagine the delirium of joy that seized upon the successful candidate as he shaved his head and painted it red. And one hesitates to think of the grief that struck so suddenly into the ranks of the defeated ones. Foreknowledge of success has definite reactions when the information turns out to have been wrong. The losers tore their hair and cut deep gashes in their breasts with obsidian spearheads. But nobody paid any attention to them inasmuch as a new and glorious hero had arisen and the populace was greeting him with glad acclaim.

The defeated *hopu* whose grief was probably less poignant than that of their masters swam hastily back to the foot of Rano Kao to take a tardy but enthusiastic part in the feasting. The custodian of the egg washed it, wrapped it in a fiber basket, tied it to his head and followed his recent companions across the little strait. After he had landed he surrendered the prize to the winner whose arm was bound with tapa-cloth while a *rongo-rongo* man recited suitable words. A fire signal was lighted on the edge of the crater, its position announcing what section of the island the winner had come from, and the contest was officially ended.

The bird man then took his egg and danced down the mountainside where he was joined by his delirious followers. In a shouting, cavorting mob the clansmen escorted him to a proper retreat. Sometimes these heroes went into their own districts and took up their abode in houses dedicated to the bird cult. But generally winners out of the western group of clans retired to Anakena and those of the eastern division to Rano Raraku.

The bird man remained a year in his retreat. For five months he lived under strict tabu. No one might enter his house without incurring the death penalty. His wife came to a near-by house but could look at him only from a distance when he emerged to sit in the shade. His followers came timidly to leave gifts of food at his doorstep. He spent the days principally in sleep or meditation. During the remaining seven months of the year he was still a holy and terrible personage but the tabu was not so strict. His wife moved into his house and soothsayers came to visit him. His egg, which had been blown on the third day, was displayed in front of his house. He was very happy.

The soothsayers whose revelations had been erroneous never suffered any dire consequences. It was too patent that the losers had done something to make the gods change their minds. With the finding of one egg the divination started all over again to determine who would be the hero of the next contest. The *ivi atua* played too important a part in the drama to be lightly discredited.

One who looks only at the surface of this shadow show is certain to see in it only another manifestation of Easter's wasted energy. There seems to be no logic or motive in the annual creation of a puppet hero and something pathetically childish in the ritual attending it. Save for the solemn aftermath one might look upon it as a carnival. But there was nothing comic in the reverence with which the finder of the first egg was treated throughout his life and even after death. One searches vainly for an explanation until one discovers a fact which in the days when the cult was an active influence on Easter, received little attention. During the five months of the bird man's isolation he was forbidden to eat eggs. Inasmuch as the hero himself was thus restricted in his diet it was only proper that the tabu should extend to everybody else on the island. By the time the bird man came out of his retirement the nesting season of the sooty tern was finished . . . the eggs were all hatched. And therein is revealed once more the intelligence that directed the destiny of these people for centuries.

Wandering sea-birds were an important source of food on this wretched island. Some one—presumably Hotu Matua—foresaw that they would return year after year only if they were unmolested in their nesting. If the populace for even a single season were allowed to gather the eggs without restriction, the sooty tern would have been exterminated. The bird cult as an instrument of food conservation that remained effective for possibly a thousand years takes on a new significance.

Chapter Twenty-Four

SUNK LYONESSE

The Lost Continent

There came men out of New Bedford and Boston and Gloucester in great white ships, a crew whose bloodshot eyes were fixed on no particular quarter of the horizon, whose port of call was the large round world. . . . Wanderers who went where the sperm whale went and never wasted a thought on the mystery of the palm islands. They swept the south seas in numerous fleets, confining themselves to no lanes of travel, drifting with the broad swift rivers that lie on the ocean surface, shifting their courses as the wind shifted.

Their navigation was something less than accurate. Their logs were seldom illuminating. But out of the mass of reports that the whalers brought back from the lower Pacific came pilot books and maps and data concerning trade winds and tides and currents. The chart of this sea had been a wide empty sheet whose whiteness was marred only by parallels of latitude and longitude and a wavering line at the right edge representing the South American coast. It began to show a stippled shading which strangely fascinating names showed to be groups of islands. On small-scale maps these little dots seemed so close together that one might have mistaken them for stepping- stones across a waste that covered half the world. One forgot that a thousand miles may add up to very little on a six-inch globe.

Hydrographic survey ships of half a dozen nations followed the whalers and new charts began to show ocean depths from New Zealand to the Aleutians and from Singapore to Valparaiso. People began to think they knew something about this Pacific. Its surface was plotted with all the detail one might expect to find in a map of city streets. Instead of a watery empire revealed to the sight of inquisitive strangers after a thousand hidden years, it became a blue space in the pages of school geographies and a table of copra tonnages in the trade reports. And then came whispers of the Lost Continent.

It rested somewhere in the region now occupied by the Society and Cook Islands, this continent—stretching in an easterly direction almost to the coast of Chile and to the north as far as Hawaii—providing a land bridge across which the sons of Ishmael might walk dry shod in their endless journey out of nowhere into the beyond. It spread to far corners the peoples and the flora and fauna of the dawning world, and having served its purpose it collapsed to strew the ocean floor with its shattered bones.

The legend of its existence came first in thin whispers from the baffled mariners who had gone vainly questing for Davis Land and the lost islands—a half-hearted explanation of their failure. The lands that had filled the horizon in latitude twenty-six degrees south no longer tossed their grim peaks into the empty sky. They were one with Lyonesse and Avalon under the waves—and imagination contemplating this awesome fact enlarged upon it to envision the cataclysm that had engulfed them. Such a yawning of the sea might have swallowed not only Davis Land but possibly vast tracts of land to the west. Perhaps the rocks of Sala-y-Gomez and the peaks of Easter, Pitcairn and Manga Reva were the surviving sentinels of a ridge that once had stood with all the majesty of the Andes. . . . Perhaps . . .

There came other murmurs, louder and more assured. Writers who had made a study of the symbolism of the temples of the Far East and the art of Polynesia and the wrecked empire of the Mayas, produced books describing not only the geography of the Lost Continent but its people, its government and its superior culture. This mysterious, not to say mythical, land came in time to be looked upon as the real site of the Garden of Eden, and the story of the flood was seized upon as a graphic account of the tidal wave that had blotted it out.

One learns to speak softly in the Pacific Islands. So little is known of them—so little is knowable—that one may not quarrel too earnestly or confidently with anybody's theories. The placid Polynesian pursuing his lazy smiling way beneath the flame trees of Tahiti must have come here from somewhere as did his blood brothers in islands thousands of miles distant. There is something homogeneous about the South Sea archipelagos despite the wide scattering of their components. It is not by accident that the sugar cane grows in all the islands, and Pandanus palm and taro and plantain and coconut. And it is certainly significant that no wild animal or snake is to be found in any of them. Their similarity in language and culture and plant and animal life places them definitely as atoms in one great unit.

But one ventures to doubt the tale of the Lost Continent. In the first place the ocean soundings so far have shown no plateau such as that which supports the theory of a sunken Atlantis north of the Azores. The tall peaks of the Pacific's high islands step right up from the floor of the sea, slim spikes of basalt, some of which are twelve thousand feet from base to summit. And the deeps that lie between them for hundreds and in some cases thousands of miles show none of the characteristic variations that one finds on the surface of existing continents between their mountain ranges.

There are peaks as high as the Himalayas under the Pacific and valleys as deep as the Grand Canyon. But at present they seem to lack coordination. The back-bone of the vanished continent which one might expect to find in a search of the bottom does not exist and one shakes one's head sadly at efforts to reconstruct it from a few widely separated vertebræ such as Easter and the Gambier.

It is with considerable regret that one discards the story of the sunken motherland of the Pacific. There is something that prods the imagination in the picture of a continent such as that on which we now are living, brought to a state of Edenic plenty by the warm kindliness of the tropic sun and peopled by a race that had never been forced to struggle for an existence and had never learned to sin, thrust into the sea in one catastrophic stroke.

The scene as it takes shape in one's mind is vivid enough to be true: The ocean, once impotent against the rocky barriers of the coast, comes farther and farther inland. It seems to be rising—each crested comber mounting higher than the last. Men and women who have lived in peaceful security in this sheltered land can not believe that it is dropping away from them. The high black cones of inland volcanoes are afire and great rivers evaporate in steam as molten lava begins to run down to the oncoming sea. The earth is trembling and stones are raining out of a hot black sky. Still the people brave the slopes of the fiery mountains, retreating in blind panic from the rushing water. The ocean has covered the farm lands and meadows and made lakes of regions where once stood tall forests. The villages are gone and thousands of bodies are being cast up by the tidal wave—a ghastly flotsam at the base of the high hills.

A person wishes he might believe what his sense of Romance tells him ought to be true. But unfortunately he can not. The traditions of Polynesia are too definitely concerned with desperate voyaging in long canoes and too definitely silent on the subject of land bridges to be ignored even were there some tangible evidence in support of the great submersion—which there is not.

L. Frank Stimson who has been conducting research work in the South Seas for the Bishop Museum of Honolulu probably has come closer to the solution of the racial puzzle of the Pacific than any other authority. In his laboratory at Papeete one may see a tall filing cabinet filled with cross-indexed notations on varying characteristics in island dialects and one will be shown a mathematical graph demonstrating visually the conclusions that may be drawn from this terrific labor. One discovers with something of a shock that the colored lines linking similarities in language variation take form as something far more important: a map of Polynesian migrations in the Pacific. And in nearly all details they bear out the legendary accounts of the Tahitians and Maoris.

For his comparisons Mr. Stimson obtained from virtually all the Polynesian Islands lists of the thirty names given to "the nights of the moon." These designations correspond in our calendar to the days of the month but had a special significance. Certain nights of the moon were religiously designated for the taking of fish. Other nights were considered most suitable for the planting of *kumara*—the sweet potato. And because of their constant repetition in ritual the names of the nights were less subject to modern corruptions than other words in the Polynesian vocabularies.

It had been known for many years that the language of Tahiti was basically similar to that of the Maoris in New

Zealand and the natives of the Hawaiian Islands and Samoa. But not until Mr. Stimson had completed his analysis was the nature of their relationship suspected. The graph told an almost unbelievable story. It demonstrated that the oldest language in the Pacific, as proved by its elision of consonants and its prodigal use of vowel sounds, was that spoken in the Society Islands including Tahiti. The newest was found in Hawaii, New Zealand and Easter Island. The dialects at these three points—the outposts of Polynesia—were more nearly similar than those of any other group in the Pacific.

The explanation of this was direct and logical.

"If you drop a pebble into a pond," said Mr. Stimson, "the place where you drop it becomes quiet after a time. But the widening ripples go on and on. So it is with a language."

He pointed to the chart which told its own story. The tongue of Tahiti had undergone the changes that come to a language with age. The dialect carried away from the island by voyagers to the north and east and south had retained its virility. It was only a step from that to the tracing of the course that the men of Polynesia had followed in their wanderings.

The bold lines of the graph started at the Indo-Chinese peninsula and marked a route which might well have been plotted from the supposedly dubious information contained in the old legends. The first Polynesians had come from the continent of Asia across the Pacific to Tahiti. From thence the diagram shows three streams of movement by which the other islands of the mid-Pacific may have been populated—one north, one south, one east.

One breathes a sigh for the theory of the land bridge as one looks at these maps. The Lost Continent would explain so many things but alas! it will not explain this. The linguistic changes among the peoples of Polynesia were caused by a race of mariners who started from a common homeland and thereafter lived in isolation. Whatever continent once filled the present emptiness of the southern ocean—if it ever existed—it was gone before the first Polynesian set out from the coast of Indo-China. And to drag it up once more from its resting-place on the bottom would be merely to present another mystery without solving those that have gone before.

Easter, more than any other island in the Pacific, has spurred the search for the Lost Continent. Many scientists have contended that the immense engineering works in this region were that of a populace much larger than any the island could ever have supported. So two theories have gained wide circulation: first, that Easter is the sole remaining peak of a vast land which now lies under water; second, that it is the only surviving member of a great archipelago.

The first theory can be held only by those who have never seen the island. One can not escape from the fact that soundings only a short distance from the shore show a depth of twelve thousand feet. If the floor of the ocean were to be lifted to the surface, then the crater of Rano Kao would be something over thirteen thousand feet above sea-level. The whole territory embraced by the island as it is to-day would be well above the snow-line for the latitude of twenty-six degrees south. One finds it difficult to envision the image-carvers and stone masons who contrived the great puzzle of Rapa Nui choosing so rarefied and chilly an atmosphere for their work.

But the argument is not needed if one pauses to look at the works whose existence this theory seeks to explain. The thirty-five-mile circumference of Easter is walled with burial cairns whose back walls parallel the present coast-line. It is fairly obvious that when they were built the coast was just as it is to-day. There has been no subsidence of any sort since the stone giants were set in place to watch over the honored dead.

The second theory is more tenable and is given considerable space by Professor J. Macmillan Brown of Wellington in his book *The Riddle of the Pacific.* Professor Brown contends that Easter was set aside as a sacred burial place by the people of the sunken archipelago. It is his argument that everything about the island indicates an organization and a populace which must have been directed and supported by fertile lands at no great distance. And he believes that Easter's sun went down and the long night of starvation and misery began when the tributary islands were engulfed.

Perhaps this is true. There are too many unexplained stories of mirages like Davis Land that were seen by many men and then lost to human ken for ever to permit of any argument with one who says that such things may happen. But as in the case of the Lost Continent one who looks at the chart of the Pacific's depth is not convinced.

Native traditions still alive when the Peruvian slavers demolished what was left of Easter's culture told in much detail of how the pioneering King Hotu Matua came to the island. Such matters as the battle between the long-ears and the short-ears were preserved in prose epics. It is significant that these legends make no mention of any homeland other than Rapa Nui. There is no tradition of foodstuffs brought from other islands close at hand though there are many stories having to do with feasts and famines of local origin.

If any vast archipelago went down it did so without ruffling the complacence of Easter Island's story-makers. The people of the island may have been stoics—in their environment they could hardly have been anything else—but it is scarcely likely that they could have displayed so magnificent an indifference to a major catastrophe.

One realizes as one stands on the quaking coast of Easter or looks into the gaping maws of the dead volcanoes that one day this island may fade from the maps as Davis Land faded. One gazes over the crumbling burial platforms and in awe and fear gropes for something that will explain this vast and futile effort. One would willingly look to the ghosts of a vanished continent or a drowned archipelago. But with Rano Kao still firm against the buffeting of the sea and the volcanic blisters of the uplands still rising against the sky, these ghosts are very nebulous and their voices very weak. Easter's mystery is no more baffling and Easter's tragedy is no less poignant because self-contained.

Chapter Twenty-Five

FEAR

The Dark Heritage of Easter

One sat on the shaded porch of the Mataveri ranch-house over the stone foundations of what, ages ago, had been a house of kings. And one gazed at a flower garden bright with hollyhocks and other blooms generally associated with domesticity in parts of the world where ships come oftener than once a year. Through the garden wandered a gravel path that presently dived under an archway of trees to the open land on the slope toward Hanga Roa village. And save for one's consciousness of complete isolation, this might have been a pleasant retreat on the south Dakota plain or for that matter a corner of the more quiet districts of the Wabash Valley.

One lolled in a wicker chair and smoked English cigarettes and talked of far places . . . the manager, the foreman, and one tired stranger just landed from a battered boat—the manager a mining engineer who before the war was one of the world's authorities on placers and dredges—the foreman who in another existence had taken gold out of the beds of unmapped streams on the west coast of Africa.

"A quiet life here," observed the manager in a matter-of-fact tone as he lighted one cigarette from the end of another. "If you don't get murdered the atmosphere is certainly fine for your nerves."

The foreman smiled and yawned. "Even getting murdered is sure to have a calming effect," he observed.

"What happened to Percy Edmunds?" inquired the visitor with a realization that neither of these men had been mentioned in reports from Easter and that all travelers had given particular notice to the kindly and somewhat harried Mr. Edmunds, one-time manager of the ranch.

"Nothing much happened to him except twenty-three years on this island," observed the new manager. "At the end of that time he thought he'd been calmed sufficiently, so he went to Chile. I took his place. I've been here a year and a half this trip. But I've been out before just to look around . . . four times altogether."

The sun had dropped behind the grove at the left of the pathway and night was slipping up through the barren valleys beyond the town. The dead hush of the island had come like an enveloping cloud.

"What on earth did you come here for?" inquired the visitor.

The manager shrugged.

"It's interesting here," he said. "There's no more interesting place in the world. I get paid as much as I'd be paid for managing a mine and I'm not bothered by a lot of silly people. I've been living so long with the old stone giants out on the hill that I feel related to them. But I'm going to chuck it. My wife is a Valparaiso girl and she doesn't think so much of the solitude as I do. I'm going away by the next boat and the good old statues will have to worry along as best they can without me."

He talked of placer mining in Spain and prospecting in New Zealand and of a lonesome trek across Lapland afoot. He filled the twilight with visions of snowy tundra and high mountain peaks and Moorish gardens in which guitars echoed and fountains played in the moonlight.

"I have always liked to travel," he said. "Before the war I was free to get around a bit. But the war did for me. I am just beginning to regain hope that I may wander about in the odd corners of the world once more."

The visitor looked at him intently but could detect nothing but sincerity in the eyes that gazed at things beyond the long road to Hanga Roa. . . . The eternal plaint of one who has known the itching foot: to be away to the lands beyond the blue! And he was voicing his plaint on Easter Island . . . last port of Adventure.

Dinner was served in a high-ceiled gray dining-room with clean paneled walls and a spotless floor. Screens, the first of their kind seen south of San Francisco, kept out the serenading insects that had gathered in grove and garden. A kerosene pressure lamp gave a light of electric brilliance and one had to glance at the framed chart on the wall to be reminded that this was Rapa Nui, Isla de Pascua, Easter Island, and not some well-kept room at home. There came the manager's wife, a dark-eyed, quiet-mannered Spanish girl who sat in a silence imposed by her meager knowledge of English; and the foreman's wife, a quick-witted, sprightly young woman formerly of London; and the foreman's two children, a boy and a girl born in Patagonia and Punta Arenas. The note of welcome was sounded instantly and effectively.

"Do they give you good meals on the boat?" inquired the foreman's wife.

"The meals don't make much difference," was the truthful answer. "We've been running through gales and small cyclones for two weeks. But if anybody should happen to be interested in the meals such as they are, he'd find that we've been pretty well reduced to good old army rations—canned corned beef and canned beans."

"Oh, dear," sighed the lady reminiscently. "To think that there really is some corned beef left in the world. What wouldn't I give for some of it!"

The guest looked up across his portion of roast lamb and salad, frankly amazed.

"If you mean that about the beef we can put some ashore for you," he said. "The beans are just about out."

"Of course I mean it," she declared. "We can't slaughter much beef here because there is no ice and meat spoils rapidly. As a result we have mutton—mutton—mutton. There seems to be no end of it." And she turned wistfully to her husband.

"You'd better make a note to order some canned beans by the next boat," she suggested. "Otherwise you'll surely forget. And we want quite a lot of them."

He nodded and made a notation in a little book. She sighed as if in consciousness of a good work well done and continued to serve the roast. The guest was silent. It came to him that the next boat would arrive in nine months. A year after that another boat would deliver what the foreman had ordered. In twenty-one months the lady who disliked mutton could have a change of fare.

That night one lay in the bedchamber behind the dining-room—the manager in one bed, his guest in another, with a wavering candle on the night table between. From afar came the pounding of the surf, a combination of artillery and escaping steam.

"It's a tough night for the west coast," said the manager, raising himself on his pillow. "It gets worse the longer the wind holds in that direction and right now it's dangerous." He sighed. "That's the trouble with this island," he commented. "There's always something going on to give your nerves an edge. . . . The place shakes all the time as if it were deathly afraid of something. The motion is so great and so continuous that the Chilean Government had to remove the seismograph they tried to set up here. The sea is always shifting and the skippers have to keep awake every minute they are off this shore. . . . And if it isn't the sea it's the natives. . . ."

"The natives look a little soiled but not alarming," said the visitor. "What's wrong with them?"

"Red cloth and phonographs—not to mention leprosy," said the manager. "They are being pauperized by well-meaning souls who might just as well be doing something for their actual benefit.

"They are a shiftless lot, probably the laziest persons on earth. They raise a few scrubby horses—that is to say they steal the horses—and they don't walk or turn a hand oftener than is absolutely necessary. And in spite of all that disease and filth and poisonous food can do for them they are multiplying at a rate too fast for their economic environment."

"What do they do for a living?"

"Ah, there you have it! What can they do? In the old days it is obvious that these people must have been agricultural. On an island this size there wasn't much but truck raising to occupy their time. They had the simple tastes of savages. They lived on yams and wild bananas and possibly sugar cane and an occasional rat or fish. And when they wanted a change of diet they ate one another.

"When this ranch started they were still living on that primitive scale. They found it easier to work for the ranch than to drag sustenance out of the soil. In that way at least civilization did something for them.

"The Peruvian slave raids and the smallpox rather took the starch out of them, I guess. And the white man's diseases added to their troubles. The only thing they can't blame the European uplift for is the leprosy. They seem to have discovered that for themselves.

"All in all they weren't so badly off a generation ago. There were few of them here, their tribal structure had been broken and their traditions had been destroyed. But there never was any real danger of their starving to death.

"There will always be people ready to criticize any exploitation project such as this ranch; but the managers here took care of the natives and at times saved them from extermination. There was plenty of work for those who wanted it—simple easy work, that involved no worse hardship than sitting down, and the people got in return better food and better clothing and more comfortable lodging than they had ever been able to get through their own unaided resources.

"Now we have an entirely different situation. This generation wants phonographs and red cloth, neither of which will grow wild as the food grows in the crater of Rano Kao. To buy phonographs it is necessary to get hold of Chilean dollars and that, of course, means either barter or work.

"There is no work on this island for which a native can possibly receive any pay except on this ranch. But the natives have established a legend of their own superiority as workmen and they have arrived, by heaven knows what process, at a scale of wages.

"They think they ought to be paid two dollars gold per diem and receive a daily ration of eight pounds of mutton. A similar scale in the United States—based on costs of living—would be about twenty-five dollars a day. The Company naturally has declined the highly paid services of this village union. To adopt the suggested scale would be merely the last step toward going out of business and giving the island back to the islanders for the raising of yams and taro.

"Inasmuch as we represent the only source of cash

on the island and maintain the only store where the natives can buy such thing as sugar and flour, we are able to get what help we need at considerably less than the rate of two dollars a day but there are plenty of die-hards at Hanga Roa who refuse to demean themselves and consequently don't do anything but stir up trouble and sleep."

"Isn't there any barter? Don't the natives make anything that is salable?"

"They do a little trading in hides and wool," murmured the manager. "It is an economic process whose simplicity would arouse the envy of an international banker. They steal sheep from us and sell us the hides. You will see that in such an arrangement waste is almost entirely eliminated."

The candle wept. The surf kept up its chant for the lonely stone gods. Rain came out of the northwest and made strange noises among the Norfolk Island pines, and put glistening beads on the upper window-panes.

"It isn't so much the loneliness," said the manager. "A man can get used to being by himself. I've been just as isolated in London as I am out here on the edge of the earth. It's the sense of constant antagonism that gets you . . . the feeling that it's you and your two fists against the world.

"The old whaling skippers used to say that this island was cursed. And after you've been here a while you get to feel that they must have been right. We have to import new sheep each year to keep up our flocks. The breed goes bad unless we do. Every now and then a good sheep just walks out into the middle of the corral and dies. Nobody knows why. Nobody knows how. . . . Bring good horses here . . . they breed down to scrubs. The pests flourish but everything else goes bad.

"A pair of domestic cats came ashore a long time ago. Somebody connected with the ranch thought they would be of some use in fighting the plague of rats. But somehow they got on to the ways of the island. I shot one of their descendants the other day—a big Tom that had been preying on our poultry. He was about four feet long from his nose to the tip of his tail and he had the frame of a black puma. These cats have gone back to their savage state and the present breed is running to size. If they keep on they'll be a genuine menace if they're not that now.... But they never bother the rats. They've declared a truce.

"Out in the hills when the sun is shining the flies will eat you alive and leave nothing of you except your shoe pegs. There is a tradition that flies are another of the white man's blessings. No matter. They're here and the history of a fly isn't so very interesting. We imported game birds in the hope that they'd help a little to keep down this pest. But the natives found out that the game birds were edible and that was that. I sometimes think that this island was created just to be a graveyard and that we're wasting our time trying to change its destiny."

Somehow there seemed to be nothing fantastic in this. The rain and the wind and the surf and the flickering candle seemed to be the correct properties for a night in the realm of unfriendly gods.

"It's bad enough to have to worry about the ranch without the natives," the manager went on. "But the natives can't be ignored. You never know just what they're going to do. There's no law out here. This place is like the American frontier in 'forty-nine."

That seemed to be a bit of exaggeration. The visitor said so.

The manager shook his head.

"Figure it out for yourself," he suggested. "These

people are savages. It's only recently that the government has placed them under any restriction whatever. Even now the restriction doesn't amount to much. We have a prefect of police who theoretically has the power to arrest them and a governor who has limited judicial authority and may fine them. But any crime greater than an ordinary simple misdemeanor was never considered possible by the administration which put this machinery here.

"On a night like this they murdered Don Sebastien . . ."

"They what?"

"They murdered him . . . these simple Kanakas. He was our overseer and a European. He made it hot for some horse thieves and they got him. They shot him right out there by the front gate and dragged him back behind the house and through the corrals. They took the body up the side of Rano Kao intending to dump it into the crater. But they got tired so they left it half-way up the hill.

"In the morning we found Don Sebastien's horse saddled at the gate. We went out to investigate. We followed a trail of blood through the grass and got the body. We found a hat which was easily identified as the property of one of the villagers. So we risked a revolutionary war and went down and got him. He confessed, implicating three other men. . . ."

"And what happened to them?"

"They were fined a couple of sheep or pigs or something. I suppose they stole the stuff from us to pay the fine. They are still on the island. One of them walked up here behind you this afternoon. He is the worst scoundrel in the South Pacific."

One felt a chill that was somehow distinct from the bite of the howling wind.

"Why do you permit these people to carry arms?" demanded the visitor.

"There you have me. It makes things a bit difficult when you know they are armed. But so far I have the edge. A few days ago I took out a stick of dynamite and blew up a rock that had blocked the road to the village since the road was a native path. For two hours it rained rock on this cursed island and for two days you couldn't have found a native with a troop of cossacks. They'd all taken to the hills. And when they came back they had the fear of God in them. They know I have plenty more dynamite."

"Not a bad weapon. Do you keep it where you can get it in a hurry?"

"Right under the house. . . . As a matter of fact it's just about under your pillow."

Chapter Twenty-Six

TOMBS

The Dead Men Lie in Regal State

LIFE was a weary thing on Easter of the image-makers—death magnificent.

The long sleep into which one sank after year upon year of wretched wet days and miserable nights and a constant struggle with starvation seems to have been no very horrible thing. The mysterious beyond in which one lingered as a shadowy but presumably contented being promised no perils or hardships worse than those which beset the living and on the other hand presented the attractions of anesthesia and forgetfulness. If the religion of Rapa Nui offered no heaven it provided at least a surcease from hell.

So it is not surprising that the island's culture concerned itself largely with the phenomenon of Death and its constructive energy focused itself upon a great work of sculpture. Every few yards as one rides across the island one comes upon the platforms of the dead. Every time one moves from the marked trails it is to stir up some new acreage of skeletons. By which necromancy one reads the story not only of a tremendous racial energy but of an unbelievable population.

These burial platforms—called *ahu* in the native dialect—were the first of Easter's queer remains to attract the attention of the early explorers. Roggeween and the long procession of mariners which followed him walked across these Cyclopean terraces without once realizing that the dust of an uncanny race and all that remained of a hope for empire lay moldering under their feet. But they saw at once in the massive masonry of the walls and the crystallized labor of generations in the buttresses and paved areas and approaches some evidence of the energy and purpose that had made Easter distinct from the other islands of Polynesia.

There was no avoiding the cairns. . . . Every little volcanic uplift, every sheltered nook along the seacoast presented one. They hugged the shore like a flotsam of stone thrown up by the Pacific. No matter where one might choose to make a landing one was always in the shadow of these vast stages on which the Easter Islanders performed that ancient tragedy with which they were most familiar—the drama of Death.

So it comes about that Roggeween's report is as much concerned with these platforms as with the statues that decorated them. Gonzalez the Spaniard and La Pérouse the Frenchman and Cook the Briton were similarly impressed. They pronounced the riddle that other voyagers have failed to answer adequately after two hundred years: Whence came these things and what do they mean?

The platforms in some instances show a greater advancement in mechanics, art and the science of building than the great stone gods although the two were always closely associated. In these works one may discover something of the development that is so noticeably absent in the statues—an evolution from piles of rough stone to well constructed walls, which, after all, represents the whole range of architecture.

The style of the sarcophagi seldom varied. They were built close to the seacoast, after the general fashion of tombs in ancient Polynesia. The side toward the sea was a solid wall generally about fifteen feet high and of a length which varied with the importance of the tomb. The surface of the platform sloped away from the top of the retaining wall toward the land side for a distance of perhaps thirty feet and in some instances gave on to a sort of paved court which extended still farther inland.

In many instances—although not always—the sea-wall was surmounted by the conventional statues. The number of images used to decorate a platform seemed to be governed by no set usage. Some cairns had only one. On others numerous images stood side by side. At Tongariki, the greatest of the burial vaults, whose tall dike stretches along the sea in the shadow of Rano Raraku, fifteen stone Titans lie face down as if in some ritual of lamentation.

The red stone hats, carved in the crater of Punapau, not far from the present village of Hanga Roa, were peculiarly the property of the mortuary images, the tops of whose heads were flattened to make a base for their odd crowns. The placing of the statues, too, was at a variance with the haphazard practises observable at Rano Raraku. Uniformly they stood with their backs to the sea, gazing inland across the platforms as if to supervise the rites for the dead.

Under the platforms were vaults, roofed with stone slabs, which crypts to this day are filled with the remains of the men, women and children who for a brief period wrested a livelihood from the desolate hills. Thousands of bodies were thrust into these charnel-houses—relics of a populace whose size must at all times have taxed the meager food supply. When the last trump sounds over Easter's ghastly coast-line it will summon a concourse which will crowd the island from Rano Kao to the eastern headland.

Two hundred and thirty platforms have been located

on the shores of the island. It was the opinion of archeologists attached to the Routledge expedition that they generally were placed near villages that disappeared long ago. Thirty vaults of fair size and workmanship are to be seen farther inland where, apparently, a second line of burial places was being constructed when the old culture flickered out. A variety of design is to be found in the platforms and it is evident even to a casual observer that while some are linked with hoary antiquity others are of comparatively modern construction. Ninety-four—all of which were decorated with images—show signs of having been in use when Roggeween came to the island. One platform discovered by investigators from the U. S. S. *Mohican* stood high on the east slope of Rano Kao. A slide from the mountain destroyed it and its scattered masonry is still to be seen on the shore at the foot of the cliff.

The Titans set to guard the dead—and as nearly as one can tell from a count of the fragments there were more than two hundred and twenty-five of them—were from twelve to twenty feet high. All now are fallen—their fine red hats tumbled far from their half-buried heads. And so one comes to another of Easter's endless enigmas: What happened to these things?

For many years the theory persisted that an earthquake had knocked them down. But it needs only a glance at the wreckage to refute such an idea. Save in one or two places the statues lie on the platforms, face down—the stone hats flung from them in the same direction. Any seismic disturbance must certainly have produced a motion that would have thrown some of the statues toward the sea and some away from it. Particularly inasmuch as the platforms were confined to no one section of the coast-line. But nothing like that happened. The images on the tombs of the south generally have fallen toward the north and those of the north grovel with their heads to the south. . . . And with very few exceptions the faces are down.

The first travelers to bring back reports of life and culture on the island mentioned that some of the statues were standing, and they seem to have remained standing until the late eighteenth century with their red hats still in place. When fifty years of the nineteenth century had gone not one remained on its pedestal. On which subject the native lore of Easter is strangely muddled.

In the little bay by which one approaches Tongariki on his way to Rano Raraku and its image quarries, the surf-boat scrapes past a head of spongy lava and then jars over hidden rocks to a cove whose encircling walls are tunneled and pitted by the waves. It is only after a second visit that one notices the peculiarity of the low dikes about the cove. One discovers with something of a shock that they are not natural formations at all, but piles of basalt cubes, matched and jointed. They are walls built by master masons and so skilfully contrived that for centuries they have withstood the pounding and grinding of surf and tide.

In many places the sea has carved out little caves, chipping away portions of two or three of the component rocks—sometimes a part of one and a part of another right at the joints. But save for the weird pattern of erosion close to the water-level the destructive force of the sea has had little effect. The top structure of the wall stands as immovable as the dikes of porphyry which Rano Kao as an active crater poured down into the Pacific.

Cubes of rock some two feet on a side—and sometimes larger—were used in the sea-walls of the platforms. One stands amazed at the engineering problems involved in raising these buttresses to a height of fifteen feet and when one considers that in some vaults—such as that of Tongariki—they were three hundred feet long the energy of the constructors seems incomprehensible.

The Tongariki *ahu* presents a pattern which seems to have been conventional in the construction of all of the larger burial platforms. The terrace sloped from the retaining wall toward ground-level in two gradients. The first extended inland thirty feet at which point it was seven feet above the base line. From that point it sloped more gently for a distance of two hundred and fifty feet.

Save for a variation in the pitch of the terraces virtually all of the platforms to be found along the shore-line are of this type although there is evidence of an earlier vault in the shape of a half-pyramid and some ruins have been found suggestive of a step pyramid. In isolated cases natural outcroppings of rock were used as retaining walls and natural caves as vaults. There was little evidence of building skill in the pyramidal cairns. For the most part they were merely rough piles of unmatched stones.

The terrace at Vinapu, just east of Rano Kao, is by no means the largest of these remains but it is undoubtedly the one which will puzzle archeologists the most inasmuch as it shows a total, and studied, departure from the design and methods employed in the construction of its neighbors.

It is built of gray stone of a sort found about Rano Raraku—although it stands in a region where the sea has exposed a stratum of red volcanic tufa. It is situated midway between two other platforms, both of which are made of red stone. And so one approaches it with some curiosity.

One stumbles across open patches strewn with boulders and comes upon it from the coast to wonder if, after all, this is still Easter Island. For the retaining wall of

A Lost Hat

This specimen was six feet in diameter and four feet high. It lies near Vinapu Terrace

Vinapu

Detail of masonry showing careful jointing of basalt blocks

Solomon Island Canoe Prows

Some authorities see a resemblance between these long-eared ornaments and the giants of Rapa Nui

New Guinea Bird Woman

The Easter *moai miro*—wooden images—have their counterparts in Melanesia where a rite similar to that of Easter's bird cult is still to be found

Tragedy in High Hats

The statues on the *ahu* depicted here were less than twenty-five feet high. Scores of the island's weird giants were taller. Thus they stood in their pride before petty warriors overturned them. (Reconstruction)

Vinapu, save for its lack of ornamentation, is distinctly Peruvian.

It is a type of masonry which the Romans built and the tireless engineers of Angkor—massive blocks matched to a fraction of an inch and polished so that the joints would admit no water. The wall is broken now—the credit for that going to the *Mohican* expedition rather than to prehistoric vandals. But there is still enough of it left to amaze investigators who will come to look at it hundreds of years from now. At the eastern end, where a huge image lies with its face in the rubble, a long stone is turned up to reveal a beautifully carved cornice. At another place, where, apparently, the corners of two cubes were broken in transit or quarrying, the irregularities have been chiseled to smooth angles and a trapezoidal stone fitted so snugly into the opening that only the weathering of the material itself has revealed its presence.

One can not but feel thrilled at the parade of the Titans under Rano Raraku, but to look at this wall and to study it is to approach bewilderment. Here, but for a matter of geography, is a piece of Baalbek or Palmyra or Luxor or Chicago. It is masonry of the finest type that man has ever learned to make and more than any number of carved stone gods it represents the striving of a people well out of savagery toward a culture that it only just failed to attain.

Roggeween came home to Europe to mention that he had seen the natives of Easter performing some rites, apparently similar to sun worship, on the terraces where stood the gods with the red hats. But subsequent investigation tended to show that the Dutch admiral must have been misinformed or mistaken in his observations. The chasm that lies between the present race and the ancients of Easter is nowhere so evident as in the attitude of the moderns toward the relics.

"The old gods are gone," remarked Timateo who came one day to act as guide over one of the broken trails into the hills. "They were not our gods anyway. . . . I have it from my grandmother's mother who was a very old woman that these gods were here always. Many people were afraid of them."

"And you were not afraid of them?"

"They are gone," he sniffed. "And anyway they were not very powerful gods. They did nothing to protect the people who did all this foolish work for them. The gods are gone. The people are gone."

"And your people never worshiped the old gods?"

"The old gods belonged to the old people. My grandmother's mother who was a very old woman said that the old gods were dead long before the white man came to this island. The old gods belonged to the old people and they also have been dead a long time."

The present natives of the island are listed in the pilot book of the British admiralty and other publications as Roman Catholics. That is because the one church in the little village of Hanga Roa has a Roman Catholic name over its blistered door. By the same process of thought if any one had built a temple of Siva at Hanga Roa the populace could be classed as Hindu.

These queer people have two new deities: One is a Chilean war-ship that now and then drops anchor in Cook's Bay . . . the other a sort of demon, neither good nor evil, called The Company. Which is to say the intangible authority under which operates the island's lone industry—the ranch. Behind this pair of gods are ancient deities which may have died before the arrival of Roggeween but whose ghosts, oddly distorted and little reverenced, still wander aimlessly through the lives of the people. The Polynesian theology has survived here in an unrecognizable form.

"My people said pooh-pooh to the old gods," said Timateo. "But the people of my mother's grandmother used to bury the dead in the vaults of the old platforms. I have heard talk of this in my own family. You would wrap the body up in rush matting and set it up on a framework of sticks on the *ahu*. Four—maybe five—relatives would sit around all day, keeping the birds away, singing old chants. All the time they stay there. Sometimes one year—sometimes two years. After long time the body all finished. . . . Nothing but bones. You pick up the bones. Maybe you bury right there in the platform. If the vault is full you carry the bones somewhere else and bury. . . ."

This ceremonial, of course, savors of something that had a basis in custom and very likely was copied, or inherited, from the early constructors of the platforms. On the other hand it may never have occurred at all. Timateo—and other natives who later repeated the same story—may have been ascribing to a fairly recent ancestry a tradition as old as Time. It is certain that in recent years there have been no burials in the terraces. The cemetery near the church presents conclusive evidence of that.

And yet, before one may hazard an opinion even on such a point he confronts the great question mark that hangs like a continuous shadow over the valley of the gods:

The platforms were in repair and the images in place within the last one hundred and fifty years. The overthrow of the Titans was accomplished not by an earthquake but by some fury of humans. One can see no reason why the heritors of the image-builders should have waited so long to destroy their work. There is no logic to this island. To answer one question is to ask another.

Chapter Twenty-Seven

UNCLEAN

Black Magic That Worked by Night

Ghosts?

The manager shook his head gravely, then smiled.

"There ought to be plenty of them hereabouts," he admitted. "Ghosts must have been the principal crop of the island in the old days and production holds up in spite of decreased facilities. After you've been here a while you have to give your mind a prod now and then to keep from believing anything anybody tells you. The natives see ghosts. Old Bornier, who is under a cairn beyond the orange grove, is always annoying them. That's one of the reasons they don't come wandering around here at night. I've never seen Bornier or any other ghost myself. I suppose that's my misfortune."

A still night had followed days of storm. The leaves of the grove beyond the porch hung limp. The pounding surf had shifted to the north side of the island and the air was quiet—breathless.

"We thought once that we were at grips with the supernatural," he said. "For days we lived in a detective story and all that held us to a sane solution of it was the broad general principle that a ghost won't steal sheep.

"Stock had begun to disappear from a corral near Vinapu where we had some prize ewes. That in itself wasn't so odd. We have to be on watch constantly to keep the ranch from moving en masse into the stomachs of Hanga Roa. It's always been a sort of game with the natives. They work for us when they have to and they steal from us when they can.

"So we put out a few more riders and charged up the missing sheep to profit and loss. We thought we had the raids stopped. But the section from which these sheep were disappearing is in rough country. The fence goes up hill and down dale and is hard to patrol. It is virtually impossible to keep a close watch on all parts of it at once. So we weren't surprised to discover three days later that more sheep had gone west.

"We had a problem on our hands. Our ranch police are natives and to increase the force meant to admit more natives to the ranges. On the other hand it was obvious that our guard wasn't strong enough.

"We went down into the village and paid a lot of social calls. There is one good thing about sheep-stealing in these parts, it is pretty hard to conceal the evidence. We knew that if the stolen stock had been eaten in the village there would be plenty of signs such as bones and fresh hides.

"And right there was where the real mystery began. There wasn't anything to indicate that the people of Hanga Roa had eaten any meat in months.

"It was a real puzzler. There was always the chance that the thieves might have disposed of the offal somewhere in the hills but it seemed scarcely likely that any native would have gone to all that trouble. In the first place he would have been unwilling to rid himself of a hide—even a stolen hide. In the second place he wouldn't have gone to the trouble to carry the bones very far when he could avoid personal connection with the crime by dumping them somewhere on the edge of the village.

"We came back to Mataveri and mulled over the thing without getting at any answer. We were still at it when one of the ranch police came in all out of breath. He said that he had come upon three men dragging a sheep through a hole in the fence northeast of the village and had lost them in a draw not far beyond.

"We didn't waste any time worrying about how he had allowed the thieves to slip through his hands. We rode right down to the governor's house and got him to turn out the local guard. We made a complete canvass of Hanga Roa—every last house. Where you know the name of everybody who ought to be home in bed at a certain hour it's a simple matter in a town so small to hold a sort of check roll-call. In fifteen minutes we had looked at the entire population. And then there was plenty of mystery. Not one man, woman or child was missing. There wasn't a single trace of a lost sheep in Hanga Roa.

"Knowing what we did about the topography of the place where the hole had been made in the fence we were certain that we had reached the village at least five minutes before the raiders could have returned. And the policeman's evidence was definite that he had seen three men. Two sheep were missing and there was the broken fence to bear him out.

"I'll confess that the puzzle was too much for me. I couldn't sleep that night. I just lay there for hours trying to figure out some explanation. Then, all at once it came to me. If the villagers hadn't stolen the sheep, then the thieves had come from outside the village. It took no Sherlock Holmes to figure that one out. . . . And what men were there on the island outside of the village?

"I turned out the foreman and we rode once more to the governor's house. I told him my theory.

" 'Ghosts don't steal sheep,' I said. 'And if you leave the ghosts out of it nobody could have gone through our fence to-night except the lepers.'

"He laughed at me.

"'You're taking leave of your senses,' he said. 'Those people are sick and dying. They haven't the energy to go out on raids. They couldn't walk from the leper colony to the ranch fence. They wouldn't have the strength to carry a sheep much less to slaughter it and I doubt if they'd be able to cook it.'

"But we rode on up the hill to the shack they call the leper hospital and there was the answer right in front of us. The lepers weren't asleep. All of them—men, women and children, were sitting around a fire wooling at half-cooked mutton. The remains of half a dozen other feasts lay strewn about the back of the house.

"How they forced disintegrating flesh and bone and muscle to carry on these raids is still a puzzle to me. I suppose the innate will to eat that was the ruling passion of Easter Island since its first settlement made them forget their miseries.

"There wasn't anything we could do about it. You can't punish a leper. We washed out the incident and set a permanent guard near the colony. There hasn't been a raid from that quarter since."

"Leprosy," the manager said, "was China's gift to this island. The Chinese gave it to Tahiti and some of the local Kanakas who came home from the Tahiti sugar plantations brought it with them.

"I hear that it isn't a virulent form of the disease. If that's so I hope I never see any of the really serious forms. It's probably the most ghastly thing on the island and everything here is pretty ghastly.

"The hospital is no hospital at all. There is no doctor here . . . no nurse. We have chaulmoogra oil and other materials for the treatment of the disease but we can't make the natives take the medicine. The stuff upsets them—especially the hypodermics—so they'd rather sit down in the shack on the hill and die.

"There are twenty-two in the colony now. The number hasn't varied much during the past few years. How many more cases are running loose in Hanga Roa I'd hesitate to guess.

"Only the other day a man came to me looking for salve. He said his wife had a trifling sore on her leg. We investigated and found her in an advanced stage of leprosy. Until that time nobody had suspected her of being in anything but the best of health. I sometimes wonder if this disease isn't going to finish the work of extermination started by the smallpox and syphilis. . . . Poor devils, no wonder they believe in ghosts."

Easter in its earlier existence shared the luck of all Polynesia in complete freedom from most diseases. Cannibalism had given the natives a fair working knowledge of human anatomy and their treatment of wounds received in war seems to have been surprisingly efficient. For the rest they had to worry about few ailments save indigestion, the inevitable result of their régime of alternate famine and feast.

But like all other Polynesians they had no resistance against the diseases of the white man. Smallpox came close to obliterating them. Venereal scourges left few, if any, of them untainted. Tuberculosis, coming on the heels of these scourges, found them ready victims and to-day an epidemic of influenza such as that which visited Tahiti would probably fill the burial cairns for the last time.

They are without adequate medical protection. Of recent years their lot has been improved through The Company's forethought in stocking the ranch with staple remedies but they are still shy about taking the white man's medicines. In a way they are worse off, psychologically at least, than they were when sorcerers assumed all the burden of fighting off Death and all disease was traceable to one common influence, the *akuakus*.

"Oddly enough," said the manager, "these soothsayers sometimes got results. In the first place they got the confidence of the person who was sick—a principle which medical practitioners recognize throughout the world. In the second place they developed an effective method of treatment.

"You don't have to believe that ghosts are the chief cause of disease and suffering. There is much to be said against that theory. But just the same the search for the *akuaku* might be put into practise at Hanga Roa to-day with excellent results.

"The soothsayers were agreed that the best way to get rid of the *akuaku* was to lure him into a hole and catch him in a net. If they got him out of the house the patient survived. If the patient didn't survive that proved merely that they had failed to trap the *akuaku*. It was certainly a simple process.

"Not all the sorcerers had a high rating in medicine. Some of them confined their talents to the casting of spells, and the foretelling of winners in the egg-hunting contest. But there was one lad whose successes were nearly a hundred per cent.

"His processes were a little different. He didn't believe in catching the *akuaku* in a hole away from the house of the patient. His theory was that a ghost has many chances to get away from even the most skilful soothsayer if allowed any latitude. So when he was called in his first act was to remove the sick person from the house to a shelter prepared in advance, or, weather permitting, into the open. Thereupon, after suitable incantations, he hung his nets over the entrance and burned the house down. Very few *akuakus* survived.

"You can see what actually happened if you consider life as it existed in those times. The houses were semi-dugouts without light, heat or ventilation. Even to-day a germ couldn't ask any better environment, and after the coming of the white man there were plenty of germs.

"When you come to think about it the actions of the soothsayer who destroyed the germ life while looking for *akuakus* weren't much different from those of the military authorities who burned down the nipa shacks on the edge of Manila to stamp out cholera. Sometimes you'd almost wonder how much black magic is science and how much science is black magic."

Chapter Twenty-Eight

WOODEN GHOSTS

The Fantasy of a Palace Builder

If one may credit the ancient legends there came to Easter with Hotu Matua not one single school of art but two, widely divergent in their product and their application. To Hotu Matua himself may be credited the quarrying of the massive gods and the engineering that set them in place. But to Tuukoihu, his wise lieutenant, is ascribed the origin of a link between the Titans and humankind, little wooden figures made to look like living creatures, whose carvers preserved their skill long after the ancient culture had disintegrated.

Tuukoihu seems to have been a ruler more readily understandable than his chief. He had no grand ideas such as the erection of massive statues along miles of seacoast. But he gave much practical thought to his own personal comfort and with some of Hotu's vigorous energy might have translated burial cairns into castles and stone gods into cities.

The standard dwelling-place of Easter Island was a canoe-shaped hole in the ground roofed over with reeds or stone. Hotu Matua, himself, apparently provided himself with no house worthy of mention in legend, and his death occurred in one of the stone-covered dugouts on Rano Kao. Tuukoihu, however, was less modest.

Hotu Matua established his seat of government at Anakena on the north side of the island and gave to his lieutenant the remaining sides of the triangle, the south and west. Tuukoihu took up his residence in his new territory and gave a utilitarian note to the engineering of Easter by erecting a palace on each coast.

These buildings probably have grown large in legend, the more so in that no ruins remain to indicate their size. But the description of them is detailed and through comparison with the burial platforms near which they stood one may arrive at the conclusion that they were more than two hundred feet long and that their walls were constructed in part at least of basalt blocks such as are to be seen to-day in the terrace at Vinapu.

The palace on the west coast was erected near a quarry where the great cubes were readily available. It was the larger of the two residences in itself and was surrounded by a group of outbuildings for his personal staff, his cooks, stores and ovens. Islanders even to-day sigh regretfully as they point out the site of the circular building that served as his kitchen. No such works have been constructed on Easter since.

The south coast residence was remarkable in that a granitic dike was used as part of it. It, too, consisted of a main palace with numerous subsidiary buildings. One who looks at the foundations near Hangahahave, which tradition identifies as the remains of this project, realizes how far the local culture had come at the very moment when its end was in sight. Had engineering and community labor continued in favor buildings like the Cyclopean works of Peru might now be puzzling visitors along with the images.

The story goes that Tuukoihu was walking overland to his western palace when, in a pass near Punapau, the little quarry hill whence had been taken the red hats for the statues on the *ahus,* he came upon two animate skeletons asleep. Tuukoihu found something ludicrous in the sight of their ribs showing through their wrinkled skin although these phenomena of starvation should have occasioned no mirth on Rapa Nui. He laughed uproariously and the two sleeping figures awakened.

The governor realized then that he had acted unwisely. These racks of skin and bones were not his own people. And they were hostile. They drew their wrappings of tapa about their emaciated bodies, picked up weapons and dashed toward him. Tuukoihu walked on through the quickly deepening shadow without indicating the fear he felt. He simulated surprise when they overtook him, striving to convey the impression that he was looking at them for the first time.

"Did you see our ribs as we lay asleep?" they inquired.

He shook his head.

"I have never seen your ribs," he answered. "I have never seen any part of you until just this minute. And I am not interested in your ribs."

Being simple-minded creatures they allowed him to go on his way. But they were not entirely convinced by his denial.

They entertained fears that Tuukoihu might have been lying to them. In which case he would undoubtedly tell his friends of what he had seen and by morning the whole island would know that these two wanderers were so thin that their ribs protruded.

The tellers of the legend gravely accept the idea that this was a very comical situation although it is by no means clear just why it should have been. Certainly in later years on Easter the sight of protruding ribs engendered no hysterics.

The emaciated ones followed Tuukoihu to his palace and for a long time afterward dogged his steps. Here again is naïve inconsistency. Tuukoihu, the mighty governor, in his own palace or on his own grounds, still feared the pair he had encountered on Punapau. He wisely refrained from mentioning them to his friends and he was careful to keep a serious mien and tell no jokes to those about him while the suspicious skeletons were loitering about.

His skilful acting had its effect. The starving men became convinced that they had been awakened by the laughter of some one else. They left him and went back into the hills. Tuukoihu suspected that he had been entertaining *akuakus.*

The memory of their pointed hip-bones and their ladder-like display of ribs remained with him long after they had gone and kept him from sleeping when at last he lay on his mat in the western palace. Thus came inspiration. He arose, found himself a piece of wood and a diorite chisel and set about producing two little images, portraits of death, which in all important details save size were duplicates of the strange beings from the hat quarry. These were the first of a long line of *moai miro*—little wooden gods.

The first products of Tuukoihu's new school of art were male images because the *akuakus* from the hills had been male. But he soon learned that this was an oversight. Death, and survival of it as a ghost, are functions not confined to either sex and the female *akuakus* were quick to resent the implied slight.

They appeared to Tuukoihu in a vision, pointed at him with scornful fingers and threatened violent alterations in his anatomy. He awoke perspiring and trembling and set to work at once to make a set of female figures no fatter than the male. The ghost-women of Easter appear to have been placated inasmuch as legend indicates that they left him in peace.

Later, for no reason that any of the native tellers of

tales know anything about, he carved some double-headed *akuakus*—a type much favored by the artists who followed him.

Tuukoihu appears to have had some object in his portraiture of the dead. It may have been that he expected the malignant ghosts to cluster about their graven images rather than about the bedsides of living beings whom they envied, or that he hoped the wooden *akuakus* might serve as decoys for their spiritual counterparts. As a secondary consideration he may have hoped that his friends would find the display of ribs and hip-bones as amusing as he had found them. If he had any such idea about the establishment of a local school of caricature he was disappointed. His people, who did not live in palaces with large cookhouses and unlimited food supplies, found nothing laughable in representations of hunger and death.

Whether because of the popular attitude toward his earlier works or because of a natural development in his art, Tuukoihu next turned his hand to the delineation of characteristics to be found in living and well-fed men and women. He built his new statues with movable arms and legs and mounted them by the dozen on pivots on top of his house. With cords he controlled their movements so that he was able to put them through the postures and turnings of the ceremonial dances. Men and women came from all over the island to look at them and until Easter Island's traditions ended in the present cultural apathy of the people Tuukoihu's fame was assured through his dancing dolls. It is casually mentioned that he was a good governor and a great builder. But these matters were nothing compared with his ability to provide amusement for the populace.

Wooden images are to be found, of course, in virtually every community under the sun. But the lineal descendants of Tuukoihu's dolls present characteristics definitely their own. They have almost uniformly large Roman noses which tradition ascribes to Tuukoihu's vain representation of his own facial ornament. Generally they have an appendage on the chin, a copy no doubt of the short beard once popular on the island. One such *moai miro* brought away by the *Ramona* was of a female figure with a bearded chin, indication that conventional symbols in these carvings no longer have any meaning.

Easter's wooden articles were few, as one might suspect. There is little surprising in the fact that Tuukoihu's people never learned to make household utensils out of wood. Rather one finds it an amazing thing that carving succeeded as an art in a region where trees were so scarce that the private possession of one has been recorded in an oft-repeated myth.

Somehow materials were found for the apprenticeship of the *moai miro* makers and this phase of Hotu Matua's culture survived all vicissitudes and came down through prehistoric times to our own day. Later, when careless whalers began to discover through experience the treachery of Rapa Nui's currents, timbers from wrecked ships furnished a supply for the carvers.

In the meantime dancing paddles were turned out in considerable numbers, as were little lizard talismans and lizard-headed clubs. Wooden rings and wooden belt ornaments and wooden rattles were highly esteemed as articles of personal use for ceremonials.

This craft never reached, even approximately, the development attained by the Maoris of New Zealand although Tuukoihu's *moai miro* look more like genuine beings than any of the fantastic three-fingered gods who stick their tongues out at the world in the neighborhood of

Rotorua. One pauses to consider what might have happened to the carving industry of Easter if there had been enough wood to encourage apprentices. But here, as always, one gets scant satisfaction from guesses. Easter's culture was remarkable chiefly because of the handicaps in the way of its development.

The part played by the *moai miro* in the life of the island is problematical. One may take it for granted that the more human of the figures merely carried on the tradition of Tuukoihu as objects of amusement. On the other hand the carving of the emaciated figures went on until the present era and they, from the very first, were linked with religion.

Brother Eyraud in his report mentions that nearly every house on the island had some form of wooden image. He observes that one might naturally take them to be idols but he declines to classify them as such.

He observed that they were treated with scant ceremony save on one or two occasions when they were set up outside of a house and remained there while the owners were performing a sort of dance. The dance ritual, he found on investigation, had no particular significance. The celebrants were doing merely what they had seen their fathers do. No one interviewed by the missionary could tell him what the little images signified or why they were kept.

It seems apropos to recall here that small likenesses of human beings have figured in primitive magic the world over and Easter Island never had any dearth of sorcerers and juju workers. Here, as elsewhere, one worked harm to one's enemy by attacking the image that was supposed to represent him. Similarly, whether the *moai miro* possessed any supernatural qualities of their own, they may quite likely have been magic links between the natives and their gods.

It has also been suggested that they may have been taken into family life originally as ancestral portraits. If so it is not difficult to see that they would speedily acquire a religious aura. Easter's legends show how readily ancestors become gods.

Tuukoihu's dolls may have seemed of no importance alongside the mightier bulk of the stone giants—mere comedy relief for a great tragedy. But it is through them rather than through the ponderous carvings of Rano Raraku that the world outside has obtained some idea of art as it obtained on Easter. The little gods have gone forth to the far corners of the world and have conveyed vividly the message that Tuukoihu's craft put into them—the imminence of death.

Chapter Twenty-Nine

WOMEN

The Social Significance of Obstetrics

"The women of Easter Island are highly immoral and the men are the greatest thieves in the world. . . ."

Thus one might condense the reports of all the voyagers who came to Hanga Roa from 1722 until the advent of the Peruvian slavers. One heard an echo of the ancient tradition when the anchor of the *Ramona* slid into Cook's Bay and the long-boats of the islanders came out through the surf:

"Batten down the hatches," said Hippolyte the Supercargo. "And lock all the chests. Here come the burglars. They are always hungry and have nothing to trade but their wives."

Hippolyte had never before laid eyes on Rapa Nui but he spoke with deep conviction. He had heard much of the island and little good of it. One marveled not so much at his intensity as at the subject matter of his discourse. It recalled so vividly the observation of another philosopher who had never looked upon Easter: "The evil that men do lives after them." The stone gods are crumbling and the scrawny heritors of the race that built them are awaiting the inevitable end but a reputation founded in 1722 shows signs of continuing for ever.

It would be difficult at this date to disprove the general indictment of Easter Island's morals even if anybody cared to try it. There is plentiful evidence that the natives received presents from La Pérouse with one hand while stealing his clothes with the other. And the bitterness of his complaint at such inhospitable treatment has found its counterpart in the reports of Gonzalez and Cook. If that were not enough of a case for the prosecution one has only to call on the manager at Mataveri and hear his ironic comment:

"The largest industry on the island is sheep-raising; the most profitable industry is sheep-stealing."

As for the promiscuity of the women, the presentation of evidence seems to be restricted only by one's personal taste. Venereal disease is prevalent and in some instances the outward marks of it are unmistakable.

To view the matter conservatively it seems scarcely likely that the ethics of Easter Island with regard to sexual relations and property rights were ever quite those of European civilization. And yet, if one studies the traditions of the island, one realizes that conditions were not always as they are now.

There was, for instance, a fixed idea concerning the importance of the family before the coming of the white man's morals and the white man's diseases. A majority of the clans may not have been, as in other communities, family groups, but one of them, the Miru, certainly was. And in all of them a man's neighbors stood ready to take up arms to avenge injuries to his wives or children.

Strict social usage bound any man to hunt down the slayer of a near relative and legend would indicate that this obligation was seldom ignored. The mythic lore of the island is filled with incident about parents who performed heroic deeds to punish sundry ogres who had murdered and devoured their children. The burial ritual of the image terraces included not only a constant watch over the exposed corpse but a search by the dead person's

The Weirdest Sky-Line in the World
The gods are forgotten but their fear is eternal

Modern Expressions

The bird, the turtle, phallic symbolism and the exposed ribs are still favored by the artistic ones of Rapa Nui. (From the collection of T. S. Earl, Mataveri)

The Work of the Master Builders

No more grandiose memorial to the dead was ever contrived by man than these massive platforms of Easter with their walls of cyclopean rock. This reconstruction, to scale of one that stood near Hanga Roa, shows a typical *ahu*

kinsfolk for the malign influences that had ended his life.

It is traditional also that the children of Easter Island, unlike those of other parts of Polynesia, were kept secluded until puberty. After this period they were examined by the priest of Orongo and tattooed with a symbol of virginity. Not until that time were they allowed to enter the choruses that sang and danced at the feasts.

In view of the moral laxity that came to the island in later years one is surprised to discover that a valuation was actually placed on chastity in both sexes. But there is plenty of lore to show that such was the case. Parents exercised complete control over the marriage of a daughter. They chose for her a mate whom they believed to match her in comeliness and physique. They demanded of him that he pass the examination of the priest. His parents, in turn, required a similar guarantee of qualifications with reference to the girl.

Marriage, as elsewhere in Polynesia, had no religious significance. There was nothing very formal about it even as a contract and no ceremonial attached to it save that the bridegroom was required to give a feast. Nor was it assured of any permanence. If a girl failed to get on with the husband who had been selected for her, there was nothing to prevent her leaving him, as, no doubt, she frequently did. Divorce implied nothing more complicated than a statement of intention. But whatever the stability of her first marriage, the details of it rested entirely with her parents and custom required her to respect their judgment until test had proved it erroneous.

Hotu Matua, the prolific father, seems to have been monogamous as was the lieutenant who accompanied him from Marae Renga to Easter. But polygamy was extensively practised by his followers and descendants. Any man was free to take as many wives as he might wish to have in his house. It is traditional that few men contrived to get along with more than three at a time. Nothing in any of the legends would indicate that there was ever a community of women in any of the clans.

There are some puzzling features in the native attitude toward personal property. A man was justly jealous of certain articles of adornment, his lizard-headed club and in some cases his *rongo-rongo* tablets. But, apparently, he realized the uselessness of trying to establish individual ownership of the crops he raised or the fish he caught. What he had in the way of food his neighbors owned, for that was the ancient custom of all Polynesia. Such a complacent attitude may have developed that acquisitive skill which, when directed toward the property of visiting explorers, was classed as theft.

The women of Easter were subject to few of the tabus found elsewhere in the South Seas. They were under male domination and, although they had the right to terminate a marriage relation if they chose, were regarded as the property of the husband. He might trade them for other property, a right which is exercised at Hanga Roa to this day, but it seems likely that their acquiescence was required to make good the bargain. In all other respects they seem to have enjoyed complete freedom. They took part in religious exercises, in some of the wars and, what was considered more important, in the feasts. The only important rite in which they seem never to have engaged was the annual competition of the bird cult. They never were admitted to the priesthood or instructed in the mysteries of the *rongo-rongo* tablets but many of them became soothsayers and as such exercised a considerable power.

In Tahiti and elsewhere in the South Seas a strict tabu was placed about women in childbirth. But not so here. The prospective mother paid a visit to Orongo as a religious ceremony and her accouchement was something of a public function. Until quite recently friends of the family were invited to attend en masse.

As an added attraction to this function the father of the child also went through all the outward manifestations of confinement along with the mother, and on some occasions does so to-day. It was a current belief that such thoughtfulness on the part of the father would insure an easy delivery and the permanent health of the infant.

Female infanticide was widely practised, especially in the days when the island was thickly populated and the menace of starvation was constantly increasing. Instances of it have been reported in recent years. And as long as any remnant of the old culture remained, childbirth was always followed by a conference of relatives to decide whether or not the baby should be kept.

As a sort of corollary to the inhuman attitude toward infants one must consider the removal of old people who had become feeble or otherwise might be considered a burden on the community. They were taken out and stoned to death. In this perhaps is the origin of a story, unsubstantiated in local legend, that the *ariki* and the *maoris* once set the limit of population on Rapa Nui at nine hundred and that to maintain this number they decreed one death for every birth. If the newborn child was permitted to live an old person was taken out and killed and if the child was smothered some ancient was thereby accorded a new lease on life.

It is quite within reason that no such improvident people as the natives of Easter Island ever lived anywhere else on the face of the earth. The instinctive fear of hunger that led them to stone their grandparents and toss their children into the sea would seem to place them instantly in the category of brute savages. And yet it is only in their candid attitude toward such practises, and the publicity with which they surrounded them, that they differ from civilized moderns who have the same attitude toward life but more discreet phraseology. Basically they seem to have preferred laughter to murder and feasting to laughter. With famine always at their elbows they tossed their stores into a common oven and banqueted. They made no attempt to establish reserves of food. What they had they devoured as soon as possible in an effort to forget the lean days whose coming they hastened.

Every death was considered an excuse for a feast. These sporadic banquets might be classed as semi-public affairs, affecting as they did only family and clan groups. But there were other feasts in which the whole population took part and these lasted for days.

One such affair, the Paina, a summer festival, was said to have been instituted by Hotu Matua himself and in the course of years had assumed a religious significance. As a general celebration it was confined to no one clan and there is a tradition that it was held at a different burial platform each year.

Originally this feast appears to have been a sort of testimonial given by some individual clansman to an admired relative. One man in the group whose turn it was to hold the Paina announced himself host and issued the general invitation. In practise it was a community picnic in which the guest of honor seems to have been totally submerged.

As on Pitcairn to-day it was customary for the invited ones to bring whatever they could muster in the way of food. For days before the date set, the sea along the coast of the island was covered with swimmers on their way to the feast pushing before them wickerwork floats filled with yams and sugar cane and taro. Many a guest brought every root he could dig out of his fields condemning himself to months of starvation that he, and others, might gorge themselves to satiation for a week. The soothsayers determined what was the best day on which to light the ovens and in some measure decided who was to act as host. In the event of competition for this honor it was arranged that the Paina could be repeated with a different host, which ruling sometimes brought about as many as five such banquets in a year.

The *rongo-rongo* men came to the Paina with their tablets which they recited with due solemnity. And the pious atmosphere was increased by the presence of the singing and dancing groups identified with all the ceremonials of the god Makemake.

An important feature of the celebration was the erection of a figure of wickerwork on top of the *ahu*. This figure was in the form of a man or woman, representing the father or mother of the host. It was generally about fifteen feet high and covered with bark, feathers and human hair. When the feasting began the host climbed up on a ladder inside the figure and passed food out through the mouth to the waiting guests. At the conclusion of the banquet it was pulled down and destroyed.

A feast of even greater importance was the Koro which, while more strictly a family affair, lasted longer and involved a more generous distribution of food. Special houses were erected for its observance, the foundations of some of which are still to be seen on the island. Guests came in platoons or in whole clans and stayed as long as they pleased, eating continuously and taking part when they were able to move in dancing and singing entertainments.

The Koro was a mark of esteem given by a son to a

living father or to the memory of one dead. And while the whole island was not included in a blanket invitation to such affairs scores of guests did come as family units bringing presents of food which were promptly redistributed and in departing made room for other scores.

On the last day all the food remaining was set out for one climacteric banquet after which wreckers with lizard-headed clubs tore down the building and laid the poles away for use at the next celebration.

Feasting was a principal part of the ritual for the dead as it was in all other religious manifestations on the island. Easter's nebulous creed was bound up with ideas of famine. Deified passion has been the basis of more than one primitive religion and in this barren land even sex was subordinate to hunger. Makemake, the god who superseded the forgotten deities of Polynesia, was revered as a preserver, a provider of food and the filling of an empty stomach was looked upon as an act in his honor.

Death, despite the pomp and circumstance surrounding it, was looked upon as a calamity. . . . An odd inconsistency in a race whose wars and cannibalism placed so low a valuation on life. The principle of a virtually indestructible spirit in the human compound was recognized inasmuch as there was a wide-spread belief in *akuakus*, or ghosts. But these *akuakus* had little to be thankful for in their life beyond the grave. They went to no special land of peace and comfort but loitered miserably about the burial cairns in which their bones had been laid, a restless, fearsome band who envied the living and worked what evil they could on their survivors. They spoke to the sorcerers—the *ivi atuas*—and revealed the names of the winners in the egg-hunting contest, which revelations were generally about ninety per cent. incorrect. And they fostered disease in a spiteful effort to add recruits to their shadowy army.

So, when a man lay dying, the *ivi atuas* were called in to do what might be done to drive away the *akuakus* or better yet to kill them. But the removal of a ghost is difficult and the killing of one more difficult still, so frequently the disease triumphed. The immediate relatives mourned perfunctorily and went through the routine observances such as seeking out the enemy who had engaged the hostile *akuaku* to bring the death about.

The body was wrapped in bark cloth and bound with braided grass after which it was carried to the *ahu* and laid on a temporary table of sticks. Members of the family took up positions on the *ahu* to keep watch night and day over the remains, a precaution practical as well as ceremonial in the case of a great man whose skull might have uses for minor sorcery. The feasting commenced with a prelude of ritual weeping which was repeated at frequent intervals. Food was issued to the mourners with a prayer which also figured in the great feasts: "Receive this for the gods and Makemake." So the observances went on through the day and in darkness far into the night. Fires and torches were tabu about the burial platforms.

After a day of this the distant relatives went home. The family of the dead man continued to keep watch by turns until the body had dried and fallen apart. The bones were then taken and thrown into the vault and the period of mourning was finished. A new *akuaku* was free to roam the treeless hills and make business for the sorcerers.

Chapter Thirty

OBSIDIAN SPEARHEADS

The Engaging Pastime Called War

All across Easter, along the seacoast, strewing the old trails through the valleys, shining through the sere grasses on the hill slopes, lies an unsprouted crop of dragon's teeth . . . obsidian spearheads, laboriously flaked to workable shapes and carefully edged. Dozens of them are to be found in half an hour's walk. Probably thousands could be gathered if any one cared to prowl the gaunt acres in search of them . . . black talismans from which, even more vividly than through native legend, one may reconstruct the island's dark past.

With them as markers one may follow Easter's tides of war from coast to coast and across the plain of the burial *ahus.* He may trace out the battle-fields in the saddles of the hills and the lines of retreat down which defeated warriors dashed in panic from an inglorious end in cannibal ovens. And he can not but stand amazed at the extent to which mortal combat involved the life of the island.

The shafts of the spears and the thongs that bound them have long since decayed but time has not altered the volcanic glass points. The marks of the stone tools with which they were chipped from their matrix are still discernible on them and their identity as weapons could never be questioned.

In other parts of Polynesia one might consider them inconclusive evidence of wide-spread warfare inasmuch as they might serve in skilful hands for hunting purposes. But there never was any hunting on Rapa Nui, no animals for the chase save human beings. All these hundreds of spade-like missiles were designed for one purpose, the killing of men . . . and there were no men to kill within a thousand miles save natives of the island.

Here, as usual in the affairs of Easter, one comes close to the inexplicable. One may recover from his shock at the discovery that bloodshed must have been the daily amusement of these people. Such a state of affairs is not without parallel in other savage communities about which more is known. But in contemplating the flotsam of battle one must return once more to the basic mystery of the island—the statues—and remember that under one ruler at least there must have been an organization too closely knit to permit of wars. Battle and riot and massacre even within clans and between related families are understandable but that a race capable of such violence could have been tamed even temporarily is almost beyond belief.

Wars on Easter, like other social functions of the island, failed to conform to outside standards for such things. Professor Macmillan Brown points out that there was no such village organization on Easter as that which provided a constant source for animosity in many of the Melanesian Islands. He cites the linguistic differences between Melanesian villages where each community had its own dialect and makes comparison with the Easter clans which had a common tongue and, when not engaged in war, mingled socially with one another. The clan arrangement of Easter was undoubtedly potent in the fostering of ill-feeling between large portions of the populace at once. But conflicts between these groups appear to have been in the nature of family squabbles on a large scale, provoked by antagonists who for a large part of their time must have been friends, and fought to the death by warriors who were well acquainted with one another. There might be something impersonal about a war between villages on some islands of the South Pacific; there could never be any detached attitude about a battle on Rapa Nui.

Causes of war were simple: personal pride and a wish for personal aggrandizement; revenge; and a need for food. Cynical observers have advanced the theory that the broad general principle of hunger led all other considerations as an excuse for a fight.

Cannibalism on Rapa Nui had none of the ceremonial, semi-religious significance that was attached to it elsewhere in the South Seas. An Easter Island warrior never cherished the belief that by eating the heart of an enemy he might strengthen himself with that enemy's moral and physical qualities. Rather he felt that by eating suitable portions of his enemy, properly cooked, he might stave off starvation a little longer. Cannibalism persisted until well into the past century and there are Easter natives alive on Tahiti to-day who can tell of the feasts on human flesh that followed the wars. But there has never been any tradition that this practise was different, save in the reluctance of the victim, from the eating of mutton.

It is said that when a clan had taken offense at another clan it sent an emissary to the village of Orongo on Rano Kao. The war-herald proceeded to the house of the statue Taura Renga which figured in ceremonials of the bird cult and there stood in silence with the feather crown of his clan upon his head. He stood there patiently until some savant of the offending clan came to the house. The newcomer did not need to be told that war was threatening. The presence of the earlier arrival with his hat on his head was tantamount to a formal declaration.

The clansmen departed without speaking to one another

and warned their people of the approaching conflict. Spearheads were sharpened, old shafts renewed, and stones small enough to be thrown by hand were collected in large numbers. Lizard-headed clubs were taken from their hiding-places. War dances were performed and fires lighted in the hills.

The armies moved to war headed by their *rongo-rongo* men carrying the sacred tablets or dancing paddles (*ao* or *rapa*) and sometimes the king, forbidden to take any part in the fighting himself, was present to lend it importance through regal patronage.

The legends of Hotu Matua tell of how he instructed the youth of the island to fight in formation. But military science, if it ever existed, went the way of the art and culture. Young men went forward as an advance guard and sometimes young women accompanied them. They made contact with the enemy and started a hand-to-hand slaughter. The main columns presently joined and after that the fight proceeded without tactics and without leadership.

The Easter Islanders even at the time when European explorers had begun to visit Rapa Nui were skilled in throwing stones. They practised this science during most of their spare time and developed an accuracy which white visitors declared to be deadly. But aside from such missiles they were virtually without long-distance weapons. They never discovered the bow and arrow, and the slingshot used to-day for the killing of birds is a modern importation. Their javelins, while no doubt deadly, were not so accurate as hand-thrown stones nor could they be used when the lines were far apart.

So the warriors found themselves toe to toe almost at once, each engaged in killing the man in front of him. The battle continued until the immediate cause of the trouble—a man who had committed a murder or otherwise injured some one in the rival clan—was killed. Instantly all hostilities ceased. The combatants still alive set about preparing an oven to accommodate the dead victims. The night was spent in feasting after which the clan armies went home to wait for the next war.

There were, of course, many wars whose causes were not ascribable to so simple a thing as murder. Raids for food, thefts of women, desecration of burial cairns in a search for wonder-working skulls . . . such things as these could not be avenged by the killing of one single miscreant. The more intangible the cause, the more deadly the insult and the more wide-spread the slaughter.

In such conflicts the fighting spread not infrequently to more than two clans and generally did not cease until the offending community was virtually wiped out—its villages, its animals and its men, women and children. Sometimes the bloodshed stopped short of the elimination of the defeated clan but that was only when the victims acknowledged their defeat and consented to spend the remainder of their lives as the slaves of the victors. On one occasion cited by Professor Brown, the beaten warriors fled from the field and hid themselves in a cave on a small island north of Hanga Roa. The successful fighters were much pleased by this solution of their problem. They maintained the island as a corral from which they took new victims as often as their dietetic requirements dictated.

Only the natural fecundity of the Polynesian race can explain how any of the population could have survived the island's unending program of massacre. It is true, of course, that not all wars had as their object the extirpation of whole sections of the community. Such undertakings

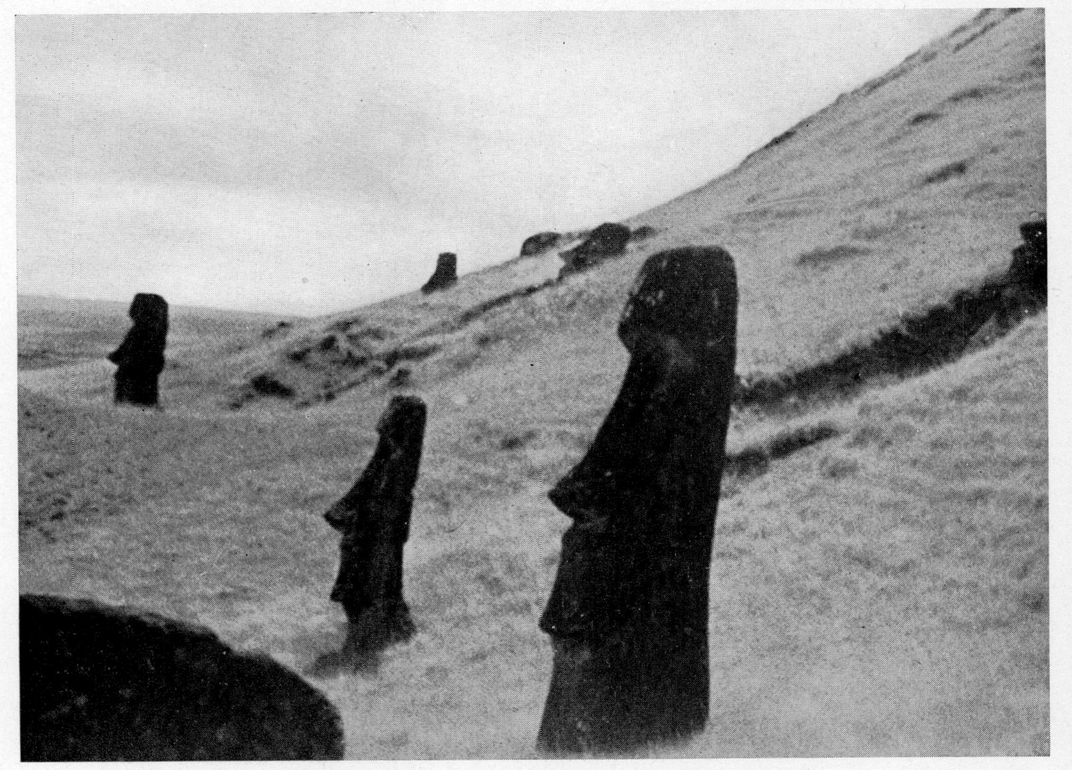

Defiant of Time

Half buried by slides from the volcano, the giants are otherwise much as they were the day they were set in place

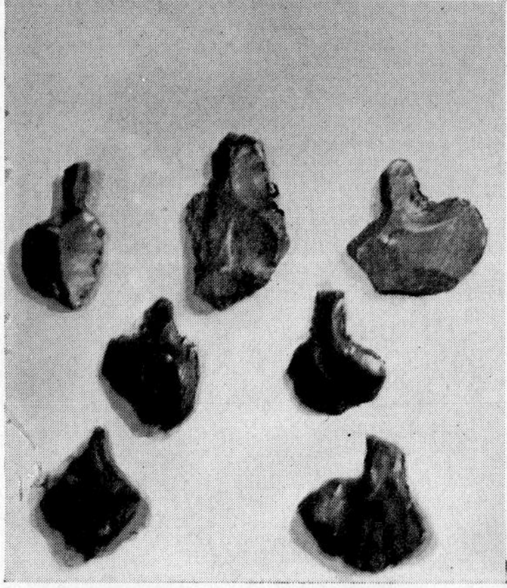

Mataa

Obsidian spearheads of the type one finds strewn all across the island. They are generally about two inches wide

Simpler Arts of Easter

A carving of red tufa (the material from which the high hats were made). This figure, five inches high, is fairly modern

Front view

Rear view

Wooden Marionettes

The two outer figures are old. The one on the left has a known history of a hundred years. The central puppet is odd in that it represents a female figure with the characteristic beard

required sustained effort and the maintenance of a high emotional pitch, both of which considerations were foreign to the normal life of Polynesia. Despite the long sagas of blood with which the ancient traditions are filled, one may take it for granted that the majority of the conflicts were hardly more than simple personal quarrels brought to a quick conclusion by outside help. The casualty lists were probably too small to have any lasting effect on the census.

On the other hand there were undoubtedly some conflicts which made the island a shambles and blackened the coves with the ashes of burned villages. There were days in the history of Easter when the deep vaults of the *ahus* could not contain the dead even had there been enough persons living to drag the corpses to the seacoast from the battle-fields in the hills. There were days when a few old men and half-crazed women stood on the rocks of Rano Kao and surveyed acres of emptiness where the slaughtered clansmen had wandered in colorful hundreds to the great feasts.

Perhaps it is because of this recurrent phenomenon that the early voyagers never seemed certain about the population of Easter—why one discoverer placed its census at a few hundred and another at thousands. There undoubtedly were periods when fewer people lived between Anakena and Hanga Roa than had landed from the boats of Hotu Matua. And repeatedly the race recovered.

There has been much speculation concerning the catastrophe that threw down the images on the burial cairns many of which were standing at the time of Roggeween's visit. The Dutch admiral's report that the platforms were in use in 1722 was verified by voyagers who came to the island in later years, though by 1840 none of the statues along the seacoast remained on its pedestal. For many years the idea was prevalent that this wholesale collapse of the Titans was due to lack of care on the part of the natives or perhaps to an earthquake such as might be expected on an island which is constantly a-tremble.

But even superficial contemplation of the ruins convinces one that no convulsion of Nature is responsible and that neglect could not have accomplished in a few short years what it had failed to accomplish in generations.

With the traditions of war in his ears a person peers across the battered remains of the burial platforms and sees a battle-field. He can not rid himself of the notion that here, at least, is evidence of a struggle which came close to bringing the great silence back to Easter. At Tongariki where the dozen or more canoe-shaped backs of the images range like fallen dominoes he sees plainly the marks of human fury. He sees how the ropes of grass were looped about the necks of the images and passed into the hands of the waiting destroyers. He sees the straining bodies and hears the crunching collapse of the stone gods. Such manifestations of warfare are not indigenous to Easter Island.

Desecration of a tomb belonging to one clan, must, of course, have brought retaliation in the desecration of another, and so in the wide-spread destruction one may discover plentiful evidence that in this, the last of the island's great conflicts, virtually the entire population must have been involved. . . . Notwithstanding which there were nearly three thousand people on the island when the slave ships of Peru came to Hanga Roa.

It seems idle to speculate concerning the causes that led to the overthrow of the images or the methods used to destroy them since ruin is always so much simpler than construction. The destruction of the culture that evolved them and the tragic disintegration of the race that lasted no longer than its own leering gods are more complex.

Chapter Thirty-One

SHIPWRECK

The Immortal Spirit of the Schooner "Falcon"

A STILL but rainy night had come at the close of a stormy day. There had been trouble in the scaling of Rano Kao. Shifting winds and treacherous currents had driven the *Ramona* out of her temporary haven in the lee of the southwestern headland and she had set out on her endless touring about the island. At the ranch there had been a heated argument between the manager and the prefect of police over the rights of the populace to clamber over the company's gates and damage the company's fences—a discussion that had come to an impasse when the manager thoughtfully picked up a branding iron.

With night came the promise of a gale but nevertheless a hint of peace. The ranch management hung up its branding iron and the important prefect went back to his headquarters behind the church at Hanga Roa. All was cheery when a nondescript group of bearers deposited a pile of motion-picture apparatus on the porch of the administration house and the weary visitor stopped for a breathing spell on the steps.

"You'll have to stay for dinner," declared the manager. "The wind will go into the northwest presently and there will be a surf like a tidal wave at Hanga Roa. Your captain will have to pick up his hook and go out to sea. You'd just waste your time if you went down to the mole and tried to get out to the schooner now. . . ."

So once more the visitor sat down and through the eyes

of the manager watched the strange gods of Easter stalking across the gaunt black hills.

The foreman and his wife had taken their children to bed. The manager's wife had retired. The dining-room table had been cleared and spread over it lay numerous photographic copies of the Rapa Nui script. The dull booming noises of Easter echoed distantly among the hills. The manager discoursed fluently on his analysis of the hieroglyphics but his attention seemed to be distracted. His head was half turned toward the open door. He seemed to be listening for something.

"It's a funny thing," he observed as if the thought had just occurred to him. "Many ships have come to this island since Roggeween discovered it, but the Chilean training ship *Baquedano* and the freighter *Antarctica* are probably the only ones that ever have come here twice."

"What's odd about that?" inquired the visitor combating a foolish sense of uneasiness.

"Nothing except that most of these good ships are somewhere on the bottom of the Pacific. . . . The *Falcon,* the *Alba,* the *Angamus,* the *Metura,* the *Esteban,* the *Jean,* the *Fortuna,* and a Chilean naval auxiliary . . ."

He paused . . . listening again. Rain was spattering on the porch, the wind was playing a dirge in the pines, the surf sounded vaguely like Romagne on the morning of the attack. But there was nothing unusual in such noises. The manager directed his attention with an effort and lighted a cigarette.

"The *Jean* and the *Fortuna* were war prizes," he went on. "I suppose they really don't belong in the hoodoo classification. The *Fortuna* was taken by Von Luckner after the wreck of the *See Adler.* She was sunk off Rano Kao. The *Jean* was a steel bark which Von Spee took for her cargo of coal at the time the Germans were using the island for a naval base.

"They took the coal out of her and then set off a bomb in her hold. She went to the bottom just off Hanga Roa. That was war and such things might have happened anywhere. But it is nice to observe that the German navy didn't escape the curse. The *Dresden, Scharnorst, Gneisenau, Nurnberg, Leipzig* and *Eitel Friederich* made this their rendezvous point in the Pacific. Most of them sailed away to be sunk off the Falklands and the *Dresden* was blown up at Juan Fernandez.

"The other ships just failed to survive the strain of the trip out. The *Falcon* was a good schooner owned by the company that operates this ranch. She came out from Valparaiso with no trouble at all and loaded at Hanga Piko, the inlet south of Hanga Roa. She was just about ready to start back for South America when a change of wind got her. She came on to the rocks as if she intended to ride on over the island. And that was the last of her.

"The *Angamus* overturned after leaving here. There were forty-three people aboard and not a soul was saved. . . . Not a bad ship either—old but seaworthy—and she was about as big as any boat that ever came out here.

"The *Alba* went home from here on one trip and landed her cargo at Valparaiso. She was sunk in a gale on her next trip out. The other ships that we've known out here are strewn up and down the coast of Chile.

"The *Alba* was fortunate in that she actually got home. I was here visiting Edmunds during her stay and I can remember the day when the captain tried to pull up his anchor and get her out of an inshore wind. I was standing on the hill beyond Hanga Roa and I could hear her winches grinding and grinding.

"Her stern began to come up out of the water and her bow began to go down. They took a list to starboard and from where I stood it looked as if she would overturn any minute. Then she righted herself and the whole process started all over again.

"It wasn't until later that I discovered what had happened. Her anchor was fouled on the wreck of the *Jean.* It came loose just in time and she got away from the wind without a minute to spare. She had swung around into shallow water and her engines weren't doing her any good. She was less than half a length off the rocks."

Once more he paused and gave an ear to the wild night. There was still no clue to what had distracted him . . . no sounds that seemed worthy of notice save the wind and the tom-toms of the reefs.

"The *Carnegie* lost an anchor here," he went on. "It was a bronze anchor worth more than an ordinary schooner. It got fouled but the skipper of the *Carnegie* wasn't like the old man on the *Alba.* He'd seen enough of Easter Island and he wasn't going to risk his ship to save an anchor. He cut it away and sailed.

"Afterward Edmunds sent down some native divers and got ropes on it. The whole population turned out and salvaged it. It's back in the States by now.

"The *Baquedano* on her last trip left a midshipman through careless handling of a pistol. We made a coffin for him and buried him in the Hanga Roa cemetery. That's the way it has always been. . . . Something happens to every ship that comes here."

He raised his head suddenly.

"Do you hear that?" he demanded.

The startled visitor listened.

"Hear what?"

"There it is again. . . ."

He leaned forward in his chair. The visitor followed his glance instinctively and saw nothing but the gray paneling of the walls, shiny in the rays of the lamp. But he heard and as his attention focused on the sound he realized that it had been present all evening, a thin obbligato to the symphony of the storm.

A prolonged creak—a crescendo squeal succeeded by a low groan—and behind it a pulsation felt rather than heard. Only one group of noises in human experience could have resembled this sequence and the resemblance was so marked that the visitor came half out of his chair. He was ashore, seated in a house on the slope of a volcano. But he was listening to sounds that everybody who has ever been to sea has heard in the corridors of a ship at night—the protest of the hull against the roll—the straining of rivets and joints, and the dull throb of the engines.

"It's just the wind," suggested the visitor, only half convinced.

The manager smiled and shook his head. "I knew you'd say that," he said. "That's why I've been waiting all evening to call your attention to it. The wind has died."

He pointed out across the veranda to one of the island's two coconut-palms. The fronds hung limp and motionless. In the lighted rectangle beyond the door the rain was falling in vertical lines.

"It's a dead calm," he said. And his voice trailed off to blend with the echoes of the rolling ship.

"After all it's a wooden house," suggested the visitor. "Probably the rain has softened the ground and it's settling."

Once more he shook his head.

"This house is on foundations that have been here at least two hundred years—maybe a thousand," he argued. "Squared rocks as big as you'll find in the burial *ahus*.

Masonry like that doesn't settle. And the house itself is made of oak planks and timbers joined ship-fashion and bolted together. It's strong enough to stand a hurricane. The material came out of the wreckage of the *Falcon.*"

The creaking rose and fell. The pulsation went on like the beating of a metronome. So vivid was the effect that the gray room, the house, the island itself seemed suddenly unreal—fantasies projecting themselves into a dream. In a moment one would open one's eyes and discover one's self strapped into a bunk in the *Ramona* with a gale tearing through the rigging and the sea breaking over the starboard bow.

"A ship at sea!" observed the manager. "The house has made those sounds ever since the hull of the *Falcon* was salvaged. . . . I've heard plenty about the ghosts of men but never anything about the ghost of a ship. . . . And that's what this is. The good old *Falcon* doesn't know she's been sunk."

Creak and groan, groan and throb, the eery echoes filled the room.

One discovered with some surprise that the old reflexes of civilization did not function so smoothly or so quickly here as they might have done in a more familiar environment. One's mind admitted at once that all of this was the sheerest nonsense and that one's convictions would presently adjust themselves to one's experience. But one was conscious nevertheless, and a bit ashamed, of a cold trickle along one's spine. Ships that lived after death were something entirely removed from one's routine.

The manager laughed harshly and broke the spell.

"It's the damned island," he said. "It shakes."

The visitor took a deep breath and suppressed a sigh of relief.

"What's the reason for that?" The question was put with considerable interest quite aside from the weird echoes of the *Falcon* as one remembered the crater of Rano Kao dominating the landscape behind the house.

"Some dispute about it," said the manager. "There was an inquiry into causes after the Chilean seismograph shook itself to pieces. One of the scientists who came here with the gunboat to take it off said that the trembling is due to external pressure of the sea rather than to any submarine disturbance. The island comes straight up from a depth of ten or twelve thousand feet and is pretty narrow for a shaft of that height. The surf battering at the top of it produces a continuous shiver. . . . At any rate that's the theory."

He found that his cigarette had gone out and relighted it.

"You've got to take a lot for granted on this island," he observed. "I probably am the least superstitious man in the whole world. I've been a mining engineer ever since I got out of the university in New Zealand and I lean toward the scientific point of view. But things like this ghost of the *Falcon* certainly furnish material for a quiet evening's discussion. The natives would read some kind of warning into these sounds if they ever heard them and all because the architect of Easter made the sea in this neighborhood just a little too deep."

He yawned and gathered up the photographs of the script. And while the *Falcon's* timbers went on with their eery song of the high seas it was a simple matter to recall the stories of Easter circulated for generations wherever wanderers sit to smoke pipes and exchange yarns—stories like that of the curse of Tut-ankh-amen, having to do with the lingering influence of vanished gods.

"Of course all these sailors' stories are a lot of poppycock," he said as if sensing his guest's unspoken thought. "The probable explanation of the disasters that have overtaken the ships we have seen out here is in the ships themselves. They nearly all were ready for the scrap heap when they took the charter to make the trip from Valparaiso. . . . But the coincidence is quite interesting, isn't it? . . . I wonder what they've been doing at the naval conference? . . ."

The ghostly engines of the wrecked *Falcon* continued to drive on through the night.

CHAPTER THIRTY-TWO

SEASCAPE

A Voyage between Two Planets

THE cameras had been taken aboard. The governor's official seal had been fixed to the ship's papers. The populace of Hanga Roa in uniforms and cutaway coats and gingham aprons and ball-gowns stood on the little mole to watch the lifting of a sail and the moving of a boat over the distant horizon.

A storm was gathering. A high wind had begun to whistle through the empty valleys and the surf had resumed its deafening cannonade. Scurrying clouds tore themselves to shreds on the grim dark summit of Rano Kao. And the menace of the Pacific, forgotten these many days, was abroad once more in the crested rollers.

The quest was ended. Inquisitive eyes had peered once more into the inscrutable faces of the Titans. Profane hands had stirred once more the rattling bones in the terraces of the dead. But now all that was finished and to-night the *akuakus* might scream their indignation into ears long attuned to their plainting.

To-morrow the gale again with the decks running water and a black sea breaking over the bows—wind in the rigging and sharks in the churning wake—and long nights broken by the clang of the pump. To-morrow the vast loneliness with dim horizons ever receding. To-morrow the anxious study of barometer and chart and the shivering consciousness of wet clothes and wet blankets.

There should be regret at leaving this island and its

creature comforts for a further venture into the wide unknown. One should be feeling a landsman's hesitance in stepping from firm ground to the nervous deck of a battered schooner, the landsman's dread of illness and water and storm. But there is no regret.

On the top of their dead volcano the giant gods leer out across the ancient desolation, their mockery more evident to-day than ever before. Another wanderer has come to look upon them in puny astonishment. Another wanderer is outward bound.

For one brief moment the sun strikes through the cumulus clouds and then is gone again, leaving the land appropriately in twilight. The surf-boat puts out. The natives peer after it, motionless, unsmiling. . . .

The anchor comes up. The prow swings around to the west. A wave comes over the port rail. The little engine begins its throb. And presently the white surf of Easter and the black headlands are lost in the gray rain.

To-morrow it will be the memory of a vivid dream. One has seen the land of the great *cauchemar*, the burying-ground of the gods, a world as distant and distinct from one's own as if it rolled in the void beyond the stars. One has walked in savage antiquity and has seen man come up from the slime, pause for one moment in the sunlight and fall back again. One looks with gratitude at the calendar and then at the chart.

Tahiti is only three thousand miles away.

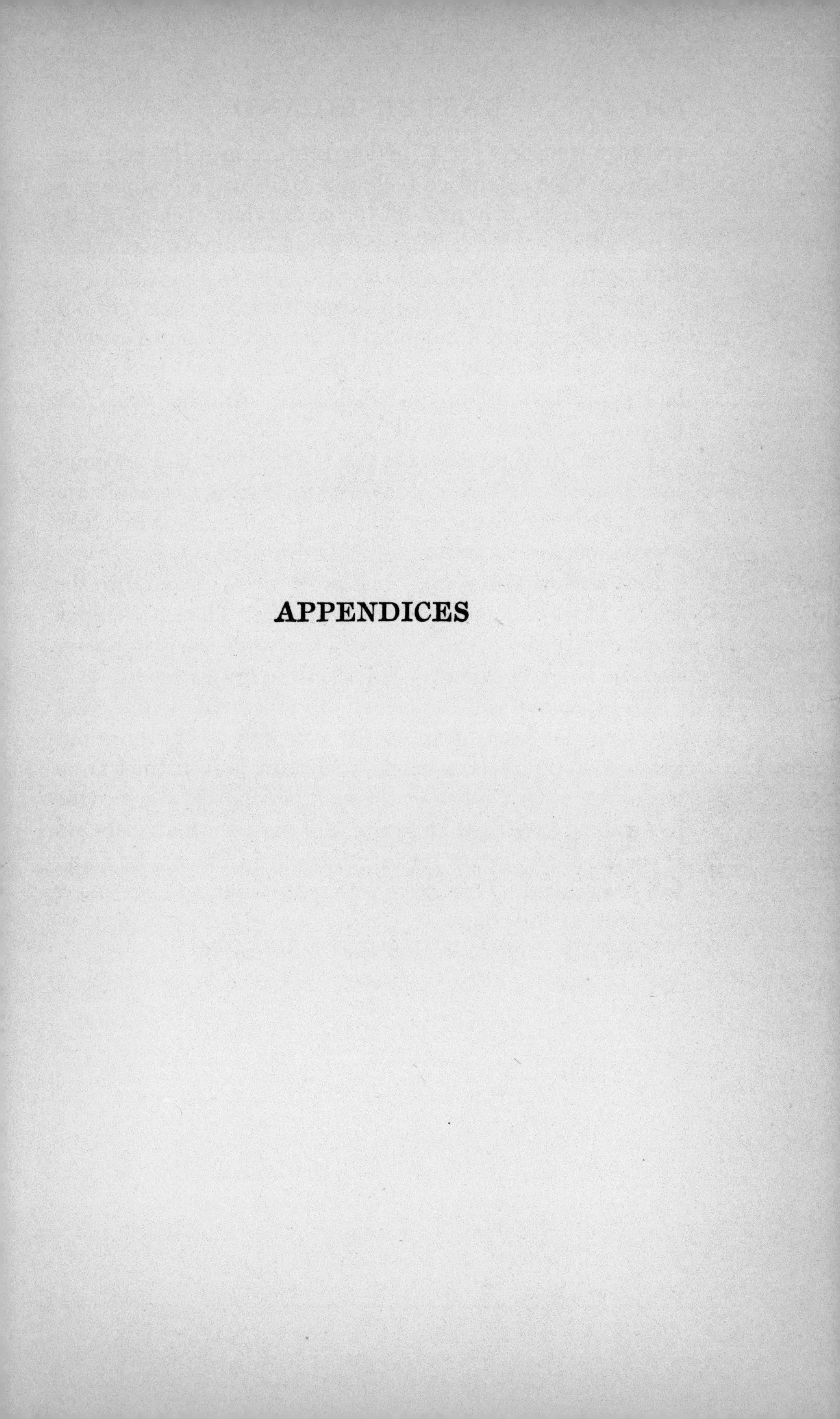

APPENDICES

I

Dutch Exploration of Easter

(From "The World Displayed; or, A Curious Collection of Voyages and Travels Selected from the Writers of all Nations." London, 1773, Vol. IX, pp. 118-25.

Mr. *Roggewein* on his leaving *Juan Fernandes,* proposed to visit a southern continent, said to have been discovered by Captain *Davis* in the year 1680, and having the benefit of a south-east monsoon, soon arrived in the latitude of 28 deg. and in 251 deg. longitude, where he expected to have met with *Davis's* land, of which every person on board had the greatest hopes, when they perceived abundance of fowls flying, and observed the frequent shifting of the winds, both of which are considered as certain signs of lands. Some of the company even flattered themselves that they saw it; but to the great mortification of the Commodore no such land was to be found, which indeed was no wonder, as according to Mr. *Wafer's* description of it, he sought it near 10° too far to the west.

Having failed 12°. west, still in sight of a vast number of birds, they arrived on the coast of a small island about sixteen leagues in extent, and as they discovered it on *Easter*-day, called it *Pasch,* or *Easter* Island. The *African* galley being the smallest, and best sailer, went first to examine this new country, and reported, that it appeared not only very fertile, but well inhabited, since the crew had seen abundance of smoke in all parts of the island. This news gave great joy to the Commodore. The next day they spent in looking for a port, when being about two miles from the shore, an *Indian* came off to them in his canoe; they made signs to him to come on board, which he very readily did, and was well received. As he was naked, the first present they made him was a piece of cloth to cover him, after which they gave him pieces of coral, beads, and other baubles, which, together with a dried fish, he hung about his neck. His body was painted all over with a variety of figures: His natural complexion appeared to be a dark brown, and his ears were so excessive large and long, that they reached to his shoulders, which was no doubt occasioned by the wearing of heavy ear-rings that had thus extended them. He was tall, well made, robust, and of a countenance expressive of great happiness. He was brisk, active, and by his gestures, and manner of speaking, appeared to be of a very merry disposition. They gave him a glass of wine to drink, which he threw away in a manner that surprized them. Our Author supposes he was afraid of being poisoned; but perhaps his being used to water, might render the smell of that liquor offensive. They next cloathed him from head to foot, and put a hat on his head, with which he was not at all pleased; but appeared aukward and uneasy. They then gave him food, which he eat heartily, but could not be persuaded to use either knife or fork. Upon their ordering the music to play, he seemed extremely delighted, and whenever they took him by the hand, would leap and dance.

Finding it impossible to come to an anchor that day, they thought proper to fend off the Indian, and, to encourage others, allowed him to keep what he had got; but to their great surprize, they found that the poor creature had no mind to go. He looked at them with regret, and held up both his hands towards his native island, crying in a very audible voice, *Odorroga! Odorroga! Odorroga!* and they had much ado to make him get into the canoe; he plainly shewing by his signs, that he had much rather they would have carried him away in their ship.

By day-break the next morning they entered a gulph, on the south-east side of the island, when great multitudes of the inhabitants came down to meet them, bringing vast quantities of fowls and roots; many came on board with these provisions, while the rest ran about from place to place. As the ships drew nearer, they crowded down to the shore, in order to have the better view of them, and at the same time lighted fires, and offered sacrifices to their idols, abundance of which were erected on the coast, probably with a view of imploring their protection. All that day the *Dutch* spent in mooring their ships, and very early the next morning observed the people again prostrated before these idols, towards the rising sun, and burning sacrifices before them. The necessary preparations being made for their landing, the friendly *Indian* who had been with them before, came on board a second time bringing with him abundance of his countrymen, who to make themselves welcome, came with their canoes loaded with plenty of live fowls, and roots dressed after their manner. Among them was a man, whose complexion was perfectly white, in whose ears hung round white pendants as big as one's fist. This person had a very devout air, and seemed to be one of their Priests. While things were in this friendly situation, one of the Islanders was by some accident shot dead in his canoe, by a musket, which threw the rest into such consternation, that most of them leaped into the sea, in order to get the sooner on shore, while the rest, who remained in their canoes, rowed with all their strength, in order to obtain a place of safety.

The *Dutch* soon after followed them, and landed 150 soldiers and seamen, among whom was the Commodore in person, and the Author, who commanded the land forces; when the people crowding upon them, they had the rashness and cruelty to make their way by force, to which they were particularly prompted, by some of these *Indians,* being so curious as to lay their hands upon their arms. The *Dutch* therefore fired, and by this single discharge, many of these innocent people were killed, and among them the poor *Indian,* who had been twice on board; but though the rest were almost frightened out of their wits, yet in a few moments they rallied again; but kept at the distance of about ten yards, probably supposing they might there be safe from the muskets. Their consternation, however, was not soon over; for they still made dismal lamentations, and purchased the dead bodies of their friends, by giving for them great plenty of provisions of all kinds. In order to pacify these invaders, both the men, women, and children, presented themselves before them, with all the signs of peace, and endeavoured to testify, by the most humble postures, how desirous they were to mollify and make them their friends.

The *Dutch* affected by their submissions, did them no farther harm, and being willing to make up all differences between them, made them a present of a painted cloth sixty yards long, and also gave them a considerable quantity of coral, beads, and small looking-glasses, with which they were much pleased. Being now convinced that the *Dutch* intended to treat them like friends, they brought them at once 500 live fowls, which exactly resembled the barn-door fowls of *Europe,* with a great quantity of red and white roots, and potatoes, some hundreds of sugar canes, and a large quantity of pisans, a sort of *Indian* figs, as big as a gourd, covered with a green rind; the pulp is as sweet as honey, and there sometimes grow an hundred of these figs upon a single bough. It is remarkable, that the leaves of this tree are six or eight feet long, and about three broad.

The *Dutch* saw no other animals in this island, but birds, which were of various sorts. However they thought it probable, that there might be cattle and other beasts in the heart of the country; because on their shewing the *Indians* some hogs on board their ships, they informed them by signs, that they had seen such animals before.

It appeared to the *Dutch,* that every family or tribe had its separate village, composed of cabins; some of which were 40, and others near 60 feet long, and six or eight broad, formed of a certain number of poles stuck upright, with the spaces between them filled with a kind of clay, and covered on the top with palm leaves. They had all little plantations staked out, and very neatly divided. At this time, almost all their fruits and plants, herbs and roots, were in full perfection, and every where appeared an air of plenty. In their houses, however, they had not many moveables, and those they had were of no great value. They had earthern pots, in which they dressed their meat, and a red and white kind of stuff, that served them when walking for clothes, and when sleeping for quilts. This stuff was as soft to the touch as silk, and was in all appearance of their own manufacture.

These Islanders were in general a slender, well made, brisk, and active people: they were very swift of foot, and of a sweet and agreeable disposition, but extremely timorous; for whenever they brought the *Dutch* either fowls or other provisions, they hastily threw themselves on their knees, and as soon as they had delivered them, retired as fast as their legs could carry them. They were generally of as brown a complexion as the *Spaniards.* They were, however, some among them almost black, others were white, and others perfectly red. Their bodies were painted over with the figures of birds and other animals, and all their women in general had an artificial bloom upon their cheeks of a crimson, far surpassing any thing known in *Europe;* nor could the *Dutch* discover of what this colour was composed. On their heads they wore a little hat, made of reeds or straw, and they had no other covering except that already mentioned. The women, however, appeared to have no great flare of modesty, for they beckoned the *Dutch* into their houses, and when they sat down by them, would throw off their mantles.

It is very remarkable, that these Islanders did not seem to have any arms among them; but whenever they were attacked, they fled for shelter and assistance to their idols, which were all of stone, of the figure of a man with great ears, and the head covered with a crown, the whole very nicely proportioned, and so highly finished, that the *Dutch* stood amazed. Round these idols were palisadoes of white stone, at the distance of 20 or 30 yards.

The *Dutch* could not distinguish among these people any appearance of government or subordination, much less any Prince, or Chief, who had dominion over the rest; but on the contrary, all seemed to speak and act with equal freedom. However, the old people wore on their heads feathered bonnets, and were obeyed with the greatest readiness.

One evening they had been on shore, and the Commodore, on the report of his officers, was determined to land the next morning with a force sufficient to make a strict examination of the whole island; but before it was light a west wind drove them from both their anchors, so that they were obliged to put to sea to avoid being wrecked. After this misfortune, they cruized some time in the same latitude, and then steering to the westward, arrived at the island discovered by *Schovten,* to which he gave the name of

Badwater, from all its springs being brackish. The *Dutch* then sailed upwards of 800 leagues without seeing land, till arriving in 15°. 30. south latitude, there appeared a low island, the coast of which was covered with a very yellow sand, and in the middle of it was a lake; it was in the latitude of 15°. 45. south, and they gave it the name of *Carlshoff,* or *Charles's* coast.

II

The English on Easter

(From "Three Voyages Round the World," by Captain James Cook. This account by an unnamed chronicler, appears in *The Second Voyage.*)

On the 25th [of February] Captain Cook was taken ill of a bilious colic which was so violent as to confine him to his bed so that the management of the ship was left to Mr. Cooper, the first lieutenant who performed his duties much to his satisfaction. It was several days before the dangerous symptoms of his disorder were removed. . . .

. . . At eight o'clock on the morning of the 11th of March, land was seen from the masthead, bearing west, about twelve leagues distant. They now tacked, and endeavored to get into what appeared to be a bay on the west side of the point; but before this could be accomplished night came upon them and they stood on and off under the land until next morning. This is called Easter Island or Davis' Land. Here a canoe, conducted by two men, came off. They brought with them a bunch of plantains, which they sent into the ship by a rope, and then returned ashore. This gave the captain a good opinion of the islanders and inspired them with hopes of getting some provisions of which they were much in want. They continued to range along the coast till they opened the northern point of the isle. While the ship was working in, a native came on board. The first thing he did was to measure the length of the ship by fathoming her from the taffrail to the stem; and as he counted the fathoms they observed that he called the numbers by the same names they do in Otaheite. Nevertheless his language was nearly unintelligible to them. Next morning the captain went ashore, accompanied by some of the gentlemen to see what the island was likely to afford. They landed on a sandy beach where some hundreds of the natives were assembled, who were so impatient to see them that many swam off to meet the boats. None of them had so much as a stick of a weapon in his hand.

After distributing a few trinkets among them, they made signs for something to eat on which they brought down a few potatoes, plantains, and sugar canes and exchanged them for nails, looking glasses and pieces of cloth. They soon discovered that they were expert thieves and as cheating in their exchanges as any people they had yet met with. It was with some difficulty that they could keep their hats on their heads but it was hardly possible to keep anything in their pockets, not even what they had just bought, for they would watch every opportunity to snatch it from them, so that they sometimes bought the same thing two or three times over and after all did not get it.

The captain was obliged to content himself with remaining at the landing place among the natives, as he had not yet recovered. They had a pretty brisk trade with them for potatoes which were dug out of an adjoining plantation but this traffic soon was put a stop to by the owner of the plantation coming down and driving all the people out of it.

By this they concluded that he had been robbed of his property and that they were not less scrupulous of stealing from one another than from their visitors on whom they practiced every little fraud they could think of, and generally with success; for they no sooner had detected them in one than they found out another.

A party who had been sent out in the morning to view the country now returned. They had not proceeded far before a middle-aged man, punctured from head to foot, and his face painted with a sort of white pigment appeared with a spear in his hand and walked alongside of them, making signs to his countrymen to keep at a distance and not to molest them. When he had pretty well effected this he hoisted a piece of white cloth on his spear, placed himself in front and led the way with this ensign of peace.

On the east side, near the sea, they met with three platforms of stone work, or rather the ruins of them, on each of which had stood four large statues, but they were also fallen down from two of the platforms and also one from the third only one was uninjured by the fall or in no degree defaced. Mr. Wales measured this one and found it to be fifteen feet in length and six feet broad over the shoulders. Each statue had on its head a large cylindrical stone of red color, wrought perfectly round. The one they measured which was not the largest, was 52 inches high and 66 inches in diameter. In some the upper corner of the cylinder was taken off by a sort of concave quarter round; but in others the cylinder was entire.

Beyond this they came to the most fertile part of the island, it being interspersed with plantations of potatoes, sugar canes and plantain trees; but they could find no water except what the natives twice or thrice brought to them, which, though brackish and stinking, was rendered acceptable by the extremity of their thirst. They also passed some huts, the owners of which met them with roasted potatoes and sugar canes; but at the very time some were relieving the thirsty and hungry, there were others who endeavored to steal from them the very things that had been given them. At last, to prevent worse consequences, they were obliged to fire a load of small shot at one of them who had been so audacious as to snatch the bags which contained everything they had brought with them. The shot hit him on the back, on which he dropped the bags, ran a little way and then fell; but he afterwards got up and walked, and what became of him they knew not, nor whether he was much wounded.

This affair occasioned some delay and drew the natives together. They presently saw the man who had hitherto led the way, and one or two more, come running toward them; but instead of stopping when they came up, they continued to run round them, repeating in a kind manner a few words, until they set forward again. Then their old guide hoisted his flag, leading the way as before and none ever attempted to steal from them the whole day afterwards.

They observed that the eastern side of the island was full of gigantic statues, some placed in groups on platforms of masonry, others single, fixed only in the earth and in general much larger than those in the groups. Having measured one which had fallen down, they found it very near 27 feet long and upwards of eight feet over the shoulders, and yet this appeared to be considerably short of one they saw standing. They saw no animals of any sort and but few birds, and Captain Cook determined to leave the island the next morning, since nothing could be obtained that made it worth his while to stay.

The produce of this island is sweet potatoes, yams, plantains, and sugar canes, all pretty good, the potatoes especially which are the best of the kind they ever tasted. They have a few tame fowls, such as cocks and hens, but they saw very little fish among the natives. The inhabitants did not seem to exceed 700 souls, above two-thirds of whom appeared to be males. They either have very few women among them or else many were restrained from making their appearance. In general the people of the isle are a slender race. They did not see a man that would measure six feet, so far are they from being giants as one of the authors of Roggeween's Voyage asserts. They are brisk and active and have good features and not disagreeable countenances, are friendly and hospitable to strangers, but as much addicted to pilfering as any of their neighbors.

The women's clothing is a piece or two of quilted cloth about six feet by four, or a mat. One piece wrapped around their loins and another over their shoulders make a complete dress. The men for the most part wear only a slip of cloth betwixt their legs, each end of which is fastened to a belt or cord about the waist.

On the 16th of March the ship stood out to sea. . . .

III

La Pérouse's Record

(From "Voyage de La Pérouse Autour du Monde")

On the eighth of April at two o'clock in the afternoon I discerned Easter Island which was twelve miles west of me and five degrees south. The sea was very rough; the winds from the north.

I lay off during the night of the eighth about three leagues from the coast of the island. The weather was clear. At daylight I made for Cook's Bay, the spot most protected from the winds of the north and south and conditions were so fine that I had hope that there would not be a blow for several days. At eleven o'clock in the morning I was not more than a league from the anchorage. The *Astrolabe* had already dropped her anchor and I anchored close to that frigate. But the slope of the bottom was so steep that the hooks failed to seize. We had to pull them up and move to regain our anchorage.

This difficulty did not cool the ardor of the Indians. They followed us to sea while we coasted a league. They came aboard with a laughing air and an assurance that gave me the highest opinion of their character. More suspicious men might have been frightened to see us hoist sail and take them away from their native land; but the spirit of these seemed entirely free from any idea of perfidy. They stood in our midst naked and without any arms of any sort. A simple cord about their loins served to hold a packet of herbs in front of them. Their physiognomy was generally agreeable but quite varied and they did not seem to have—like the Malays, Chinese or Chileans—any character distinctly their own.

I made many presents to these Indians. They preferred bits of figured cloth to nails or knives. But they desired above all else our hats. We had too small a quantity to give hats to many of them.

At eight o'clock in the evening I said farewell to my new hosts, indicating to them by signs that I should disembark at daybreak. They went dancing to their canoes, throwing themselves into the sea about two pistol shots from the shore over which the surf broke with considerable force. They had taken the precaution to make little packets of my presents and each had set his packet on his head to protect it from the water.

Cook's Bay, of Easter Island or Ile de Pâques, is situated in 27 degrees 11 minutes south and 111 degrees, 55 minutes, 30 seconds west. It is the only anchorage which protects from the winds of the southeast and the east which are the prevailing winds in this quarter. The bay is easily recognized. After having rounded the headland on the south corner of the island you follow the land about a mile and see presently a little inlet which makes identification certain. Landing is easy at the feet of one of the statues of which I shall speak presently.

At daybreak I prepared for our debarcation. I flattered myself that we would be among friends inasmuch as I had heaped with presents all those who had come aboard the preceding evening. But I had given too much thought to the reports of other voyagers not to know that the Indians are big children and that the sight of our equipment would so excite their cupidity that they would use every wile to possess themselves of it. I believed that they could be held in check by fear and I ordered that a few implements of war be taken ashore with us. In all we dispatched four canoes with a dozen armed men. M. de Langle and I followed with all the passengers and officers with the exception of those who were required for service aboard the two frigates. We numbered about seventy persons.

Four or five hundred Indians awaited us on the shore. They were without arms. Some of them were covered with pieces of white or yellow cloth but the greater number were naked. Many were tattooed and had painted their faces a red color. Their shouts and their faces expressed pleasure. They came forward to offer a hand in our descent.

The island at this point has an elevation of about twenty feet. The mountains are about seven or eight hundred toises (about 1400 to 1600 meters) in the interior. The terrain slopes gently toward the sea, which space is covered with grass and seems suitable as forage for cattle. The grass covers large rocks not imbedded in the earth and these rocks which we found such an inconvenience in walking are really a blessing of nature in that they preserve the freshness and moisture of the earth and in some measure provide a substitute for the shade of trees which the natives have had the imprudence to cut down at some time long past; an imprudence which exposed their soil to the baking influence of the sun. As a result they have neither brooks nor springs. They are ignorant of the fact that in these little islands in the middle of the ocean a fresh earth covered with trees is able to attract and condense the moisture of clouds and set up on the mountains a continuous rain which manifests itself in springs or in creeks in the different quarters. Islands deprived of this advantage are reduced to a horrible dryness which little by little destroys the plant life and makes the land virtually uninhabitable. M. de Langle and I did not doubt that these people owed their wretched plight to the lack of forethought of their ancestors. And it is believable that other isles of the South Seas are more happily placed because of their inaccessible mountains on which it was impossible to cut the wood. . . . The inhabitants of this island have less to complain about in the eruptions of their volcanoes, extinct for many years, than in their own imprudence.

But as man is of all beings best capable of adapting himself to all sorts of circumstances, these people appeared to me less miserable than they had appeared to Captain Cook and M. Forster. When these men arrived on the island after a long and difficult voyage, lacking every sort of supply, ill with scurvy, they found no water nor wood nor pigs; a few chickens, bananas and yams were at best meager resources under such circumstances. Their reports reflect the mental attitude induced by their situation. Our lot was immeasurably better. Our crews enjoyed perfect health. We had taken aboard at Chile enough supplies to last us for months and we desired nothing of these people except a chance to help them.

We gave them goats, sheep and pigs and we had for distribution the seeds of oranges and lemons and cotton and corn and generally all species of plant life which might flourish on the island.

Our first care on landing was to establish a barrier with the armed soldiers arranged in a circle. We ordered the natives to leave a space free and in this space we erected a tent. I had the presents intended for them brought ashore together with the live stock. But as I had expressly ordered the men to refrain from firing and to push back only with the butts of their rifles such Indians as became unruly, the soldiers themselves were presently exposed to the rapacity of the islanders whose numbers were steadily increasing.

By this time there were at least eight hundred and in the number were certainly one hundred and fifty women. The physique of many of these women was pleasing. They offered their favors to anyone who would make them a present. The Indians pressed us to take them . . . and pending the importunities of the women they stole the hats from our heads and the kerchiefs from our pockets. All appeared to be accomplices in these thefts; for no sooner had one been committed than, like a bird flight, they all fled at the same instant. But seeing that we did not resort to our fire arms they returned some minutes afterward. They renewed their caresses and waited opportunity for new larceny. This trickery went on throughout the morning. As we were going away that night and had so short a time in which to undertake their education, we played the part of being amused by the ruses which the islanders employed to rob us. The Indians were without arms. Three or four among the great number had a sort of wooden club quite formidable. Certain ones seemed to have a light authority over the others. I took these for chiefs and gave them medals which I attached to their necks with chains; but I soon discovered that these were the most distinguished thieves. And when they assumed the rôle of chasing after those who had stolen our handkerchiefs it was easy to see that they had no intent to overtake them.

We had only eight or ten hours to remain on the island and we had no wish to waste our time. I confided the tent and all our effects to my lieutenant M. d'Escures. We then divided into two parties; the first in command of M. de Langle was to penetrate as far as possible into the interior, plant the seeds in all places where it seemed likely that they might grow, examine the soil and the plants, the culture, the population, the monuments, and generally everything of interest among these extraordinary people. The second group, to which I attached myself, contented itself with visiting the monuments, houses and plantations near our headquarters. M. Forster believed that the monuments were the work of a people very much more numerous than those who exist to-day. But his opinion does not seem to me to be well founded. The greatest of the busts which were on the platforms measured by us are not more than fourteen feet, six inches in height. These busts, I say, could be the work of the existing generation which I believe can, without any exaggeration, show a population of two thousand persons. The number of women seemed to me to be very close to that of the men. The babies here seemed to be the same as those in other islands, and since among about twelve hundred natives whom our arrival assembled about the bay there were at most three hundred women, I can draw no other conclusion than that islanders from the extremities of the land came to see our vessels and that the women remained in their houses. We all went into the caverns in which M. Forster and some officers of Captain Cook believed the women might have concealed themselves. They are subterranean dwellings of the same form as those of which I shall presently write. In them we found little faggots, the largest piece being not more than five feet long.

All the monuments which exist to-day, of which M. Duche has made a very exact drawing, seem to be quite ancient. They are placed on marae—as we were able to judge from the numbers of bones found beside them. . . . We did not see any trace of a cult. I do not believe that anyone could take the statues for idols although the Indians display a sort of veneration before them. These busts of colossal cut, showing the progress these people have made in sculpture, are of a volcanic production known to naturalists under the name of lapillo.

I can only hazard conjectures concerning the customs of these people whose language I do not understand and whom I saw only for a day. But I had the experience of the voyagers who preceded me. I knew their reports perfectly and was able to join their experiences with my own.

The tenth part of the land is cultivated and I am persuaded that three days of work is sufficient to procure for each Indian his subsistence for a year. This facility in providing for vital necessities led me to believe that the products of the land were held in common. Moreover I am fairly certain that some houses are used in common at least by all of a village or a district. I measured one of these houses near our headquarters. It was three hundred and ten feet long, ten feet wide and ten feet high. It had the form of an overturned canoe. One cannot enter at the two doors—two feet in height, except by crawling on his hands and knees. This house could contain two hundred persons. It was not the dwelling of a chief, since it contained no furnishings . . . it formed, with two or three little houses some distance away, an entire village.

It is reasonable to suppose that there is in each district a chief whose concern it is to watch over the plantations. As for the women I cannot say whether or not they are the common property of the whole district and their children belong to the republic. It is certain that no Indian appeared to exercise over any one woman the authority of a husband.

Some houses are subterranean as I have said; but there are others constructed of reeds—which proves that there must be marshy places in the interior of the island. The reeds are artistically arranged and furnish adequate protection against the rain. . . . The edifice is carried on a foundation of stone. . . .

One cannot doubt, as Captain Cook observed, that these

people are identified with those of other islands in the South Sea. They have the same language, the same physiognomy. Their cloth is also made from mulberry bark. But it is very rare on account of the dryness which destroys the trees. Those of this species which have survived are not more than three feet in height and the natives have had to build walls about them to protect them from the winds. It is significant that the trees never exceed in height the walls which surround them.

I have no doubt that in other epochs the islanders had the same products as the Society Islands. The fruit trees have been killed by drouth as well as the pigs and dogs for whom water is an absolute necessity. But man, who in the Hudson straits drank whale oil, accustoms himself to everything. I have seen the natives of Ile de Pâques drink sea water like the albatross of Cape Horn. We were in the wet season. They found a little water in hollows along the seacoast and offered it to us in gourds. But it would have disgusted the most hardened. I do flatter myself that the pigs I presented them will multiply but I hope that the hares and the sheep which love salt will turn out well.

At one o'clock in the afternoon I returned to my tent intending to go back on board so that M. de Clonard, my second in command, might come ashore. I found everybody without hats or handkerchiefs. Our docility had encouraged the thieves. One Indian who had helped me to descend from a platform—after he had rendered me this service,—seized my hat and fled at all speed, followed as usual by the others. I did not pursue him, not wishing to have the exclusive right to protection against the sun in view of the fact that we were nearly all without hats. I continued to examine this platform. It is the monument which gave me the highest opinion of the talents of these people for masonry. It appears that they knew nothing of any cement. But they cut and squared the rocks perfectly and jointed them according to all the rules of the art.

The revetment which is on the side toward the sea is made of compact lava to endure for a long time and I do not know of any implement or material among these islanders hard enough to cut these stones. Perhaps a longer sojourn would have given some explanation of these subjects. At two o'clock I returned on board and M. de Clonard came ashore. Presently two officers of the *Astrolabe* arrived to report to me that the Indians had committed a new theft which had occasioned a fine row. Divers had cut the cable of the boat of the *Astrolabe* under the water and had picked up the hook. This was not discovered until the thieves were well on their way to the interior of the isle. As the hook was necessary to us two officers and some soldiers pursued them but were met with a shower of stones. A shot fired into the air had no effect. They were obliged finally to discharge a load of buckshot of which some of the grains, no doubt, reached one of the Indians for the stoning ceased and the officers were able to regain the tent peaceably. But it was impossible to catch the thieves who could well be astonished at not having destroyed our patience.

They soon came back to our establishment. They began again to offer their women and we were just as good friends as we had been at the first interview. Finally at six o'clock all returned on board and I gave the signal to prepare to depart. M. de Langle gave me an account of his voyage into the interior of the island.

He had sown seeds all along the route, he had given the islanders marks of extreme kindness. I believe I can convey a picture of his beneficiaries in reporting that one chief to whom M. de Langle had made a present of a pair of goats—male and female—received them with one hand and stole his handkerchief with the other.

Nobody who has read the accounts of recent voyagers can take the Indians of the South Sea for savages. They have, to the contrary, made great progress in civilization and I believe them to be as corrupt as they could be in the circumstances in which they find themselves. My opinion is not founded on the robberies they have committed but upon the manner in which they take things. The most impudent rogues in Europe are less hypocritical.

They displayed violence toward young girls of thirteen or fourteen years to send them after us in the hope of receiving their wage. The repugnance of the Indian maidens was proof that this, in their view, was a violation of the law of the country.

I found in this land all the arts of the Society Islands but much curtailed because of the lack of raw material. The canoes were of the same form but they were built of very narrow boards of four or five feet in length. They were able to carry four men or more. I only saw three in this part of the island and I should not be surprised if presently, thanks to the lack of wood, not one remains. They are such excellent swimmers that in the roughest sea they will venture two leagues out and search out for sport on returning the spot where the surf breaks with the greatest force.

There seem to be few fish along the shore. The inhabitants live on potatoes, roots, bananas and sugar cane and a little fruit that grows in the rocks on the edge of the sea, a fruit like the grapes one finds in the tropics in the Atlantic ocean. One cannot regard as a resource the fowl which are very rare in this island. Our voyagers did not see one land bird and those of the sea were not common.

The fields are cultivated with considerable intelligence.

The islanders pick herbs, burn them and fertilize the earth with their ashes. The banana plants are set out in rows.

The care with which they measured my vessel proved to me that they have not seen our arts sufficiently to be unmoved. They examined our cables, our anchors, our compass, our wheel; and they came back on the next occasion with a string to take measurements, which led me to believe that they had had some discussions on the subject ashore and that they were in doubt. I esteem them considerably less since they seem to me to be capable of reflection. . . .

Here is the report of the little journey of M. de Langle and his companions into the interior:

"We set out at eight o'clock in the morning and were shortly two leagues to the east toward the interior. The march was very difficult over knolls covered with volcanic rocks. But I perceived that there are paths by which the natives can easily communicate with one another. We visited several plantations of taro and potatoes. The soil of these plantations is a vegetable earth quite rich, which the gardener judged to be suitable for the growing of our seeds.

"We sowed cabbage, carrots, beets, corn etc. and we tried to make the islanders understand that these seeds would produce fruits which they could eat. They understood us perfectly and when they showed us the best lands they indicated to us the spots where they wished to see our new productions. We added to leguminous plants the seeds of the orange, lemon and cotton and we made them understand that these were trees and that what we had previously sown were plants.

"We found no trees other than the paper mulberry and the mimosa and we took our course toward the mountain. After we had gone two leagues to the East we turned to the south toward the south-east coast where we saw many monuments of which a large number were overturned.

"Having seen an assembly of cabins I directed my route toward that village. It appears that this part of the island is more cultivated and better populated than in the neighborhood of Cook's Bay. The monuments on the platforms were also multiplied. We saw skeletons on several of the rocks of which the platforms are composed and we discovered that clefts which we had thought to communicate with caves were filled with the bodies of the dead. One Indian explained to us by means of expressive signs that those who entered here went presently to heaven. We saw on the edge of the sea pyramids of stones arranged like the balls in an artillery park. We saw some human bones near these pyramids and statues all of which had their backs to the ocean. Time had made more or less inroads on them depending on their antiquity. We found on one of them a sort of mannequin of reeds about ten feet high. It was covered with white native cloth.

"The head was of natural size, the body narrow, the legs were sufficiently well proportioned. About the neck hung a panier which seemed to us to contain grass. Beside this sack was the figure of an infant two feet long. . . . This mannequin could not have existed for many years. It is perhaps a model of one of the statues that they erect for the chiefs. Not far from here was one platform whose two parapets formed an enceinte three hundred and eighty-four feet long and three hundred and twenty-four feet wide. We could not tell if it were a reservoir for water or the beginning of a fortress.

"At the extremity of the south point of the island we saw the crater of an old volcano whose width, depth and regularity excited our admiration. . . .

"Upon returning to the tent I gave to three different

natives the three species of animals we had brought for them. These islanders are apparently hospitable and well meaning. They gave us several times potatoes and sugar cane. In the meantime they never overlooked an opportunity to rob us.

"We were in the wet season. We found the moist earth a foot in depth. Some holes in the hills contained a little fresh water but we encountered no running streams. The land appears to be of good quality. . . .

"If the islanders had the industry to build cisterns they could remedy by this means one of the greatest evils of their situation and prolong, perhaps, their span of life. One does not see in this island any man whose age appears to be more than sixty years, if one may judge the age of a people he knows so slightly and whose mode of life is so different from ours."

In departing from Cook's Bay on the evening of the tenth I took the route to the north and followed the coast of the island at a distance of a league in the light of the moon. . . .

IV

Popular Error

For many years the belief was current among people who had heard of the island at all that the stone of the images was of a variety not indigenous to Easter. As the text shows, this tufa is plentiful on Rano Raraku and would be conclusive evidence of the source of the statues even were the hillside not covered with the niches whence the carvings were taken.

There was a report also that the ancient Rapa Nuis possessed remarkable surgical powers as evidenced by trepanned skulls brought from the island by voyagers in the last century.

If such skulls are in existence no mention is made of them by any of the observers who have written reports on Easter Island, nor is anything known about them by the present inhabitants. It is conceivable that some observer mistook for the mark of trepanning a conventional symbol incised in the forehead of the skull of a chief of the Miru clan. The Mirus in life were creatures apart from the rest of the islanders, people of the royal line who walked in an atmosphere of awe and magic. Their chiefs were the great "medicine men," keepers of the culture of the *rongo-rongo* and gifted with charms to make hens lay eggs. Some of their *mana* or supernatural skill lingered about them after death so their skulls were sometimes etched with an emblem of fertility and used as amulets.

V

Phallic Symbolism

There is plentiful evidence that the images of Easter may have been phallic figures. Save for one isolated and somewhat dubious example they are universally male. Inasmuch as virtually all of the statues of the *ahus* have fallen on their faces and those of the hills are generally buried to the shoulders they are difficult to examine. But all which it was possible to study showed a significant mutilation. The male markings, once pronounced, were chiseled off at some time before the destruction of the *ahus*—which is to say well in advance of any European influence. This wide-spread—probably general—effort to censor the art of the carvings was not prompted by any change of creed or any imported sense of shame. The cause can only be guessed but it is within reason to suppose that overpopulation of the island or some sudden decrease in resources made fecundity undesirable and changed the public attitude toward emblems of fertility.

The female symbol was in wide use throughout the island until recent times. It was marked on boundary stones, on the magic working skulls of the Miru clansmen and on the virgins passed by the examining priest on Rano Kao.

VI

THE WRECK OF THE "EL DORADO"

IN JUNE, 1913, the *El Dorado* bound from Oregon to Antifogasto was caught in a gale. Her deckload shifted and she started to founder. Captain Benson and his crew took to the ship's boat losing their chronometer in the transfer.

The captain knew that they were only about seven hundred miles from Easter Island but without a chronometer he was compelled to steer a course north to the latitude of the island. This maneuvering forced them to travel an additional two hundred miles through stormy seas without a sail. Eventually they reached Hanga Roa landing.

Captain Benson who feared that he would lose a home which he was buying on the instalment plan in San Francisco, patched up his boat, fitted it with a sail and embarked once more taking two men and leaving eight on the island. He borrowed a watch from Manager Percy Edmunds for use as a chronometer and this time set a straight course. He reached Manga Reva in sixteen days, stayed two days, and accomplished the remaining nine hundred miles to Tahiti in eleven days.

This feat of oarsmanship has frequently been quoted in answer to theories that Polynesian voyagers could not have reached Easter Island except by a land bridge.

BIBLIOGRAPHY

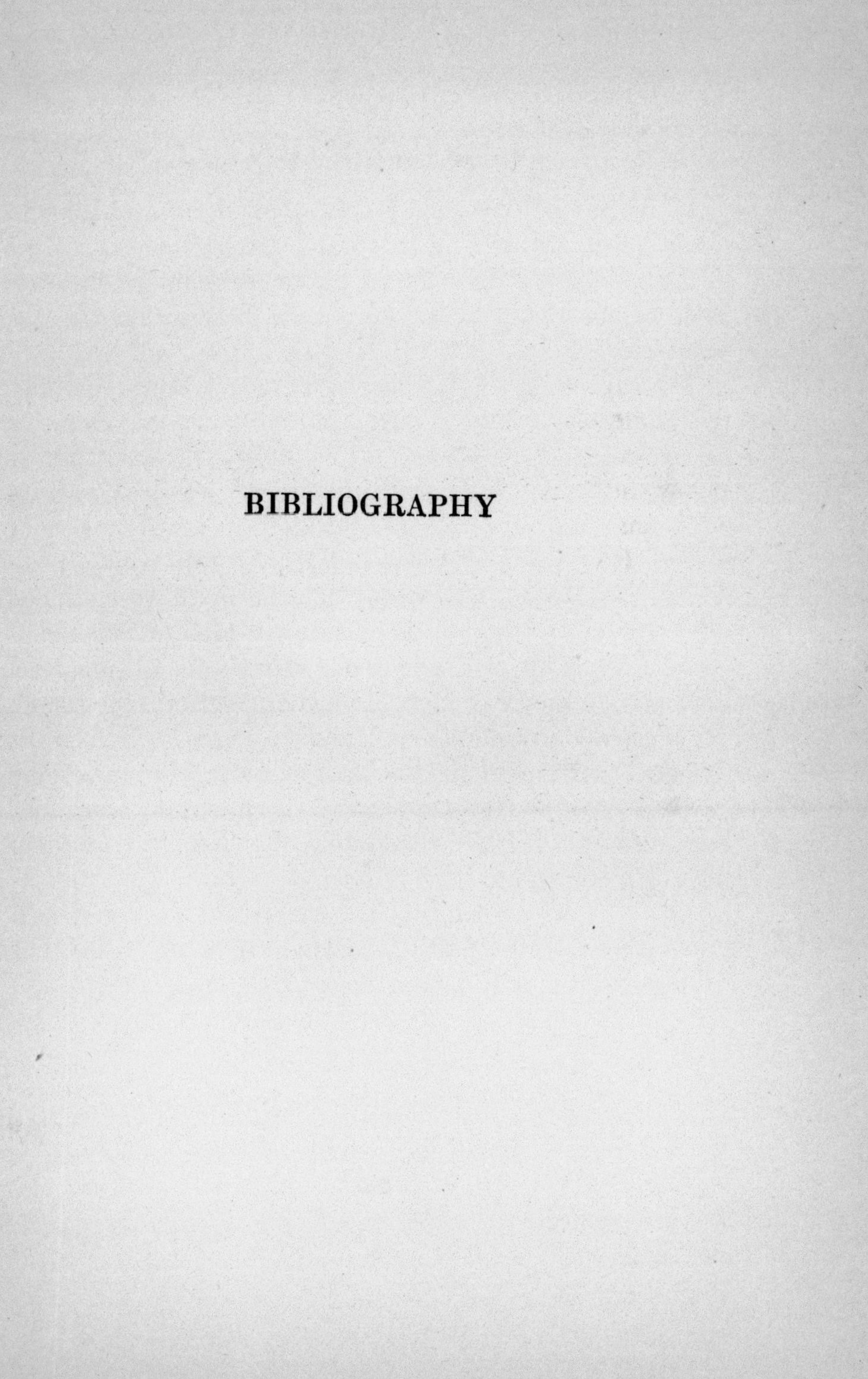

BIBLIOGRAPHY

Voyage of Gonzalez—Hakluyt Society.

The Riddle of the Pacific, J. Macmillan Brown.

Peoples and Problems of the Pacific, J. Macmillan Brown.

The Mystery of Easter Island, Mrs. Scoresby Routledge.

A Voyage toward the South Pole and round the World, Capt. James Cook.

A Voyage round the World, George Forster.

Voyage de La Pérouse autour du Monde—Editions du Carrefour.

Voyage round the World in the Ship "Neva," Lisiansky.

Voyage to the Pacific, H.M.S. Blossom.

Smithsonian Report, U.S.S. Mohican, Paymaster Thompson.

L'Ile de Pâques, (Bulletin Géographique, 1893) M. Tepano Jaussen.

The Maori as He Was, Elsdon Best (New Zealand Dominion Museum).

Polynesian Voyagers, Elsdon Best.

Spiritual and Mental Concepts of the Maori, Elsdon Best.

Astronomical Knowledge of the Maori, Elsdon Best.

Melanesians and Polynesians, George Brown.

The World Displayed; or, A Curious Collection of Voyages and Travels Selected from the Writers of All Nations, Vol. IX, pp. 118-125.

GLOSSARY

GLOSSARY

Ahu (Lit.: A pile): burial cairn.
Akuaku: ghost; evil spirit.
Ana: cave.
Ao: paddle for ceremonies; bird cult celebrants.
Ariki: chief.
Atua: a god.
Hanga: bay.
Hapopo: material for cannibal feast.
Hare: house.
Hau: feather hat.
Henua: land—the world.
Hopu: servant.
Iti: small.
Ivi Atua: sorcerer.
Kai Kai: eat.
Kaunga: feast for a mother.
Koro: feast for a father.
Maori: priest.
Makemake: god of the sea.
Mana: supernatural power.
Manu: bird.
Mata: clan.
Mataa: obsidian spear point.
Miro: wood.
Moai: image.
Motu: island.
Nui: large.
Paina: summer festival.
Pareu: loin cloth.
Pito: navel.
Poki: child.
Puhi: female symbol.
Raa: sun.
Rano: crater lake.
Rapa: dancing paddle.
Roa: long.
Rongo-rongo: the script.
Tangata: man.
Te: definite article.
Umi: oven.

From *Voyage de La Pérouse autour du Monde*